A PASSION FOR
PARIS

ALSO BY DAVID DOWNIE

Paris to the Pyrenees:
A Skeptic Pilgrim Walks the Way of Saint James

Paris, Paris: Journey into the City of Light

Quiet Corners of Rome

Paris City of Night

Food Wine Burgundy

Food Wine Rome

Food Wine Italian Riviera & Genoa

Cooking the Roman Way:
Authentic Recipes from the Home Cooks and
Trattorias of Rome

Enchanted Liguria:
A Celebration of the Culture, Lifestyle and
Food of the Italian Riviera

La Tour de l'Immonde

The Irreverent Guide to Amsterdam

Un'altra Parigi
(with Ulderico Munzi)

A PASSION FOR
PARIS

Romanticism and Romance
in the City of Light

DAVID DOWNIE

ST. MARTIN'S PRESS
New York

www.stmartins.com

Designed by Kathryn Parise

The Library of Congress Cataloging-in-Publication Data
is available upon request.

ISBN 978-1-250-04315-3 (hardcover)
ISBN 978-1-4668-4125-3 (e-book)

St. Martin's Press books may be purchased for educational, business, or
promotional use. For information on bulk purchases, please contact the
Macmillan Corporate and Premium Sales Department at 1-800-221-7945,
extension 5442, or write to specialmarkets@macmillan.com.

First Edition: April 2015

10 9 8 7 6 5 4 3 2 1

This book is dedicated to all those who are passionate about Paris, and in particular to the memory of two formidable spirits who spent decades glorying in, deciphering, and dissecting the City of Light and its inhabitants: Anne M. Harris and Mavis Gallant.

Paris that eternal monstrous marvel . . . the city of a hundred-thousand novels . . . a living creature, the great courtesan whose face and heart and mind-boggling morals they know: "They" are the lovers of Paris.

—Honoré de Balzac

CONTENTS

PART SIX

QUAI VOLTAIRE

PART SEVEN

THE NEW ATHENS AND MONTMARTRE

PART EIGHT

OPEN ENDINGS

THANKS AND ACKNOWLEDGMENTS

Special thanks are due my genial editor, Charles Spicer, and my peerless agent, Alice Martell, for their contagious enthusiasm, skill, and friendship; my wife, Alison Harris, for her encouragement and helpful suggestions, her splendid photographs and photo research; novelist and translator Marie-Pierre Emery, for her astute comments and steadfast *amitié*; and David Malone, for providing a restful retreat where I was able to do much of the research for this book.

I also wish to thank Julia Harris-Voss for her wisdom regarding photo sourcing; April Osborn and Stephanie Finman for their diligence and professionalism; Marie-Claude Sabouret of the Musée de la Vie Romantique, Candice Brunerie of the Musée Balzac, Marie-Laurence Marco and Alexandrine Achille of the Maison de Victor Hugo; Marie-Thérèse Even of La Documentation Française at the Hôtel de Mailly-Nesle, and Bruno Blasselle, director of the Arsenal Library, for opening the archives, back rooms, secret passageways, and subterranean mazes of the magnificent museums and monuments they represent; and Angelique Chenin, former manager of the café-restaurant La Frégate on quai Voltaire, for her cordiality and for leading me into the café's time-tunnel cellar. Thanks to Susan Coll and Janet Hulstrand of Politics & Prose, Elaine and Bill Petrocelli and Karen West of Book Passage, Jeremy Garber of Powell's Books, Karen Maede Allman of Elliot Bay Book, Alice Whitwham of McNally-Jackson, Carol Troxell of New Dominion Bookshop, Alex Meriwether of Harvard Book Store, Cristina Nosti of Books & Books, Mia Anzola (of Coral Gables), Jamie De-

Ment and Richard Holcomb, Linda Watanabe McFerrin and Joanna Biggar of Left Coast Writers, Roger Howlett of the Saint Botolph Club, Mary Allen of Northshire Books, Douglas Rankin of the Irving Barclay Theater, my publicists Kathryn Hough and Alastair Hayes, and Adrienne Kimball for their logistical help, enthusiasm, and support.

A long-overdue outsize merci to my sister, Diane Downie, and brother-in-law, Paul Shelley, and to Jean Kahn, Liza and Andrew Labadie, Elizabeth and Nevin Kuhl, Susan Loewenberg, Gloria Spivak, Russ Schleipman, Lou and Dan Jordan, Steven Barclay and Garth Bixler, Abbie Salny, and Sandra Gilbert, for their unflagging generosity, hospitality, and support on this and many earlier projects; and to my lexophobic pals Jay Smith, Paul Taylor, and Carl Ipsen, traveling companions in the Paris of our now-distant youth.

PART ONE

Romantic Encounters in a
Maid's Room,

or how the innocent author from San Francisco
followed Félix Nadar to Paris and was seduced by the
city, becoming obsessed by the world's obsessions and
fantasies about romance in the City of Light

The Seine, Seven Bridges, and Hôtel de Ville

1

OVERHEAD IN A BALLOON

It was a chill spring dawn in the mid-1800s when a tattered gas-filled balloon heaved into the sky outside the bastions of Paris. Quivering, the sphere's onion-shaped, tasseled silhouette floated toward the sprawl of glistening tin and tile roofs. Rain, hail, and the year's last snow had swept Paris clean during the night.

A crumpled chessboard of canyons crawling with pawns, knights, and castles appeared below the balloon's dangling wicker basket. In it a lone passenger crouched, shivering, stunned by the view. As the light grew, the mist dispersed. The chess pieces focused themselves into miniature men and women, toy horses and carriages. The canyons turned into a strangely wonderful cityscape of dusty work sites, half-ruined churches, half-built boulevards or train stations, medieval turrets, towers and gargoyles. Symmetrical, freshly finished off-white apartment houses and massive old ocher monuments spiraled outward from the Seine.

Sinuous and slow, the river wore the same indefinite blue-gray tint as the sky. Instead of clouds, whitecaps flecked the surface. The river broke around islands, rejoined itself, split again around riverboats and bridge pilings, and then curved out of the camera frame to east and west.

From under a black canvas hood the young Gaspard-Félix Tournachon, better known as Félix Nadar, released the shutter, counted, then twisted around quickly, developing his photographic plates. After a half-dozen failures from a tethered balloon, he had puzzled out the problem. The process worked, the plates retained their ghostly images, and his balloon could float free.

The most daring of early photographers, an unapologetic Romantic, Nadar had decided one day in 1855 that it was time someone invented aerial photography and that he would be the man. A gifted jack-of-all-trades full of impractical ideas, he had evolved from bookseller, smuggler, spy, caricaturist, painter, novelist, and journalist to would-be revolutionary, marching from Paris to Warsaw in 1848 to fight for Polish independence—though he had no connection to the country. With equally madcap passion he had mastered the art of photography and reached the top of his newborn trade in less than five years. Then he had taken to the sky. Ballooning was big. Why not turn a

Nadar overhead in his balloon (as imagined by Daumier)

wicker basket into a photo studio and lab?

As sensitive as his plates, Nadar had Paris on the brain. He sometimes imagined the city from romantic heights— but with no skyscrapers or Eiffel Tower to look down from. With a pigeon's-eye view in his head, he had prowled the streets, alleys, and parks, then had climbed down and explored the catacombs and the sewers of Paris—and one day would invent flash photography to record their lightless depths.

Nadar Self-Portrait as Mischievous Seducer

Nadar was also famous as a professional nomad and heartbreaker. Standing six feet tall when other Frenchmen were a head shorter, he habitually tossed his head to keep his luxuriant russet hair out of his slightly walleyes. Life was a lark, an endless chase. He had changed his name to Nadar after the Gothic fashion. It sounded vaguely medieval, bohemian, and provocative, and went with his lifestyle. He and his unruly comrades decamped from one dive to the next a day ahead of the eviction squad.

It was Félix Nadar who starred in the original cast of *La Bohème* before it migrated from Paris garrets to the realm of operatic art. He loved and immortalized the flesh-and-blood Mimi, the consumptive beauty of Puccini's masterpiece—or one of her many sisters. Mimi was a made-up name. Nadar and his comrades the poet Charles Baudelaire and the novelists Théophile Gautier and Alexandre Dumas knew the artists' studios and unheated rooftop rooms of Paris better than just about anyone.

Nadar's life inspired legions of latter-day romantics, among them a kindred spirit from San Francisco: me. Nadar was my hero. When I first saw his photographs and learned about his life I did not know I was a Romantic. But I felt an affinity for the Old World and its characters, a world of old monuments, old books, old photos, and old movies, a sophisticated world of exquisite naughtiness filled with romantic garrets and ruined castles surrounded by wineries and restaurants serving sinfully delicious food Europeans enjoyed without guilt.

Like them, I did not understand the meaning of guilt. I also suspected there might be more to the Old World than hedonism or nostalgia for times past, though I could not articulate why.

When not waiting on tables at a self-consciously romantic French restaurant in the San Francisco Bay Area, or clumsily overexposing rolls of black-and-white film in a fruitless effort to become a photographer, I wrote never-to-be-published stories set in European locales and indulged my fulsome imagination. One summer I volunteered as an usher at the San Francisco Opera and was swept up and away by *La Bohème*. I followed its roots from Puccini to its origins and discovered *Scenes from Bohemian Life*, author Henri Murger's bittersweet autobiographical book the opera was based on. Then I found the connection between Mimi and Murger and their friend Nadar. I dreamed of merging life and art, the romantic world of these long-dead men and women, a world of books and photography and wayward balloons in a black-and-white Paris where flowers when distilled into poetry by Charles Baudelaire could be both sweet-smelling and evil. I began to wake up at night with my arms thrown out, calling for Mimi.

Like others in San Francisco I watched vintage movies about Paris when they came to town or ran on late-night TV. I wore a beret, bought baguettes, and considered buying an old Citroën 2CV. Troubled by constant drought and blinded by unrelenting sunshine, I imagined myself singing in the rain on a Paris street full of bobbing old cars with yellow headlights. In my head I was the bad guy played by Jean-Paul Belmondo seducing Jean Seberg on the Champs-Élysées in *Breathless*, or Jean Gabin trailing Michèle Morgan on the quai des Brumes. I devoured secondhand French books. Their lusty, lichen-frosted fantasies featuring Gustave Flaubert's heroine Madame Bovary ravished in a bouncing carriage, or Victor Hugo's Quasimodo and Esmeralda entangled among the gargoyles of Notre Dame, seemed engrossing, outlandish, and mercifully disconnected from the deregulatory orgy that had overtaken California.

Then one day I made my way east across America and did not stop traveling until years and several putative career changes later, I crossed the Seine on the Pont des Arts and moved into my own opera-set, seventh-floor walk-up cold-water garret on the Right Bank in rue Laugier. Too excited to unpack, I found a wooden ladder in the plank-floored hallway and propped it into the shaft below a small rectangular skylight. Clutching a map of Paris, I climbed up and stuck my head out.

Transfixed, surrounded by pigeons, I balanced on the ladder and blinked. Snow fell. It was April 5, 1986, April in Paris. That tune played in my head but was soon replaced by a Puccini aria. My room was windowless and even smaller and colder than the one in *La Bohème*.

The scene seemed strangely wonderful. The only thing missing was an apparition—Nadar in his balloon, for instance, with Mimi in his arms. No balloons were overhead, however, not even the little helium-filled character from the short movie shown to us in kindergarten, *The Red Balloon*. This short movie had provided my first vision of Paris, lodging in my brain.

Summoned by sympathetic magic, a blimp eventually glided into view. Advertisements flashed on its flanks. Following its trajectory I made out the crown of the Arc de Triomphe: Belching chimney pots, black iron balconies, and pockmarked Art Nouveau turrets gently crumbled into the gutters between me and the Champs-Élysées. Farther out on the south side of the Seine stretched the lacy swan's neck of the Eiffel Tower. I blinked the snowflakes out of my eyes. The light was soft, the air

La Bohème, *based on Henri Murger's novel (poster by Adolph Hohenstein)*

scented by baguettes and croissants, coffee beans and chickens roasting—
and fuel oil and cabbages from the other maid's rooms on my floor.

The blimp's vapor trail joined the dots between the sights of Paris, the
same ones Nadar had seen from his balloon. They were still here. I unfolded
my map and traced lines to Montmartre and Belleville, the Marais, the banks
of the Seine, the graveyard at Père-Lachaise, the Latin Quarter, and Luxembourg Garden. They were places I had read about or seen on celluloid,
places I had passed through on other short visits to Paris in the 1970s and
early '80s. Now I could possess them. Paris would be mine.

I wonder if I knew on that first April morning that this would be it: I was
stuck and could not leave, indeed would spend decades prowling the streets
seeking Félix Nadar's gallery of images—the romantic men and women of
Paris' finest hour. Did I realize I would lose myself in libraries, cemeteries,
house museums and administrative offices, pestering bureaucrats, getting
married, battling the spinners of red tape over birth certificates and driver's
licenses, voter registration and noisy neighbors, unwittingly attempting to
penetrate the mysteries, the secrets of what might well be the world's most
enigmatic, compelling, paradoxical, maddening yet seductive city?

2

DECIPHERING THE PARIS PALIMPSEST

Of course I couldn't have known anything of the kind. But I must have had some inkling the first time I climbed the seven stories to my maid's room that the allure of Paris might derive as much from hidden sources as it did from the physical beauty and quality of life of the city, and that to discover them would take time.

At first I either didn't think about the magic behind the spell or attributed it to the obvious—the art and architecture, the cityscape, riverbanks and parks, cafés and outdoor restaurants; accordions in cobbled squares, Chopin in mossy churches, or Coltrane in smoky, underground clubs. Not to mention the spectacle of stylish, modish, often haughty, self-adoring, handsome or gorgeous, perversely svelte natives who were capable of challenging conventional notions about almost everything—including courtesy, metabolism, gender, morality, and hygiene.

Combine these piquant ingredients with the barrage by Hollywood, and what more need explain Paris' bizarre black-and-white magic, why look further than the mesmerizing, hedonistic surface, the great conspiracy to enjoy life that we seemed to have suspended back home?

Despite my love affair with Mimi and other romantic phantoms, I had not entirely lost my senses, nor was I easily seduced by manufactured dreams. The French had not invented love. Paris had no monopoly on romance. I knew that firsthand. The San Francisco I'd savored was undeniably bohemian and in a roughshod way romantic; Rome and Venice were supremely so. Many of the cities I'd known were as well endowed as Paris. Some were even more spectacular or exciting. They had rivers or canals, bays or waterfronts, hills and dales or real mountains. Most had stunning architecture; some had sublime weather, beautiful, stylish, sexy, friendly inhabitants, great food and abundant wine, history, mystery, and more.

So what was it about Paris? Did the yeast of romance grow on the puckered plaster like sourdough leaven? Was constant rain romantic?

During my first months in town I strolled blissfully past the foundations, the roots of romance, the big buried dark secret things that really count— the lifeblood of Paris and Parisians.

Then something clicked and I realized nothing comes from nowhere. Symptoms have a cause. Puccini's opera, Flaubert's and Victor Hugo's novels, Hollywood movies and the photos of Nadar, Brassaï, Doisneau, and Cartier-Bresson capture romance; they make people *think* Paris is romantic. They don't *make* Paris romantic.

After this revelation, everything seemed different. I saw the banks of the Seine and quays of the Canal Saint-Martin in 4-D and knew they were not fashioned in primordial times for the delectation of visitors. They were shaped by Parisians, generations of fishermen, boatmen, whores, engineers, speculators, and despots—above all, despots—each with an agenda.

The same went for the handsome old buildings on the chaotic medieval streets or the Second Empire avenues of the city rebuilt by Napoléon III and Haussmann in the mid-1800s: They had not sprouted overnight like champignons de Paris. Little was left to chance. Stagecraft was all. The components of the city would not spontaneously combust to create the urban crucible of seductive mood, the *Paris When It Sizzles* backdrop, the subtle, studied nighttime apparition of urban perfection enlivened by song, wine, and roses that everyone everywhere seemed passionate about, ready to love, sometimes to the point of delusion or obsession.

With the tingling sensation that Paris was *Paris* thanks in large part to its querulous inhabitants and bizarre culture, its literature and history, and that it might actually supply a lifetime of enigmas, pleasures, and challenges, I began a quixotic quest to uncover the romantic secrets of the City of Light.

3

A TRAMP STEAMER
TO PÈRE-LACHAISE CEMETERY

My first stop and favorite spot almost from the day I arrived was Père-Lachaise Cemetery. A direct ride on Métro line 2 or a long meandering walk from my garret, it provided air, greenery, silence, and solitude. None were available in my crow's nest in rue Laugier.

The top floor of a luxury apartment house designed by Henri Sauvage in 1904 at the pinnacle of Art Nouveau, above the apartments of the wealthy lived a stratum of squalor. This was a blend of Maxim Gorky's *The Lower Depths* and the upper deck of a vintage tramp steamer. The stained-glass windows separating the service stairway from the elevator—which was of course reserved for apartment dwellers—rattled with the shaking of each scalloped wooden tread on the seven serpentine flights of stairs. There were no Frenchmen, let alone women, on this upper deck. A dozen Moroccan and Tunisian guest workers and I lived in atonal harmony, our rooms separated by plaster panels covered with mildewed posters of palm trees and camels or *Playboy* pinups. We shared three squat toilets and a cold-water tap. Transistor radios were tuned 24-7 to dueling stations. My Mozart and Coltrane were drowned out by Maghreb ululations or Edith Piaf crooning on radio Nostalgie. I was the only tenant with a secondary education, a typewriter, or that marvel of technology, a cassette player.

I paid a year's rent up front. Beyond being cheap, these lodgings offered hidden advantages. The lack of hot running water and bathing facilities was an incentive to exploration. On my second day I bought a pass to the municipal swimming pools of Paris. This led me to discover parts of the city I might never have seen. I had no kitchen, so I got to know cafés and bistros in each arrondissement. The rooftop view from my ladder was magical, yet the lack of a proper window encouraged me to walk, read, or write outdoors much of the day, often in the Parc Monceau a few blocks away or at Père-Lachaise.

The first time I entered the monumental gateway of the cemetery, I felt part of me had always been there. I don't suffer from necrophilia and am not particularly nostalgic, but it was as if an alter ego lived a parallel existence under the climbing, winding ranges of horse chestnut trees. Père-Lachaise is where I first heard voices from Paris' past, voices eager to share secrets. They were not speaking to me but to one another, their words carrying over the off-kilter tombstones and ivy festoons.

After a few visits I decided to make a map of the graveyard's hills, roads, and pathways. I used Xs and Ys to show the essential tombs like Nadar's—surprisingly bourgeois, carefully hedged and cleaned—but also the best grave-eating trees, the best benches and views. From a spot in front of the chapel you could see across Paris. Away and below in the mist and smog were the red-and-blue piping of the Centre Pompidou, the H-shaped towers of Notre Dame, and the hovering dome of the Panthéon.

My holy of holies was a hundred yards northwest of the chapel. Readers of Balzac know the greatest moment in the early life of Balzac's most famous character, the clever, ambitious arriviste Rastignac, takes place here somewhere on the south-facing slope of the cemetery. This is where the pugnacious provincial gazes down on Paris and exclaims, "It's between you and me now!"

That spot, I reasoned, must be where Balzac is buried. His tomb is decorated with a bronze bust and a hefty bronze book to symbolize his lifelong achievement, *The Human Comedy*. Directly across the cobbled path lies Gérard de Nerval, the original Surrealist. Nerval was the genial madman who walked his pet lobster on a leash and hanged himself at the moment of his greatest glory.

Who would have guessed Charles Nodier resided only five tombs uphill from them? He gazed placidly at Balzac's left ear. Nodier was another proto-Surrealist, the patron saint of Romanticism who had written some of

Honoré de Balzac's tomb at Père-Lachaise Cemetery

my favorite stories of all time. He had welcomed Balzac, Hugo, Dumas, and others into his salon, where the Romantic movement—and the notion of modern romance—was born.

Around the corner the painter Eugène Delacroix stretched out in a black funeral barge carved with Ionic scrolls. It looked as old and mossy as Delacroix himself, a wizened centenarian the day he was born. It seemed ironic to me that

The tomb of Eugène Delacroix at Père-Lachaise Cemetery

Alfred de Musset at Père-Lachaise Cemetery

the master of modern color, the Romantic painter par excellence, was destined to spend eternity, or whatever portion of it he could claim, clad in black.

Along the winding, cobbled lanes and gravel paths lined by 70,000 tombs I gradually discovered Colette, Oscar Wilde, and Marcel Proust not to mention the proto-Romantic couple Abélard and Héloïse in a faux Gothic shrine the size of a country chapel. After more forays I followed the scent of whiskey and hash to the post-Romantic nihilist Jim Morrison of The Doors. His trashed, littered tomb was topped by a kitschy bust—later stolen.

At a shady crossroads with a fine view of the Panthéon a modest obelisk marked the home of the Hugo clan, without Victor Hugo or his wife, Adèle. I soon stumbled upon Chopin, his flower-covered tomb in deep woods, and Alfred de Musset, his sculpted effigy flanked by a weeping willow, as he had requested. Both men were jilted by the cigar-smoking, crossdressing George Sand, a prolific storyteller and the godhead of Parisian proto-feminists. Where was Sand buried? I wondered. And where was Mimi of *La Bohème*?

The men were easy to find. But where were the romantic heroines, Nerval's Jenny Colon, for instance, or Louise Colet, the poet-mistress and muse of Flaubert, Musset, and Hugo—and other sensitive souls she stalked and seduced? Where was Juliette Drouet, Victor Hugo's lifelong love?

Beyond Wilde and Proust, where were the same-sex pioneers—Joris-Karl Huysmans, for example? He was the mystic savant who had plumbed the mysteries of Paris' streets and Parisians' souls, leading Romanticism from Baudelaire across the frivolous Second Empire and Belle Époque into the modernist world of the twentieth century.

There was time. I would find them all. When I closed my eyes, a choir of voices sang in my head. They sang of love, passion, eternity, finitude, and the passage of days, months, and years. I'd never heard anything like it back home. Could the dead really sing?

On my map I drew in arrows and question marks and noted dates of birth and death, dates of shared passion and of separation. I added an N to the ones Nadar had photographed and soon realized he had known nearly all of them. From the secondhand booksellers along the Seine I bought dusty biographies and dog-eared classics. When I had done Père-Lachaise, I began exploring the other great repositories of memory at Montmartre and Montparnasse. It could take years to find all the Romantic men and women of Paris, and it would take a lifetime to read about them. More than their works, I craved to know their lives. But I had just arrived. Why hurry?

PART TWO

Discovering the First Great Romantic Circle in My New Backyard, the Marais and Ile Saint Louis

4

BASTILLE DAY

What was Henri Murger's famous line? "Bohemia is a stage in artistic life; it's the preface to the Academy, the hospital or the morgue." Félix Nadar too had seen the hungry, cold, nomadic dead end of bohemia and its "absolute, precise, and unpoetic details." It was time for me to move on.

Where to? A friend of a friend was vacating a studio apartment in the Marais. It had indoor plumbing, windows, and a kitchen and was on the first-floor French.

In an echoing courtyard behind the four-hundred-year-old Protestant church of Sainte-Marie on rue Saint-Antoine near the Bastille I climbed a cramped staircase next to a lampshade store. Then I squeezed into a hole-in-the-wall devised several centuries ago for trolls. The spot seemed cozy enough. The courtyard was shoehorned into the ruined cloister of a convent destroyed in the French Revolution. Tragedy and romance dripped like the grass-grown gutters. It seemed too good to be true.

The neighborhood I already loved. A seasonal floodplain on the Seine circa the time of Julius Caesar, it had been drained by monks, walled in, and reshaped time and again by riotous laborers. King Charles V in the mid-1300s had built bastions and the Bastille fortress to protect the eastern entry point. Then he had added two royal palaces near the Marais' wide, gently curving main street, rue Saint-Antoine. Since 1365, with a few centuries of slump, the area has been a desirable arty address with a chicken-claw medieval street plan dotted with aristocratic mansions from the late 1500s onward.

In my courtyard behind the church of Sainte-Marie another of my heroes, Théophile Gautier, author of the libretto for the ballet *Giselle* and of the first known history of Romanticism, had studied painting in an art studio. A few blocks away, on the corner of rue de la Cerisaie and rue de Lesdiguières, Balzac had lived under the eaves and honed his skills by writing potboilers. Victor Hugo's apartment on the Place des Vosges, now a house museum, was even closer to my new digs, and Gautier's parents had lived next door. I could practically reach out my window and lift the latch of Hugo's secret studio for illicit trysts. It was less than a block away. The Marais was like that—filled with hidden literary and artistic pilgrimage sites.

Certainly Balzac, Baudelaire, and Nadar would have liked my new apartment. All were famous for decamping, leaving behind unpaid debts. A back door led from my courtyard to a side street, in case the landlords or repo men arrived. Better yet, the courtyard turned out to be a *lieu de mémoire*, a historic memorial site. Reportedly it was haunted by the ghosts of nuns and the pregnant mistresses and "embarrassed" unmarried ladies sequestered in the Convent of the Visitation, the church's former name. In pre-Revolutionary days, the fruit of illicit unions was deposited at such places. Despite occasional moans from living tenants, at night the courtyard was as silent as the graves under the cobbles or the flagstones of the church next door. The ramshackle building where I lived sprouted from the buttressing like burl on a redwood.

My first night was eerily quiet. Then came morning and discovery: The lampshade store was a lampshade factory. *Brrrr, zzzzzic, tack!* Now I understood why the landlady showed the place to me in the evening. The two-story tenement shook at the firing of pneumatic staplers. Syncopated, the concert continued for eight hours a day six days a week with an hour off for lunch. Wrapped in a mummy bag and wearing earplugs I understood what twelve-tone music and mimetic prose were about. I could not help thinking of Gertrude Stein.

There was a kind of perverse romance even in my discomfort. I had not yet read either the Marquis de Sade or *The Romantic Agony*, a landmark study of Romanticism by Mario Praz, but as a lifelong lover of crime and detective novels and a fan of Alfred Hitchcock, I was predisposed to understand self-laceration, joyful misery, and other noir undercurrents.

They linked the skeletons under the church to my Revolutionary-era rooms, then ran to the phantom of the Divine Marquis, as De Sade is known to acolytes. He had been a guest from 1784 to 1789 down the road at the Bastille. The secret tunnels of noir then branched to the abodes of nearly all the great Romantic writers and many artists, including the paradoxically anti-Romantic romantic Gustave Flaubert. He had delighted in the description of Emma Bovary's death by poisoning and had defined the human heart as a "necropolis of memories." He had also famously said that when he saw a crib he imagined a tomb, and the naked body of a lovely woman evoked a cadaver. Happily I did not share Flaubert's visions but was captivated.

Even better was Charles *Flowers of Evil* Baudelaire, a pioneer of modernism, if that word means a world stripped of the superfluous and ephemeral, a lightless place where myths, superstition, and religion fail as crutches and training wheels.

Both had lived nearby—Flaubert on Boulevard du Temple a few blocks northeast, Baudelaire in at least two apartments on the Ile Saint-Louis a quarter mile away.

As the months wore on, those tunnels of bright darkness seemed to me to extend to ostensibly normal Frenchmen and -women I had met during my first year in Paris, and others I had read or heard about in the city. Noir was half of black-and-white. If any city was a study in *noir et blanc*—be it black-and-white photography, film, or literature—Paris was it. The French versions of all three techniques were born during the Age of Romanticism. So was the concept of the daredevil avenger-antihero of the noir crime novel genre, the so-called *polar,* a Parisian specialty I learned to love.

Nurtured by the bile and black milk of Byron and Blake, Paris' phantoms of the opera, its werewolves and vampires of both sexes abounded a hundred and fifty years ago, and as far as I could see were plentiful now on screen and in the streets, somehow adding to the romantic charge. They had populated the "Capital of the Nineteenth Century," as the tragic theorist of modernity Walter Benjamin had called it, a city poised on the cusp of a grown-up, godless future. Strangely, with all those skeletons and secret passageways underneath me, I had never felt so happy or at home.

5

GUEST APPEARANCES

Shortly after I moved to the Marais, I was summoned by a friend to a birthday party to celebrate the last year in my third decade. It coincided roughly with the obsolescence of my first Paris calendar. The other guests drank tea or coffee. Since it was winter and because I had been living for several months inside a mummy bag without heat in subzero weather, I sipped scotch and took a third helping of thickly frosted homemade chocolate cake.

As the party was breaking up, a knock came at the door. There followed a tall, slim, surprisingly healthy young woman with glowing cheeks and big blue eyes framed by a thatch of brown hair streaked prematurely with gray. This was no Mimi. She did not smoke, pout, or scowl, nor did she strike superior poses. She wore no makeup or nail polish and was shod in sensible shoes instead of provocative pumps or booties. Smiling, she explained she had walked across Paris and apologized for being late. She could not be French.

My guess was only part right: The mystery guest turned out to have been born in Paris and to have spent much of her life in the Marais. She had been more of a nomad than I, living and traveling worldwide. She was not a real Parisian, not to the French: She did not descend from a Gallic warrior such as Vercingétorix or Charlemagne, or some other mythical forebear. The same friend had summoned her. It was a setup. She had been living for decades a few blocks from my new apartment, was enthusiastic about photography and literature, had missed the movie but loved *The Red Balloon* as a photo book, spoke Italian, French, and English, and stood little chance of escaping my attentions. They appeared to be unwanted.

Spurred by her indifference, I gave pursuit in the style of Nadar, Hugo, Balzac, and Baudelaire, not to mention Alfred de Musset, the most debauched poet, playwright, and novelist of them all. Each is a role model to Parisian males whether

Alphonse Karr: the changelessness of change

they know it or not. After a suite of book exchanges, romantic dinners, walks in cemeteries and parks or on the quays of the Seine, followed by years of cohabitation and several blundered proposals of marriage, she at last agreed to hyphenate her last name on official French documents, a rash but so far enduring arrangement.

Like the changeless cityscape of Paris, little outwardly has changed in our lives since then except perhaps a degree of mellowing and in my case the ravages of time. As the archetypal Parisian Romantic Age writer Alphonse Karr quipped in 1848 after yet another revolution and change in regime, "The more things change, the more they stay the same."

Karr's remark was profound, with great philosophical, political, and cultural implications. In certain cases, however, his formula applies to lifestyle. It sums up why if I raise my eyes today from my computer screen, I no longer see the garret in rue Laugier or the icicle-hung ruined cloister behind the church of Sainte-Marie, where I once lived and from which I was evicted less than two years after moving in. I now gaze at the tall bronze column on Place de la Bastille a few blocks farther east. In other words, I have shifted a hundred paces in about thirty years. After moving from Right Bank to Left,

then back to the Right, from the Marais to Saint-Germain to the edge of
Père-Lachaise, where I perched above the tombs for nearly twenty years,
my office of late is once again in a garret, atop a vintage building in the
Marais a few blocks from the early addresses of Balzac, Baudelaire, Gautier,
and Hugo.

6

THE ROMANCE OF
REBELLIOUSNESS

Paris is a city of symbols and allegories. Crowning the column that I stare at daily in the center of the busy traffic circle beyond my skylights is the gilded *Spirit of Freedom*. This elegant statue depicts a winged androgynous homoerotic youth grasping a torch in one hand. In the other are the broken chains of despotism. The sculpture represents the spirit of revolution and resistance now institutionalized in France. Tamed by prosperity, that spirit remains inspiringly romantic and uncannily contemporary. Every French man, woman, and child is and will forever be a David fighting the great global Goliath.

The monster is bent on standardizing the world and dethroning the French language, French culture, French food, French national identity, and the "French model"—or so it seems to many of the French. Why else would you try to pass laws to define what French "national identity" means or lobby to get UNESCO to declare French cuisine and the French way of eating worthy of protection on the list of World Heritage "intangibles"?

Running across and up and down the Bastille column in gold lettering I can read the engraved names of the hundreds who died fighting for liberty in Paris—liberty of expression, opinion, and thought; freedom of the press; freedom from oppression, homegrown or external; the freedom to choose to have or not to have a religion and a monarchy or a republic, to believe in God, existentialism, or the absurd. Many of the fallen are entombed under

Place de la Bastille and the "Spirit of Freedom"

the column's massive plinth, which is undermined by several Métro lines and the Canal Saint-Martin. During revolutions, umpteen barricades have been erected near the column, and riotous behavior continues at the Bastille today. The column is the starting or ending point of marches and demonstrations traditionally emanating from the political left. Bastille Day and May Day are the main official celebrations, but life in Paris often starts where official events end.

That's why the column also stands unofficially nowadays for sexual freedom, women's rights, freedom of choice, freedom to marry for love and not biology, freedom to organize workers and strike against the one percent who don't pay taxes, and a myriad of other freedoms and rights. Such freedoms and rights are fought for by trade unions, progressive politicians, subsidized moviemakers, actors and students, unemployed youths, retirees without a trace of gray hair, and the city's phalanxes of modern-day romantic bourgeois bohemians. All expect to receive child subsidies for creating large families, day care for one and all, and grants for an array of essential human activities meant to impose or maintain social justice and the revered

French model. This model has nothing to do with the fashion industry, which is also subsidized. Vociferous protesting and occasional violence are de rigueur. In Paris the pursuit of happiness and the expression of romantic feelings often involve misery, anger, altercation, anxiety, melancholy, and histrionics—with plenty of metaphorical heads on pikes.

Sculpted in extra-large font on the column are three dates: July 27, 28, and 29, 1830. They refer not to the first great French Revolution of 1789 that brought down King Louis XVI and the Bastille and ushered in the Terror and the tyrant Napoléon the Great. Rather they commemorate that other French revolution, one of the biggest of the tumultuous nineteenth century, the so-called Three Glorious Days of 1830.

This was the brief but bloody summertime struggle that ousted the Bourbon monarchy and France's last absolutist theocrat, Charles X. As was to be expected, hoped-for democratic republicanism was stifled, and the outcome was the reign of the "Citizen King" Louis Philippe, who ruled until ousted in 1848. The revolutionary spirit went underground into its network of bright tunnels, springing up again at midcentury and once more during the 1871 Commune struggle. Each time the violence was greater than before.

A barricade in 1848 (as drawn by Adolphe Hervier)

Paris escaped largely unscathed from the two world wars. But it took a beating in 1848, with 20,000 killed in four days—10,000 of the corpses dumped in the Seine. During the winter and spring of 1870 and 1871, the city was wrecked by Prussian artillery and civil war, with tens of thousands dead. The scars from both conflicts are still visible.

Why does this matter? The political and military upheavals in July 1830, February 1848, and the winter and spring of 1870–1871 might never have happened if another kind of revolt, an unexpected literary, theatrical, and artistic revolution, had not occurred earlier in 1830, in the month of February. It was this cultural revolt that turned Paris into the capital of Romanticism and began the march to the City of Light and love, the city of romance.

7

DEFINING THE UNDEFINABLE:
ROMANTICISM

What exactly is Romanticism, and when was it born? Historians will remind you that the roots of the movement reach far down into the loam of time, but the fact remains that 1830 was the year a motley group of French Romantics gathered around Victor Hugo and his friends and rivals and swept Paris into the paradoxically romantic modern age, or the unexpectedly modern Romantic Age. Their meeting place each Sunday during the 1820s and early 1830s was a few blocks from the Place de la Bastille on the Seine at the Arsenal Library. Then, as now, this repository of manuscripts, incunabula, and books, haunted by darting shadows, sits astride remnants of the seven-hundred-year-old fortifications that culminated in the Bastille fortress, the two-sided symbol of oppression and freedom.

The Bastille and Arsenal have a great deal to do with twenty-first-century romance, I have learned. Take the simple fact that the city's allure is felt everywhere, but nowhere more strongly than in the United States. The laundry list of reasons includes the proverbial attraction of opposites, the American love-hate affair with France and the French. But it starts with a clear-cut historical fact: France and America are children of the Age of Enlightenment and of revolutions. One major difference marks the infancy and adolescence of these revolutionary nations. America had George Washington and Thomas Jefferson, France Napoléon Bonaparte and Robespierre.

From the American Revolution of 1776 sprang pragmatic optimism and democratic continuity in a "New World" with lots of room to roam, a place free from European historical baggage. From the French Revolution of 1789 grew the cult of perpetual struggle and world-weary pessimism, the guillotine, and Romanticism, the ambiguous creature facing both backward and forward, like the ancient Roman god Janus. He is alive and well today in the heart of every French citizen.

Visitors are understandably enraptured by the public displays of affection, lust, or anger in Paris, exhibitions unlike anything in the Anglo-Saxon, African, or Asian worlds. Sitting in cafés, they may happily reread *A Moveable Feast* or enjoy on their handheld devices their favorite scenes from *Breathless* or Billy Wilder's *Sabrina* or something more recent—*Ratatouille* or *Midnight in Paris*. They might melt with delight into the Impressionist canvases at the Musée d'Orsay. Rarely do they suspect the glamour and chic and the carefree atmosphere of the City of Light grew from and still feed off the dark fountainheads of riot, rebellion, mayhem, and melancholy—and the subversive literature, art, and music of the Romantic Age.

Depending on which flavor of academic scholarship you prefer, that age had its roots in the Renaissance or Mannerist periods in Germany, England, and Italy. It first bloomed in France in the garden of Jean-Jacques Rousseau in the 1780s. Others point to François-René de Chateaubriand's château circa 1800 or Victor Hugo's Paris apartments in the 1820s and '30s. The time frame depends on who you ask. All agree Romanticism reached its apogee in Paris in the 1820s to 1840s before fading, according to some circa 1850 to make way for the anti-Romantic Napoléon III and the Second Empire, according to others in the 1880s when the late Romantic Decadents took over. Yet others say the period stretched until 1914—conveniently enduring through the debauched Belle Époque before expiring in time for World War I and the arrival of that other perennial of the pigeonhole specialists, modernism.

There are those, however, who look beyond dates and tags and believe the Romantic spirit never died, that it overflowed, spread, fractured, came back together again like the Seine around its islands, morphed into other isms, changed its name and address dozens of times as Nadar and Balzac did and, like a phantom or vampire or other supernatural invention of the Romantic Age, it thrives today in billions of brains and hearts. The mother ship, the source, the living shrine of Romanticism remains the city of Paris.

8

AN ARSENAL OF
POETIC WEAPONRY

"Everybody knows the long, gloomy-looking building called the Arsenal, aligned with the quai des Célestins at the bottom of rue de Morland, overlooking the river," wrote Alexandre Dumas in his memoirs.

Well, maybe not everyone, not now, even though the Arsenal Library hasn't changed much since the 1820s. That is when the long, gloomy building of pale limestone with a series of suites of gilded, paneled salons became the workshop of the early Romantics—nearly all of them.

The crowd that climbed the carved-wood and brick back staircase with its thick pirate-ship banister was often headed by Alexandre Dumas. Still in his twenties, he had not yet written *The Three Musketeers* or become rich, famous, and immensely fat. He was the protégé of Charles Nodier, the Arsenal's eclectic

Alexandre Dumas when young (by Achille Devéria)

Charles Nodier at Père-Lachaise Cemetery

Charles X, the kinky absolutist dandy (attributed to Elizabeth Latimer)

librarian, himself a renowned writer of stories and novels. Among Nodier's best are *Le Vampire* and *Night Demons*, collections of fantastic tales, and the quirky novel that gave Parisian bohemianism its name, *The Story of the King of Bohemia and his Seven Castles*. Paris' artistic bohemia and its Romantics are if not inseparable at least closely linked.

Open-ended, nonsense, and fantasy fiction was Charles Nodier's specialty. "If he didn't know something, he invented," Dumas recalled. But Nodier's inventions were "far more likely, far more ingenious and romantic . . . and far nearer the truth than the reality itself."

For Nodier, reality was *not* stranger than fiction. Fiction was unquestionably more startling, shocking, and disconcerting than oppressive, predictable reality.

Reality meant the rituals and traditions of the restored Bourbon monarchy, which lasted from 1814 to 1830—with a tragicomic interval of a hundred days when Emperor Napoléon returned to power in 1815 before being crushed at Waterloo. Ruling over this reactionary regime were the surviving younger brothers of Louis XVI: Louis XVIII, then Charles X. Their goal was to turn the grandfather clock back to the days of the Sun King—the

Balzac, as a beardless youth and in his prime (attributed to Achille Devéria)

despot Louis XIV, who ruled by divine right. The goal of the Romantics among many other things was to defeat them.

Artistic and literary traditionalism under France's restored monarchs was about conforming to the classical and neoclassical precepts of beauty, symmetry, and order. These had been built up from the Renaissance to the Revolution of 1789. But the revolutionary genie of freedom, the one dancing naked atop the Bastille column, had slipped out of its bottle.

That's why from the beginning Romanticism was more than a literary or artistic movement and why it endures today. It was political—though some of its main figures were unwitting or unwilling activists. Many of the Romantics had their works censored. All lived under the threat of losing their livelihood or going to prison. With few exceptions they wrote ostensibly innocuous tales or set stories and plays in the past or in a foreign country, to be able to mock the status quo and the Classicists who dominated the French Academy and ran the theaters, magazines, and publishing houses.

· BALZAC ·

The notable exception to this rule was Honoré de Balzac, an unkempt, often reclusive provincial who looked like a caricature and was a rebel and reckless adventurer from cradle to grave. His self-imposed mission was to paint a vast, minutely detailed fresco in words of his times, exploring French society from gutter to gilded salon and grave, with a cast of over two thousand characters. The real star of his show was Paris, the city, in all its muck and splendor. Playing variations on themes by Dante (the *Divine Comedy* had recently been translated into French), Balzac called his multiple-part series the *Human Comedy*.

Though Balzac and Dumas remain giants, the greatest and still the best-known among Nodier's flock was the supremely ambitious Victor Hugo. He was a regular at the Arsenal dinners and literary salon called Le Cénacle. The word evoked antiquity and gatherings of noble minds but also the Last Supper. At the Arsenal, everyone could be an apostle of art and literature.

Unlike a Parisian soirée today, dinner in those days would begin promptly and last from six to eight o'clock—unthinkably early and suspiciously Anglo-Saxon by modern Paris standards. The young, slim Dumas had the place of honor, between Madame Nodier and her daughter Marie. After delicious food and abundant wine, the supper club adjourned and the salon began. The flamboyant pianist and composer Franz Liszt brought his lover Marie Flavigny d'Agoult. She was a popular novelist who wrote under a pseudonym, Daniel Stern; the knowledge of this was Paris' worst-kept secret. The peacock-like poet and future statesman Alphonse de Lamartine, the budding blond poet and celebrated womanizer Alfred de Musset, the moody painter Eugène Delacroix, the explosive, expansive Balzac and gentle Théophile Gautier, the cryptic literary critic and novelist Charles-Augustin Sainte-Beuve, the vain playwright De Vigny and his voracious actress-mistress Marie Dorval, the talented writer of fantastic tales and future preserver of France's Gothic heritage Prosper Mérimée, and a dozen other potentates and prima donnas might put in an appearance.

Two hours, from eight to ten, were devoted to conversation and readings of poetry or novels. Afterward, the guests danced quadrilles and waltzes. It seemed a study in art-loving innocence. Yet had he attended, the wickedly perspicacious King Charles X might have realized he was underwriting a terrorist cell, a group of young revolutionaries destined to inspire, aid, and abet those who would dethrone him.

I had never heard of the Arsenal until I moved to Paris. Only by pulling up the roots of a dozen Romantics did I discover they were growing from under this apparently unremarkable building I had passed by a hundred times.

Wending my way down the familiar curving streets of the Marais en route to the Arsenal not long ago, I rounded a gendarmes' barracks, then mounted the imposing back staircase of the library, with its massive carved banister nearly four hundred years old. It was the same staircase the Romantics had climbed before me.

Waiting upstairs was not Charles Nodier but his current successor, the library's director Bruno Blasselle. His mild manners and courtesy, even his dark good looks and tall, thin frame, were uncanny reminders of the enigmatic Nodier.

"You shall soon see," said Blasselle when I asked whether the Arsenal was haunted, as I'd heard.

Ushering me through stuffy rooms now open only to library personnel, the director acknowledged that he had occupied Nodier's apartment for a number of years but no longer lived in it. Closing the creaking doors behind us as we progressed over waxed parquet floors, Blasselle paused and indicated a fireplace. It was the twin of the one in my bedroom, installed in 1784.

"This is the salon," Blasselle said, "and that is where Nodier would stand, leaning on the chimneypiece."

The sounds of traffic faded. Time suspended its flight. As I took in the paintings, books, and objects Nodier had lived with, breathing in the rich loamy atmosphere layered with memories and dust, I summoned to mind Dumas' famous description of an evening at the salon.

"[T]he light illuminated white paneled walls with Louis XV moldings, and furniture of extreme simplicity, comprising a dozen chairs or easy-chairs and a sofa covered with red cashmere, the hangings being of the same color," Dumas detailed. At the time there was a bust of Victor Hugo, who was already famous, and a statue of King Henri IV. I could not see the bust of Hugo or the portrait of Nodier and the landscape of a view in the Alps that Dumas described. But the panels and moldings and the statue of Henri IV were still here.

I asked where Mademoiselle Nodier's piano had been. Bruno Blasselle showed me the spot, on the south side of the salon near a door to Nodier's

Role model: Lamartine the Romantic poet, statesman, narcissist (attributed to Elizabeth Latimer)

bedroom. "The salon looks much bigger in the drawings of the time," Blasselle remarked, perhaps sensing my surprise. "The room was uncluttered then."

The people of the time were also much shorter and smaller than we are today.

"When he leaned against the chimneypiece," Blasselle added, apparently referring to Dumas' account, "it meant he was going to tell a story."

Victor Hugo leads the Romantics holding a banner that reads: "Ugly Is Beautiful" (caricature by Benjamin Roubaud)

The quirky Nodier was a spellbinder. Latecomers bowed silently and sat or leaned against the paneled walls until Nodier had finished. "We did not applaud," remembered Dumas. "Do we applaud the murmur of a stream, the song of a bird, the perfume of a flower?"

Applause followed the readings by others. Alphonse Prat de Lamartine, now little read outside France, had ousted Chateaubriand and established himself as the national poet-god, the master of melancholy, wistfulness, lost love, and hopeless battles heroically fought to defend king and country and then later the secularized French republic he briefly led. Lamartine's ego was even larger than that of Chateaubriand or Victor Hugo, the rising demigod with an unnaturally bulging brow, the man for whom the term *highbrow* seems to have been coined.

Awarded a government stipend when barely twenty, the prodigious Hugo wrote reams of lyrical poetry and provocative anticlassical plays full

of passionate love and murder, betrayal, and royal buffoonery in the style of Shakespeare. It was the mocking of kings—even those long dead—that got him in trouble. He would soon write his sprawling evergreen novels with plots that exalted the horrors and torturous passions of the Middle Ages, a time that seemed reassuringly predictable to inhabitants of the frenzied nineteenth century. Gothic was the rage thanks largely to Hugo. He quickly outshined Chateaubriand, Lamartine, and Nodier, bringing on their wrath.

The brash twenty-five-year-old Hugo wrote the manifesto of Romanticism, included in the preface to his play *Cromwell*. It thrilled friends, family, and august assemblies when he read it aloud. "Another era is about to begin, for the world and for poetry," Hugo declaimed, "the fundamental difference that separates modern from ancient art, the present form from the defunct form or, to use less definite but more popular terms, *romantic* literature from *classical* literature." He continued with striking self-confidence and segued to the phrase "the grotesque and the sublime," attributing to these "types" the birth of "modern genius." The kicker came with Hugo's famous heartfelt cry, "The beautiful has but one type, the ugly has a thousand."

Modernism, the Age of the Ugly, the age of anti-everything, the age we still inhabit, had entered the world disguised in the dark robes of Romanticism. The year was 1827, the place Paris.

Waltzing in and out of the salon alongside Hugo and his beloved wife Adèle was a sometime guest, the round-shouldered, long-nosed, self-consciously unprepossessing and abrasively irreverent Sainte-Beuve, a cross of Judas and Faust.

As I stood now in the cluttered salon dreamily pondering, I was tempted to take the ghost of Adèle by the hand. But there was no music and no room to waltz amid the file boxes.

I followed Bruno Blasselle through handsome seventeenth-century rooms. We descended a rough staircase into the basement and stopped short facing the foundations. Made of massive, closely fitted blocks, the foundations ran for a hundred yards to the east, disappearing into darkness.

"The city walls of the 1360s," Blasselle said, "built by King Charles V, the same walls that ran along the Seine, up the Arsenal Basin to the Bastille,

Adèle Hugo, model wife and adulteress (drawn by Célestin Nanteuil)

and all the way around the Right Bank of Paris under the Grands Boulevards."

"So they really are still here."

"They really are."

Much in Paris, Blasselle agreed, is hidden from view.

"Isn't it interesting," he added, letting the sentence hang.

"What?" I asked. "That the Place de la Bastille is where the Revolution began and the barricades are still built nowadays?" I paused to observe his placid expression. "And the boulevards are where the theaters were and still are today, the theaters where the subversive plays were produced."

In a pleasant daze, on the way back home from the Arsenal I detoured to rue Saint-Paul and stood beneath the cracked, leaning sixteenth-century turret that juts from the corner of rue des Lions, a Marais landmark.

"It was here," I said to myself and an imaginary interlocutor, staring up, "the secret room Sainte-Beuve rented to complete the seduction of Adèle Hugo. That's what drove Victor Hugo to greatness, they say—the pain, the suffering, the humiliation of adultery and betrayal transformed him from a mere narcissist into a literary genius."

Were adultery, betrayal, and licentiousness part of the romantic spell of Paris?

I blinked in the gathering darkness at the unlikely love nest. The rectangular tower dates to the late 1500s and has tiny windows once used by archers during the Wars of Religion. "To think," I mused, "it was all the fault of *Cromwell* and *Hernani*."

This required explanation.

It took me about seven minutes to walk northeast via rue Saint-Antoine to the barrel-vaulted carriage entrance of Hôtel de Sully, a mansion celebrated for its beauty and its history of perfidious love and faithless passion.

As I passed over the heavy cobblestones through the first monumental courtyard—the one between the busy street and the south-facing wings of the mansion—I admired the carved sculptures. They represent the four elements and two seasons, fall and winter. The tan-colored limestone crawled with ornament and caught the dying light. The shadows, long on the stonework, caused the sensual four elements and the vigorous, grape-laden figure of fall to smile. Even shivering old man winter looked less cold than normal.

This palace, which was built in the 1620s, is the finest baroque town house in Paris and was occupied by the family of the staggeringly wealthy duc de Sully, Henri IV's minister of finance. Sully helped the king dream up the scheme of Place des Vosges, the Marais' centerpiece square. Restored with passion and fidelity over several decades, the town house was the perfect backdrop in the late 1980s for the film version of Choderlos de Laclos' scandalous late-1700s novel *Dangerous Liaisons*. Along with the Marquis de Sade's *Justine*, that cult book distilled the cynicism and decadence of the end of the ancien régime. But was it really entirely over?

I recalled now having watched the cast and director of *Dangerous Liaisons* at work here in the 1980s and thinking then how wonderfully appropriate the location was. Sully lived to be very old and was married to a much younger woman who openly cuckolded him, bringing her lovers to dinner. The novel was about deception and adultery, the use of love and passion to punish, torture, and debauch a ravishing adolescent and ruin the lives of others, all the while "enjoying" life and lust to the hilt. It was quintessentially French.

Dangerous Liaisons had also been the most obvious literary inspiration for Sainte-Beuve's affair with Adèle Hugo. During the affair he wrote an outrageously romantic novel, *Volupté*, about it. The novel, a transparent roman à clef, must have seemed especially offensive to Victor Hugo. Everyone knew the true identities of the characters.

Glancing at the mansion's sculptures as I walked north, I turned to see youthful spring and bounteous summer staring down from the rear façade facing the back garden courtyard and its tall slate-roofed free-standing *orangerie*, the oldest in Paris. Leaving this garden of sensual provocations through the unmarked back door, I emerged under the arcades of Place des Vosges. I checked my watch while crossing the square under the canopy of trimmed linden trees. It had taken me another three minutes. Added to the seven minutes from the turret to the mansion's rear door, I guessed it would have taken Adèle Hugo or Sainte-Beuve a total of nine or ten minutes of transit to affect a tryst.

My imaginary interlocutor was perplexed. I had refused to say a thing to her until we sat on a bench, half hidden by the leafy symmetry of the trees, and faced the Hugo apartment. It is now the Musée Victor Hugo, a house museum. Victor and Adèle had lived and loved in this royal address before the treacherous Sainte-Beuve set them drifting apart.

The spot was a risky place to sit with your beloved. Everyone in Paris knows this square and its thirty-six brick-and-stone pavilions built between 1605 and 1612. They also know that illicit couples have used Place des Vosges as a favorite rendezvous since the days of the supreme philanderer, the garlic-eating, wine-swilling good king Henri IV—a man the French to this day rate among the top ten most popular of historical figures. Henri IV had the square built. Henri IV was the king who sent messengers a week before his arrival to order his lady friends to cease bathing. Henri IV lives on.

9

LOVE TRIANGLE: VICTOR, ADÈLE, AND SAINTE-BEUVE

Victor Hugo and Adèle Foucher met and fell in love as children. Actually their romance was planned by their fathers before either was born, in 1802 and 1803 respectively.

Step back in time. At the turn of the nineteenth century when Napoléon ruled France as first consul, then emperor, one of his top generals was Joseph Léopold Sigisbert Hugo, Victor's father. Léopold's best friend was a certain Pierre Foucher, a high-level bureaucrat in the revolutionary and then Napoléonic regimes. Buddies but also neighbors, Léo and Pierre egged each other on to produce children who could in turn marry and continue the friendship down the generations.

This thoroughly romantic, preposterous plan occurred to General Hugo before Romanticism had a proper name. Admittedly the celebrated woman of letters Madame de Staël first addressed the topic of *romantisme* around 1800, so the notion was in the air. About the same time the poet, novelist, and future statesman François-René de Chateaubriand was penning his first melancholic autobiographical tales, including *René*:

"*Arise quickly oh ye desired winds, which shall waft René into the regions of another life!*" wrote Chateaubriand. "Speaking thus I walked with hasty strides, my countenance inflamed, the wind whistling in my hair, regardless of the storm; and the frost, enchanted and tormented as if possessed by the demon of my heart."

Chateaubriand shaped or warped the minds of a generation, starting with Victor Hugo. Hugo declared, "It's Chateaubriand or bust." Hugo's fellow Romantic novelist George Sand similarly exclaimed, "I was René." She turned out to be much more. Even Charles Baudelaire, a generation later, was still infected by the eternal and cosmopolitan René.

In those days of Sturm und Drang, the doctrine of happiness springing from tortured unhappiness filled the air, a tantalizing zeitgeist heralded by Beethoven and Schubert blowing south from Germany. Goethe's suicidal Young Werther remained the rage, and the fantastical Faust, like the demonic characters in the tales of E. T. A. Hoffmann, added supernatural spice. The end of absolutism, the French Revolution, the Terror, and the never-ending Europe-wide Napoleonic Wars that followed were soaking the continent in blood.

As the child of a medal-spangled general who rose to be governor of Napoleonic provinces in Italy and Spain, Victor saw with his own eyes the hangings and butchery depicted by Goya, and knew when very young what it was to be a respected, feared, yet detested conqueror of nations. France was at its military zenith, sending hundreds of thousands of young men to the slaughter. After multiple separations and reunions, Victor's mercurial parents split for good. Napoléon fell. France was prostrate under the heels of the Bourbons again.

Adèle Foucher's dark looks and mass of black hair reminded Victor of a girl he'd loved in Spain, his first great unfulfilled passion. Unlike Victor's mysterious dream girl or the characters described by Goethe, however, the young Adèle was an energetic tomboy and anything but sexy, voluptuous, or melancholic. Her life and her imagination were flatlands compared to Victor's thunder-swept peaks and valleys. She seemed the straightforward product of a loving family and was in no particular rush to grow up or marry. Flattered by his chaste devotion and proclamations, she didn't share Victor's violent adolescent passions; in fact she didn't even like his poetry. Adèle told him this, but after years of siege he battered down her defenses and dragged her into church.

Still in their teens, they tied the knot in massive Saint-Sulpice in Paris' fashionable Saint-Germain-des-Prés neighborhood, producing four children in rapid succession. They lived nearby in rue de Vaugirard, then moved a few blocks away, beyond the south side of the Luxembourg Garden to a handsome house on rue Notre Dame des Champs. Their happiness seemed guaranteed, but it was short lived.

Victor's fame, fortune, and outsize ego swelled like Nadar's balloon. Adèle wound up chained to the nursery in the shadows of the great man. As time went by, Victor metamorphosed into a priapic beast. Some of his biographers describe him as a Minotaur, the natural son of his oversexed father, racked by insatiable urges but otherwise gentle and kind. Adèle was worn out and in need of tenderness. When reports of his sorties with bohemian artists' models reached her, she was wounded but secretly relieved.

Enter Sainte-Beuve.

France's premier critic, the young Charles-Augustin Sainte-Beuve had fallen in love with Adèle before setting eyes on her, through Victor's poems. They portrayed her as an angel, a Madonna, a dark-haired Spanish beauty with pale skin and big black eyes. Sainte-Beuve had also fallen in love in a brotherly, asexual way with Victor: Was he not the heroic leader of the Romantics?

It was Victor who sought out Sainte-Beuve to thank him for his favorable review in *Le Globe*. It was Victor who insisted Sainte-Beuve visit them at home, a few doors down from Sainte-Beuve's own apartment, and become part of Hugo's personal Cénacle, share their table and become the godfather of their last child. Victor, Adèle, Sainte-Beuve, and the four Hugo children became inseparable. When the Hugo family moved, Sainte-Beuve did as well, renting an apartment a few doors away.

Later, while Victor was busily writing, casting, and directing his plays, Sainte-Beuve watched over the Hugo household. He played with the children, becoming Adèle's confidant, confessor, and mentor. He paid attention. He complimented her. He adored and revered her and wrote her love poems and passionate letters. And she began to feel affection and pity for him. He was physically weak, small, ugly, unloved and vulnerable. Yet he had a brilliant mind and a hungry heart and was as desperate for tenderness as she.

Their affair took years to mature. Adèle was torn. With cool efficiency she mastered the arts of perfidy. Sainte-Beuve was formidable, maintaining a friendship with Victor while seducing his wife and openly admitting his conflicted love for her—protected by chivalric French notions of gallantry and the so-called *droit à la passion*, notions that live on today.

The toad, the hideous hunchback who later became Quasimodo in Hugo's great novel, gradually won Adèle away. Hugo had proclaimed the doctrine of "ugly is beautiful," had he not? When Victor, Adèle, and their children moved to the Place des Vosges, the stalker Sainte-Beuve rented rooms in the bulging old building with the turret teetering over rue Saint-Paul.

"And then what happened?" asks my imaginary interlocutor.

"*Hernani* happened," I whisper conspiratorially, "and *Lucrèce Borgia*, and the great cultural Revolution of 1830."

10

THE BATTLE OF HERNANI

As the melodrama of Adèle and Sainte-Beuve was unfolding before the incredulous eyes of Victor Hugo, he was furiously penning poems, a novel, and the play that would transform him into a superstar and set Paris on fire—literally.

During the interminable rehearsals—nearly sixty—did anyone in Hugo's entourage notice the eerie parallel: The climax of *Hernani*, a convoluted tale of passion, power, revenge, and honor, came in the last act when the newlyweds commit suicide together? Hugo's heroine was an Adèle look-like—secretly an avatar of the Spanish girl he'd dreamed of when young. The name Hernani was a bastardization of the real Ernani, the town in Basque country Victor had traveled through en route to his father's palace in Spain.

Knowing these spine-tingling details, did the two-faced Sainte-Beuve worry about the future of his friend Victor and his lover Adèle, the frustrated mother of four, about to be killed on stage in fiction?

The play's heady cocktail of doomed, tainted love and political rebellion are what drive the action and are the reason *Hernani* is still performed today, as I was able to witness. If you missed the play, you might have seen the opera: Verdi's even more popular, romantic, and less believable *Ernani*.

How to summarize an overblown, intricately plotted historical tragicomedy that originally called for twenty-five actors and ran a seat-numbing several hours?

Dateline Spain in the early 1500s. The banished nobleman-brigand Hernani plots to avenge his father's death, ordained by the despotic Spanish king, soon to be crowned Holy Roman Emperor Charles V. Hernani and the king are besotted with the same femme fatale, Doña Sol. But she is promised to her lustful uncle, Ruy Gomez, also infatuated and bloody minded.

Beyond the implausibility of the love trapezoid of three men and one woman, even more implausibly Hernani agrees to kill himself by drinking poison from a horn if his jailer lets him kill the king first. The king discovers the plot, unexpectedly pardons the conspirators, Hernani and Doña Sol are married, and then even more inexplicably, the horn sounds from off-stage. Doña Sol sees that her consort is going to drink poison and snatches the horn from his hands. She gulps half the contents before he can stop her, then dies as Hernani drains the dregs and keels over.

Opening night was February 25, 1830, the venue the Comédie-Française. Built in the 1790s, the venerable quilted jewel box of a theater faces Palais Royal to this day. As I lined up to buy tickets to a recent production, I discovered it would be performed across town at the Théâtre du Vieux-Colombier. I wondered why the play was to run until February 18. Why not celebrate the anniversary night of February 25? Then I remembered the original opening was chaotic and violent, and the theater was trashed. Surely *Hernani* couldn't wreck a theater all these years later? It's among the most performed French plays of all time alongside that late Romantic warhorse *Cyrano de Bergerac*, another soul-satisfying tragicomic masterpiece with an unhappy ending.

Luckily the director had edited down the lines, pared out two acts, and trimmed the cast to five. He had also placed the stage crosswise with the audience on both sides. Before three of the performances a series of thematic debates featured administrators, a philosopher, and a historian of theater. The theme was the theater as battlefield. This followed the themes of faithfulness (meaning unfaithfulness) and time, discussed earlier. I attended the debate about political, moral, and social battles.

Disappointingly people did not come to blows. But the talk was pugnacious in a perfectly French highbrow way—and was thoroughly Romantic. The themes, aspirations, fears, hopes, and dreams of many Parisians today are

still the same as those of the
visionary Victor Hugo. They
confirm what I have come to
call the Alphonse Karr Principle: Things change, yet
they stay the same, and for
things to remain the same
they must appear to have
changed.

There are multiple ver-
sions of the opening night in
1830, the opening shot in the
war the Romantics waged on
the Classicists. That war spread
to the streets of the city and
flared into a full-blown revolution after press censorship was

An exciting night at the theater (as seen by Daumier)

put into effect in late July. This night at the Paris opera has gone down in
history as the Battle of Hernani.

Alexandre Dumas' account is not exciting—the musketeer engaged in
shouting matches but downplayed his role: He was a friend, rival, and peer
of Hugo, not an acolyte. Several years earlier Dumas had authored an equally
revolutionary play, *Henri III*, that paved the way for *Hernani*.

Théophile Gautier instead played a leading role in the battle, serving as
a lieutenant in Hugo's rowdy Romantic Army. His incomplete account is
high color. It was left unfinished, tragically, because Gautier, moved to excess by his recollections, slumped over and died while writing it. That
chapter was the last passionate torrent of ink spilled in the course of a long,
extraordinary life of love and letters.

"The rehearsals were going on," Gautier recalled. "Judging by the ex-
citement already aroused it was easy to foresee the first performances would
be riotous. My dearest wish, my highest ambition was to be at the battle."
But how to get tickets? Victor Hugo was doling them out. Gautier was unknown, a teenage art student—his first vocation was painting and he famously coined the phrase "art for art's sake."

Enter the child prodigy Gérard de Nerval—a brilliant manic-depressive with a pet lobster, the man who at age seventeen translated Goethe into French so brilliantly that Goethe wrote to thank him. Nerval, a former schoolmate of Gautier's, was a friend of Hugo's. Mischievous Nerval appeared clutching a set of square red tickets with "Hierro" scrawled on them. It was the code word. In Spanish—Hugo's second language—*hierro* means iron, but this was actually an order to show strength and courage in the coming battle.

It's well nigh inconceivable today, but Hugo had recruited Nerval and others to assemble militant modernist Romantics to wage guerrilla warfare against the Classicists. The Classicists had their paid storm troopers—the claques—ready to attack. The theater world was notoriously violent. Rumor had it Hugo's play was subversive, a paean to the ugliness of modern verse—and dangerously anti-Bourbon.

"There was talk of cabals, of intrigues secretly entered upon, of snares and traps laid to kill the play and get rid of the new school," wrote Gautier. "Literary hatred is fiercer by far than political hatred, setting in motion the most sensitive fibers of self-love, and the triumph of the adversary proclaims the other man a fool." He could just as well have been writing today.

Anyone who thinks the 1950s Beat Generation or the 1960s counterculture invented the first armies of drug-taking subversive longhairs in outlandish clothes behaving like animals while attacking the establishment should think again. The fringe movements of my youth were a revival of rebellions wilder and more dangerous in their day.

"Was it not natural that youth should be opposed to old age," Gautier asked provocatively (and I say provocatively because by the time he wrote his memoirs he was himself old), "the long-haired heads to the bald ones,

Nerval memorial at Parc de la Tour Saint-Jacques

The Battle of Hernani (drawn by J. J. Grandville)

enthusiasm to routine, the future to the past?" Gautier quickly recruited "ferocious Romantics who would willingly have fed upon the body of a member of the Academy," plus two young poets and a cousin. They armed themselves with garlicky snacks and bottles of wine. Their real weapons were derision, humor, studied irreverence, unfashionably long locks, and colorful, crazy outfits to shock the bourgeoisie.

Trendsetting Gautier wore light sea-green pants with a black band down the outer seam, a black coat with wide velvet lapels, and a heavy gray overcoat lined in green satin. Around his neck, almost hidden by his tumbling ginger hair, was a moiré ribbon, not a collar or tie. Atop his head sat the kind of wide-brimmed flat hat Rembrandt's figures wore. What stood out was the red vest—a crimson doublet. Gautier had it made. The doublet entered Romantic history not just because the handsome rebel-dandy was striking but mainly because ever since 1789, red was the color of revolution. "This getup was devised to irritate and scandalize the Philistines," Gautier gloated. It did.

The theater impresario feared brawls or raids, so Hugo's army was made to enter the theater eight hours early. That did not prevent Balzac from being pelted with cabbages. Nerval was also attacked. Verbal abuse rained down on the recruits. Inside there was no water, the bathrooms were locked, and the auditorium was unheated and unlit, creating a Piranesi-like effect.

After seven hours in a pungent twilight pumped with adrenaline and wine, they were ready to spring. When the gas-lit chandelier came down and the curtain went up, all hell broke loose.

"In my heart burned a fierce longing to scalp these larvae of the past with my tomahawk and to hang these trophies on my belt," Gautier recalled. "Had I tried, however, I was more likely to harvest toupees than heads of hair."

When the claques could not be silenced, a kerfuffle ensued. One of the rhyming lines causing the uproar—it seems innocuous today—was about an *escalier dérobé*, meaning a secret private staircase. It was the ungrammatical breaking of the verse between the two words that galled the Classicists, plus the lack of a cohesive, traditional structure—a beginning, middle, and end—to the play. *Dérobé* turned out to be the key word: secret. Did Victor Hugo sense he would become a habitué of secret staircases, living a double or triple life, and that this evening would mark a watershed for him and the course of French history?

To escape the brawling, between the fourth and fifth acts Hugo and Adèle stepped into what's now Place Colette, named for the lusty bisexual novelist who lived in Palais Royal in the mid-twentieth century. Was Adèle Hugo meanwhile secretly searching for Sainte-Beuve? He had told her he disliked the play and was nowhere to be seen. As Victor wondered about his wife and backstabbing friend, a distinguished man with muttonchop whiskers strode up. It was Alfred Mame, the publisher. He clutched a wad of thousand-franc bills, a small fortune at the time. He wanted to buy the rights to *Hernani*.

"During the second act I was going to offer you two thousand francs," Adèle in her memoirs remembers Mame saying. "At the third, two thousand francs, Now I'm offering you five thousand francs because after the fifth act I might have to offer you ten thousand." Mame thrust out the wad. The playwright hesitated, then pocketed the bills and marched back inside.

Mame guessed right. The play ran with full houses for forty-five raucous nights and raked in the revenues. It is still raking in revenues today. The printed version of *Hernani* sold through three printings in a few days. Tout Paris was still coming to blows about *Hernani* in the spring when Charles X reinstated a theocracy. As the sweltering summer of 1830 approached and France fell into dangerous disquiet, the political factions split along lines drawn in the orchestra pit at the Théâtre-Français. The conservatives supported Classicism, the king's divine right to rule, and press censorship. The Romantics and proponents of the "new school" and modernity demanded freedom of speech and a republic or a constitutional monarchy. Real battle lines were drawn. The barricades went up on the night of July 27, the first date carved on the Bastille column, the landmark of liberty and lust for life I gaze upon daily beyond my skylight window.

Is this really so unimaginable? Think *Hair, The Last Temptation of Christ,* Madonna, Lady Gaga, or Pussy Riot. Think of the Arab Spring, Syria, and Ukraine.

Rebellion is the child of Romanticism and freedom remains a risky business in the twenty-first century.

Stifling the Freedom of the Press

11

ROMEO SEEKS JULIETTE

Quick," I said to my imaginary interlocutor, "let's cross the gardens before they lock us in."

I got up from the bench in the park in the center of Place des Vosges just as the guards' whistles blew. It had taken me nine minutes to get to the square from Sainte-Beuve's turreted love nest in rue Saint-Paul. I checked my watch and set off past a splashing birdbath fountain. How long would it take from Place des Vosges to Juliette's abode, and which route would Victor have habitually followed?

Couples were scattered in the shadows of the linden trees, their limbs entwined like the branches above. How many were illicit? If all is fair in love and war, as the cliché goes, then all is always fair in Paris. Every exchange in life is a war, skirmish, or battle, be it to buy bananas, order coffee, or get a marriage license. Even the most coddled French child attends the school of rough love. The struggle to survive in what's often an oppressive hierarchy translates in adult life to the battlefield of bedroom and hearth. Make war—it *is* love.

As to the flaunting of amorous passion on city streets, the record is clear. Fairness and the *droit à la passion*—a license to wander—are guaranteed by unwritten laws a thousand years old. Lovemaking is as honorable, pleasurable, public, and ostentatious an activity as are, say, raucously wining and dining outdoors under the arcades of Place des Vosges and in approximately ten thousand restaurants and cafés in Paris, or smoking in nonsmoking areas everywhere, or insouciantly running red lights. Paris has been a permanent sexual revolution, game of chicken, driving violation, ritualized rebellion, and kissing fest for centuries. That's part of the romance.

When Victor Hugo set out from his apartment to see his mistress Juliette, crossing this square several times daily and above all nightly for over a decade, he was as we are today observed by effigies and escorted by spirits. The effigies are those of Henri IV, the Evergreen Gallant Seducer, and his sexually conflicted son Louis XIII.

Henri stares down from the King's Pavilion on the south side of the square, Louis XIII from the tall stone plinth topped by an equestrian statue portraying the monarch. Henri had at least half a hundred mistresses—and countless milkmaids, peasants, and other objects of his winy, garlicky, insatiable desire. Louis XIII loved horses, hunting, and men but was made to marry a woman he could not abide and happily acceded to being cuckolded in order to procure an heir: Louis XIV.

In the moody Place des Vosges, the spirits of countless illicit yet respected, revered, adored lovers, mistresses, philanderers, and unfaithful wives flit around the bull's-eye dormers and shepherd's crook lampposts with their outsize lanterns from the reign of Louis XVIII.

It's curious that before writing *Hernani* Victor Hugo had dreamed up another outlandish historical tragicomedy inspired by this square and its adulterers. It was a tale of orgiastic free love and couple-swapping. The play, *Marion de Lorme*, told the story of the famous real-life seventeenth-century mistress of the aristocracy who reportedly bedded every nobleman then living on the square, including Cardinal Richelieu and others hailing from far beyond the Marais. Before it was produced, the play was acclaimed at Hugo's own private salon, which had gradually replaced Charles Nodier's gatherings at the Arsenal Library. From the start Dumas insisted that of the two, he preferred *Marion de Lorme* over *Hernani*, and that wasn't because his sometime lover Marie Dorval was cast in the lead role. But *Marion de Lorme* was censored and banned. Hugo salvaged its themes and by working around the clock in a matter of weeks wrote his Spanish fantasy.

With the specters of Marion de Lorme and Marie Dorval whispering in our ears, we walked in Hugo's footsteps past Louis XIII, his silly pencil-thin mustache erect, his big wig of stone hiding his balding scalp, the kind of wig Gautier would have loved to attach to his belt as a trophy. We exited the tall black gates and walked north on rue de Béarn—another reminder of Henri IV, who was born in that Pyrenean region of France. At busy rue Saint-Gilles we turned left, walked one block, turned north on the quiet, narrow rue Villehardouin, did a dogleg west beneath leprous buildings four hundred years old, and paused on the corner of rue de Turenne.

Seven minutes so far.

I gazed up at the windows of the house where the disfigured but brilliant burlesque poet Paul Scarron had lived with his lovely wife, decades his junior, the irresistible Françoise d'Aub-

Juliette Drouet (by Alphonse-Léon Noël)

igné. Louis XIV found her irresistible. He ousted Madame de Montespan and transformed the penniless widow of Scarron into Madame de Maintenon, possibly his most formidable mistress, the woman who secretly became the king's second, morganatic wife.

Mother, wife, mistresses: The lives of millions of plucky little Louis XIVs then and now have long been defined and often ruled by a powerful female presence. Victor Hugo, the prototypical Frenchman, the hero of millions, was no exception. His mother was an autocrat, a domestic tyrant who wrestled a general into submission, and Victor married her in the guise of Adèle.

Three minutes later I walked up another street of medieval origin, rue Sainte-Anastase. I lost count of the number of celebrated adulterers, cuckolds, mistresses, and other French heroes and heroines I'd passed en route. My imaginary interlocutor was becoming concerned about the nature of my quest.

On a modest building at 12 rue Sainte-Anastase, a plaque confirms that the artist's model, actress, and career mistress Juliette Drouet, officially Hugo's private secretary, lived here, on the fourth floor. Juliette's Spartan gilded prison was an eleven-minute walk at a leisurely pace from Hugo's sumptuous pavilion at 6 Place des Vosges. Her rooms were cramped. His vast apartment, built in 1605 for the oligarchic clan of Rohan-Guéménée, was the proverbial treasure house stuffed with rare books and baubles, Gothic and Renaissance furniture, and precious wall hangings. Juliette was not allowed to visit Hugo at home.

Victor Hugo made this short run on foot hundreds, perhaps thousands of times. His love affair with Juliette, though discreet, was another of the worst kept secrets in Paris. By the time the item went public, Victor and Adèle had agreed upon a discreet open marriage, exactly as his own parents had, a thoroughly contemporary arrangement. She slipped off through the *escalier dérobé* to see Sainte-Beuve and Victor left the front door to meet Juliette— and others.

The Hugo myth has it that whereas he naturally betrayed Adèle, his wife, while of course still loving her for eternity, he was faithful to Juliette, his muse and true love for fifty years. The day Juliette died, the story goes, he retired his quills, pining for the rest of his days. The reality is more interesting and inspiring to Parisians in its dark convolutions: Half of Victor's soul went to his wife, the other half plus his heart and loins to his mistress. Why just one mistress? What could be better than multiple mistresses, multiple lives, and secret stairways everywhere?

Hugo's astonishingly Technicolor existence is never shown in the movies because it was too racy. His was a life of glory, uxorious devotion and serial adultery, fame, treachery, admirable heroism, enduring priapism, towering talent, altruism, narcissism and conspicuous consumption alternated with hair-raising escapes, exile, discomfort, and genuine danger. If you were allowed only one romantic French hero, the outsize bearded sphinx Hugo would be a fine choice.

The cult of ravishing Juliette Drouet is nearly as fervent among insiders as the government-sponsored official cult of Victor Hugo. Poor Juliette was the kindhearted martyr of love and Hugo's biggest booster. She will never be transferred to the Panthéon by the poet's side—but Adèle Hugo isn't there either. Juliette lives on in the hearts and minds of many admirers and in pixelated form on the Internet.

12

THE CONQUEST OF VICTOR

By the fall of 1832, Victor Hugo had survived Paris' great cholera epidemic and was riding high on plays, poetry, and the mega-bestselling *Notre Dame de Paris*—aka *The Hunchback of Notre Dame*—which was published in 1831. He had transformed Sainte-Beuve into Quasimodo—not without pathos, it must be said. With rare benevolence he had dealt sympathetically with the once-revered Adèle, turning her into lovely Esmeralda. But he was still hurting. A workaholic, Hugo was glad to busy himself with another historical tragicomedy about passion, betrayal, and power titled *Lucrèce Borgia*. It kept his mind off home.

A minor actress with heavy backing wound up in January 1833 cast as Princess Negroni, a small part in *Lucrèce Borgia*. This had major consequences. That actress was the twenty-six-year-old Juliette Drouet, a famous beauty and bedmate of Paris' artistic elite. "She had two lines and didn't do much more than cross the stage," Théophile Gautier recalled naughtily in his profile of her, "but she cut a ravishing figure."

An orphan, a survivor of the school of hard knocks and a spell in a convent, Juliette had made it through by posing in the nude for James Pradier, then the capital's leading sculptor and later an august member of the French Academy. Pradier immortalized her romantic beauty in artworks across Paris, notably in the statue symbolizing the city of Strasbourg in the northeast corner of Place de la Concorde. The uniform coloration of the sculpture gives no idea of the contrast between Juliette's black hair and the delicate paleness of her skin, and her haughty pose suggests petulance. If you see wreaths or flowers at the base of that stern, shapely figure, they have been left by the growing number of admirers of Juliette Drouet.

James Pradier became her first serious lover and the father of her child. Claire, an only child, lived a short and unhappy life. In keeping with the custom of the time, Pradier refused to marry Juliette,

Juliette Drouet as Strasbourg, by James Pradier

recognize Claire as his child, or pay child support: He wanted a bourgeois wife to aid his social climb. With studied indifference he pointed the plucky teenage Juliette toward the stage and shoved. She made ends meet, as most models and actresses did, by becoming a courtesan, a polite term for prostitute. Juliette was more successful than most, a coveted prize. The more sought after she became, the further in debt she fell.

Draped with sparkling jewelry and wrapped in the latest, most expensive Paris fashions, Juliette was a prisoner to her own debauched lifestyle. Her spending stretched well beyond her means. Even after Victor Hugo took over as her protector, she continued to finance her expenditures by receiving others in her boudoir. Among the regulars were the rich but violent Prince Anatole Demidoff and the affable scoundrel Alphonse Karr, an influential journalist and publisher reportedly into kinky sex.

Hot-tempered and tough, Juliette was a good enough actress to disguise her powers as an enchantress, perhaps even a dominatrix, the kind who doesn't need whips, chains, or handcuffs. Her seductiveness spooked the sensitive Hugo. He resisted her for six months, fearing he'd be one more besotted admirer overwhelmed by passion and then ruined by her ways.

But she had his number. Others raised him to Olympian heights and called him by the nickname Olympio, but Juliette called him Toto. She mothered him. This may have been the key to her success, given the French penchant for mother worship and Hugo's family background. He had fallen under her spell the moment she walked into the theater, he admitted. Was it her celebrated "Praxiteles physique" or the perfect oval of her face, her steely, sparkling blue eyes and small moist round mouth, or the mane of inky black hair tumbling over porcelain shoulders and arms?

That would be underestimating Victor Hugo and Juliette, especially Juliette. By all reports she was formidable in myriad ways, a competent actress but also a talented writer of pithy quips and no one's air-headed bimbo. Though the fact has never been confirmed, she may have written theater reviews later signed and published by Alphonse Karr. For decades she copied and sometimes gently corrected Victor Hugo's manuscripts, providing unexpurgated running commentary. She penned at least 22,000 letters to him, several per day, in a determined, elegant hand. In them, her wicked sense of humor and playful wit are matched by wisdom, patience, and sagacity—and her sincere deep love for the poet. How else could she have outlasted and outmaneuvered the resurgent Adèle and dozens of other demanding lovers? The combination of her physical beauty, magnetism, and mysterious inner strength eventually overwhelmed the hesitant Hugo— and kept him in thrall for decades.

Hugo wasn't a looker, but Juliette found Victor inspiringly deep, scary smart, lyrical, romantic—and vulnerable. He had been weakened by injuries to his amour propre. Karr, a friend of both Hugo and Sainte-Beuve, had shared with Juliette the story of Adèle's defection. The infidelity was bad enough for a narcissist like Victor Hugo. But for Adèle to then fall desperately *in love* with the devious homunculus was devastating. The publication of *Volupté* drove the dagger in all the way. The wounded poet needed Juliette as much as she needed a savior.

Victor's fears proved right, however. He wound up having to pay off her colossal debts and support her and her daughter for as long as they lived. But the parsimonious poet also browbeat James Pradier (and got him a sculpture commission) until he agreed to cough up some money. Hugo paid the rest. Then he lifted Juliette out of prostitution for good and gave her a job for life. In exchange, the white knight imposed harsh conditions. He gave her a metaphorical chastity belt and leash. She was to lead a cloistered, lonely, frugal, nearly chaste life of "mystery, solitude, and love." She agreed never to go out unaccompanied by him. The fallen convent girl, a Mary Magdalene, took her vows, becoming the high priestess in the cult of Victor Hugo. She remained loyal to him until she died, or so the story goes. Those who have read all 22,000 letters swear it. If she did play around, she was more discreet than he.

13

KNIGHT TEMPLAR

The belt and leash did not keep Juliette from sneaking out. For propriety's sake, she was not invited into the Hugo family temple on the Place des Vosges. Her letters tell of heartbreakingly lonely nights wandering the dark Marais, drawn by the sparkling French windows in the royal square, a magic lantern show she desperately wanted to play a part in.

Juliette sometimes stood on the square without being seen, watching the goings-on in Victor's vast apartment. On warm nights when the windows were thrown open, she looked up from the arcade under the pavilion where Théophile Gautier had once lived. Guests laughed, ate, smoked, and leaned with their champagne flutes over the elaborate ironwork railings. She wondered, "Will I be recognized, welcomed, an equal to the 'real wife'?"

In the apartment were Gautier bubbling with bonhomie, Dumas, Balzac, Gérard de Nerval, and the rest of the gang, the literary lights of France, as well as politicians and industrialists, the men—they were all men—who were the movers and shakers in the world and were in turn moved and shaken by the women in their lives, their mothers, wives, and mistresses. Grotesquely Sainte-Beuve sometimes also appeared at these gatherings, a poisonous toad perched on the windowsill. Wasn't that an insult to propriety? Clearly not: Sainte-Beuve was famous, powerful, and from a good family, and he was above all a man, not a mistress.

Despite Hugo's progressive, even futuristic convictions, propriety did matter to him. He had made his reputation as the ideal father, the

Victor Hugo's house and salon on Place des Vosges

poet-husband incurably in love with his childhood sweetheart. There would be no airing of dirty laundry. He would not play the cuckold and demand a duel. Hugo was beyond that, more evolved and forgiving than that. His not-so-secret ambition was to join the French Academy. Once in, you were always in. From inside the academy, he stood a better chance of realizing his artistic and political agenda. "Chateaubriand or bust" had been his motto in adolescence. To be France's leading playwright, poet, and author was

not enough now. A top-level government post—as minister or special advisor to the king—was what he wanted. How else could he militate for free education, universal suffrage and women's rights, or the abolition of poverty, slavery, and the death penalty, not to mention the creation of a United States of Europe—the only way, he argued, to avoid repeat European wars?

Hugo's social agenda frightened many, especially royalists and nationalists. How, they asked, had the son of a general with a pension from the Bourbon kings, a favorite of King Louis Philippe, how had this prodigy become a one-man revolution? But Hugo was at least a century ahead of his time—one reason he is so relevant today.

Juliette, in the dark, gazing up from the square, did not know it then, but she would enter the Hugo house on Place des Vosges one day when Adèle was out of town with Sainte-Beuve. Later, after both were dead, she would enter with full rights.

Whether Juliette went in the front door for her surreptitious first visit or climbed the service stairs to his bedroom is unknown. The service entrance today still lets out on the ground floor, with a back door opening into the courtyard. The courtyard is now a public elementary school playground. How many times did Hugo or Adèle use that staircase and back door?

On the second floor, an unmarked door opens to the left into a small, dimly lit room. It is filled with the furniture found in Victor's bedroom in the house on Avenue Victor Hugo where he died in 1885, at the age of eighty-three. Made of dark, heavy wood, the bed is Gothic in style. It is a single bed. Adèle, then Juliette predeceased Hugo, as did most of his children. Next to the bed against the wall nearest the staircase is an unusual writing desk. On it Hugo wrote *Les Misérables* and poetry, plays, and other novels. He designed the desk himself and had it built by the same carpenter who built so many of the tables, desks, chairs, cupboards, and even the wood paneling in the apartment today. Hugo, like Hemingway decades after him, faced a wall and stood while he wrote, at least some of the time, and he wrote with a particular set of goose-quill pens now treasured by the museum and rarely displayed. I saw them once. Hugo framed them, six short, well-used quills held by string to a sheet of wrinkled paper marked "Plumes des *Misérables*." The ink has dried on them, staining the feathers.

Juliette Drouet's job as secretary for over four decades was to make exact copies of Hugo's manuscripts. Before, during, and after the copy work, she wrote her letters—all of them preserved, a sign of Hugo's idiosyncratic devotion.

No one is allowed to use the back stairs to the Hugo museum except in an emergency. But when the weather is hot, a guard sometimes opens the doors and occasionally, in a slack moment on a sleepy August day when the visitors are rare, if you happen to be standing nearby and are as curious and possessed as I am, you might step over the threshold onto the landing and glance up and down and then spend months or years afterward speculating. Was this the *escalier dérobé?*

A small, narrow room is now used to display illustrations or graphic works from Hugo's books and the bronze bust Rodin made of him in the early 1880s. The bust is dedicated, with typical understatement, "to the Illustrious Master." Apparently Rodin was made to follow the aged Hugo wherever he went, sketchbook in hand, because the restless illustrious master was unwilling to sit for yet another portrait, one of hundreds. Rodin's bust is different from the others, a particularly fine piece. The likeness is more than just a likeness; it's the essence of Hugo, a distillation of the pathos, the grandeur of the soul. Hugo's eyes are deep and all-seeing; his thick hair breaks like whitecaps above a massive brow.

Filling what's now the dining room is more of the odd, dark faux Gothic or Renaissance furniture Hugo assembled from antiques he and Juliette bought. He did not troll for antiques with Adèle, only with Juliette. In the main salon, two French

Rodin with his sculpture of Victor Hugo, Edward Steichen, 1903

windows overlook the Place des Vosges. The chinoiserie paneling and gar-
ish bowls, plates, and platters displayed here were also created by Hugo
with help from Juliette. If you look carefully, you will see, playfully hidden,
the initials *V.H.* disguised, for instance, as the shadow of a Chinese acrobat
and a chair. The master's ego was monumental.

When you learn, as I did, that many of the objects in these rooms and in
the museum's reserves were made for Juliette, you realize that ultimately
she did prevail; she dethroned Adèle and the others. It was she who saved
Hugo as he fled from the police of Louis Napoléon Bonaparte, the future
Napoléon III, following him into an exile lasting two decades, and finally,
late in life, after Adèle's death, openly moving into the apartment where he
later died.

When you tour the Hugo house on Place des Vosges in summer and
fans blow hot air on you, their caress gives you gooseflesh. You are feeling
Juliette's fingers, Juliette's breath.

The second salon confirms Juliette's triumph but hints at a further mystery. In this room hangs the portrait of Juliette Drouet painted in 1827, six
years before Victor met her. Young, seductive, and fresh-faced, she seems
to be wearing a shawl wrapped around her hair or a mink hat, or maybe it's
simply her thick, dark mane. Her cheeks are flushed as if she's just made
love with Champmartin, the painter of the portrait, one of her many admirers. There is nothing Gioconda-like in the impish smile of her round, rose-
hued lips. But the eyes, those large, dark, almost almond-shaped eyes could
have been lifted from Leonardo da Vinci's enigmatic masterpiece in the
Louvre. You can almost hear the portrait whispering: "From courtesan I
will grow into the muse of the century's greatest literary genius."

Though the painting is small and hangs in a corner, all eyes are instantly
drawn to it, often skipping the full-length portrait of matronly Adèle, a portrait with pride of place near pictures and a statue of the young Hugo and
their children, including the unfortunate Léopoldine, who died tragically
when newly wed.

A mystery lingers here, a chapter left out of most tales of Hugo's life.
One portrait is missing, an important portrait. After years of wondering
about this, I had to know why. So one day I made an appointment and
climbed to the top floor, to the level of the bull's-eye dormers where Victor

had his private office, and rang the bell. The museum librarian, a small, courteous, and thoughtful woman, welcomed me. She has delved into and archived the life of Victor Hugo for decades.

Seated at a long wooden table under the steep roof, surrounded by bookshelves and filing cabinets, we spoke of romance and Romanticism, of Paris then and now, of Adèle and Sainte-Beuve, Victor and Juliette, and I asked how she felt not as a historian but as a woman, a private person, about Victor's tempestuous life, his sex life and serial philandering in particular. The public hero lived a life of private lies, I remarked. Yet he was a role model for Frenchmen, his name appearing daily in newspapers and magazines and on television or the Internet a hundred and thirty years after his death; his image everywhere in France; scores of streets, squares, parks, auditoriums, and schools named for him around the world; his plays still produced; his novels, poetry, and works for the theater routinely revived and adapted for the stage, screen, television, and radio; his drawings and engravings exhibited; music festivals held in his honor to honor the composers he admired; and so on. He might very well be the most revered and influential Frenchman of all time. If he was the prototype for many Frenchmen, as seems uncontroversial, was Adèle somehow if not a model then at least a typical Frenchwoman who could be alive today?

The librarian said quietly that nothing in Hugo's or Adèle's lives troubled her. It was true he was and is ubiquitous and probably a model for others in many places, particularly France, perhaps subconsciously, because of the country's educational system. Even more so than Adèle, though, it was Hugo's mother Sophie Trébuchet who seemed the role model for today's Frenchwoman—a strong, outspoken, perhaps even domineering liberated woman who challenged her husband, the great general, took as lover the man she really loved, and brought up the children without him. Sophie had sought and found freedom in an oppressive male universe. Her struggle continues today in France and elsewhere.

The librarian agreed, as I have long suspected, that despite the outwardly patriarchal nature of the nation, women secretly rule, women who run households and influence men in family matters, business, and politics and always have, at least since the Merovingian dynasty of medieval kings, that string of notoriously ineffective "long-haired" barbarian Franks flanked by remarkably strong queens and queen mothers who ruled from the wings.

That was over a thousand years ago. But traditions die hard in this ancient civilization. The librarian could not help but agree.

"A century ago seems like yesterday," she mused. "Romanticism is recent, alive today."

"So what of Hugo's second great mistress," I finally asked, "the mystery woman no one talks about, the one who almost unseated Juliette Drouet? Why is there no portrait of her here?"

"Léonie d'Aunet." The librarian smiled. "Madame Biard."

The librarian was referring to a beautifully coiffed woman ten years younger than Juliette, with chestnut hair and intelligent eyes, a woman who, unlike Juliette, came from an aristocratic family and was a thoroughgoing Romantic and talented writer. Léonie d'Aunet, I soon learned, was as fearless and determined and passionate as Juliette or Hugo, and their secret liaison lasted a full seven years while Hugo was still married and Juliette his official mistress.

Who was she? When still very young, Léonie d'Aunet married an academic painter of historical landscapes, François-Auguste Biard, twenty years her senior. He was successful and adventurous but clearly did not satisfy her. In the mid-1830s he was sent to record the exploits of a scientific expedition to the Spitsberg Peninsula. Léonie tagged along, much to the surprise and chagrin of the crew. She would not be deterred. She not only survived but thrived and returned to write travel essays, stories, plays, and novels. Some years later, at a celebrated salon run by the famous beauty Fortunée Hamelin, one of Paris' great courtesans, she caught the roving eye of Victor Hugo.

When Adèle learned of Victor's new love interest, she was jealous and thrilled in equal measure: She had found an ally in the battle against Juliette Drouet. Instead of shunning Léonie, she invited her to the family home on Place des Vosges and even employed her. Adèle and Victor helped Léonie with her writing projects. Everyone in Paris but the cloistered Juliette seemed to know, including Léonie's husband. He was not amused. He did not behave like most cuckolded Frenchmen of his day, ignoring the liaison or demanding a duel. He blew the whistle.

Monsieur Biard summoned the morals police. After the embarrassing, humiliating discovery of the adulterous couple caught in flagrante, even Juliette knew—but not the whole truth. Hugo downplayed the affair.

Juliette believed him. Léonie went to jail, then to a convent. Victor, a Peer of France, invoked his immunity from arrest and prosecution. He walked free. The pair's affair continued, with Victor lying to Juliette and finessing her ultimatums. Léonie also demanded he choose an official mistress and retire Juliette. So he lied to Léonie, too. Adèle viewed Léonie as the enemy of her enemy, and therefore her friend. She aided and abetted her. Léonie proved skillful and cruel. To break the deadlock, she made a bundle of Victor's love letters, tied them with a ribbon, and sent them to Juliette.

"Yes," said the librarian with a knowing smile, "that is perfectly, absolutely something a Frenchwoman would do today."

The most striking thing about the relationship is the way Victor reused the same phrases in his love letters and poems to Juliette and Léonie, and the way these two very different but equally passionate affairs buoyed him, lifting him from depression. With Juliette, the source of woe was Adèle's infidelity. With Léonie, it was the death of Léopoldine, his beloved daughter.

"What of the missing portrait of Léonie?" I asked.

The librarian shook her head. It was not really a mystery. There is only one known good portrait of her. It was painted by her husband and hangs in the Château de Versailles, like the landscapes Biard painted for King Louis Philippe. The Victor Hugo Museum actually does have a portrait copied from an engraving, but it is never displayed because of its fragile condition.

As to efforts to paper over the story of Hugo and Léonie's affair, the librarian assured me prudery and puritanical censorship are not on the agenda—not anymore, that is. A century ago the Hugo family tried to excise Léonie from his biography, but those fruitless attempts at sanitation were ancient history. School groups visit the museum, and Hugo is studied in all French schools. French students learn everything there is to know about Hugo's life, works, and loves, with no detail too unseemly to examine, though the tale of Léonie is still not widely known.

I was also surprised to learn that adultery was accepted, normal behavior from the legal standpoint. Many bourgeois or aristocratic marriage contracts in the nineteenth century imposed fidelity for a limited duration only, usually five years. In theory, that was time enough to engender an heir with a reliable genetic patrimony, or so it was believed. Love marriages were rare. Once the business of breeding was over, both partners could stray—discreetly, especially in the case of women, who had to be careful. In the world of today's haute bourgeoisie and titled nobility, things have not necessarily evolved. Adultery is the national pastime.

I continued wondering aloud if anyone at the museum or in the National Archives or the National Library of France, a scholar or a biographer or journalist, had counted the number of lovers Hugo had had. Henri IV's lovers and Dumas' lovers had been identified and catalogued. So had their illegitimate children, recognized or not. Hugo kept careful, detailed notebooks, his so-called *carnets intimes*. The numbers should be there, albeit written in Spanish. He annotated his sexual affairs in Spanish, to keep them secret.

"No one has tabulated his conquests to my knowledge," said the librarian. "Now that you mention the *carnets*, there is one curious example we have in the reserves," she added. "One notebook's significance is still a mystery."

Hugo had filled the pages of a notebook from 1873 with accounting, personal notes and observations, visiting cards and photographic portraits. The photo cards were the kind Nadar and other photographers made at the time. Do the photos and cards tally the women he had pursued and conquered? I asked. Was it a "Catalogue Aria" of a French Don Giovanni? The librarian said she did not know. There seemed no way of finding out other than reading through the *carnet* line by line and matching the dates to events in his life. "Therein," she said, "lies the charm of the object."

I return to the library once the notebook has been retrieved and I have been given authorization to consult it and also see Hugo's famous quills. I watch eagerly as the librarian slowly turns the pages, pausing long enough to read snippets here and there, or gaze at the photos and cards, the bus or trolley stubs, the tickets to the premiere of the revival of *Ruy Blas*, one of Hugo's most successful plays, the death notices and endless accounts of petty cash, and the names and addresses of friends and of course of many ladies. Were they all conquests? Perhaps they were, but not necessarily.

The notebook is the size of a small book bound in thick Basane leather tanned a dark mahogany. I quickly realized this was an English or American-style scrapbook, possibly inspired by Hugo's time in exile on the Channel Islands, where he would have known such objects, which are not typically French. It was more than a simple listing of his lovers. The charm resided in the eclectic mystery of the collages, the little ink sketches, the pressed flowers, those names, addresses, and images of visiting cards, and the neat, surprisingly small handwriting. Some pages are dotted with inkblots and a few have blacked-out words or sentences, but as a general rule Hugo, using his primitive quills, was a model of precision. The words are written from the top to the very bottom of each page—a sign, it struck me, of parsimony.

On one page, underlined, Hugo wrote: "I drink to the health of the republic, and drink to the ill health of the monarchy." That must have been when, in the 1870s, the fledgling Third Republic was nearly torpedoed in favor of the last Bonaparte or a Bourbon pretender to the throne.

Who was Eugénie Guinault in the rue Fontaines du Temple? I wondered.

"A novelist and democratic militant who wrote *Un républicain au village*," said the librarian. She was also a feminist in the mold of George Sand, it turns out. Her other famous book was *La France républicaine et les femmes*. Did Hugo sleep with her, too? It would take lots of research to find out, and then?

What about Jane Essler, resident at 86 rue Miromesnil?

"An actress and demi-*horizontale*," the librarian remarked, meaning a courtesan. Jane was set to play the queen in *Ruy Blas*, and she almost beat out the young Sarah Bernhardt for the role, but then something happened. Bernhardt remembered Essler poisonously as "a little vulgar," and better positioned than the unknown Bernhardt to win the role. Why? That was a horizontal mystery even I could figure out.

Later, Hugo reconsidered and summoned Bernhardt to his private apartment for an "audition." Warned by those in the know, the young enchantress refused to go, auditioning at the theater like everyone else. Hugo's appetite for conquest was by then notorious. Eventually she was swept away by the old man's irresistible charm and gave in to "the monster," as she called him. She was nearly forty years his junior.

"The monster was charming," she wrote in her autobiography, "so witty and refined, and so gallant, with a gallantry that was an homage and not an insult. He was so good, too, to the humble, and always so gay."

The librarian flipped more pages, and as if by magic, there appeared the visiting card of Sarah Bernhardt.

Sarah Bernhardt in a familiar position

14

THE HISTORIC PRESENT

How many times, in the rue de Sévigné, in the heart of the Marais, have I halted near the Lycée Victor Hugo to admire the sculpted wooden carriage doors of the Hôtel Carnavalet? The seventeenth-century mansion and its neighbors house the museum of the history of Paris, a repository of Romanticism as precious as Père-Lachaise. This museum was created by Jules Cousin, who served as the Arsenal's librarian after Charles Nodier and was the founder of the Paris Historic Library. Cousin's museum, like his libraries, is thoroughly Romantic: a monument to the living past, the nurse of present generations and guardian of the future. The layout is equally Romantic and as difficult to understand or follow as Hugo's *Hernani*.

Vast and splendid, the Carnavalet is also where Madame de Sévigné lived for decades. A great proto-Romantic figure, she was born on the Place des Vosges in 1626 next door to the king's pavilion, nine doors west of Victor Hugo's house. The Sévigné clan's portraits hang in her private second-story apartment. Madame de Sévigné's husband, a marquis, died young in a duel defending the honor of a lady of the Marais. He was buried under the paving stones of the little domed church next door to where my unheated apartment atop the lampshade factory once stood, a quarter mile away from the museum. The marquis slept soundly alongside the nuns, embarrassed ladies, inconvenient infants, and other victims of childbirth, his presence benign, even affable, as I recall.

He lived long enough to give his wife two children, a son of no consequence and a bright, smart daughter she loved and corresponded with, sometimes daily. Tough, pragmatic, and handsome, with Cupid's bow lips and a mass of blonde curls, the widowed Madame la Marquise de Sévigné bounced back smartly and lived gaily on without her husband. She was more than ten years older than Louis XIV but shared the king's bed, though it may well have been her even prettier young daughter Françoise-Marguerite, later the Comtesse de Grignan, who enjoyed that honor. The letters exchanged by the marquise and the countess were redacted by their heirs, and some were "lost." The delectable truth may never be known. But as her hundreds of surviving letters reveal, for the length of her long life the marquise followed from deep inside the intrigues and affairs of France's Golden Age of absolutism, the age the restored monarchs of the 1800s tried to re-create.

With a small effort of the imagination Madame de Sévigné's large pale-blue eyes can be made to peer down from their picture frame through the thick stone walls into the cobbled entrance court of the Musée Carnavalet. There stands a fine full-length bronze statue of her lover, the masculine young Louis XIV, the only original bronze of the king to survive the Revolution of 1789. Bewigged and mustachioed, he is cast as Hercules, complete with club and lion's skin. He's not depicted busily completing the seven Herculean tasks. He's slaying the great man-made threat to the Mother Church and his throne: Protestantism. During the sixteenth, seventeenth, and eighteenth centuries, the great bogey of the French was Martin Luther and his adepts. During the nineteenth and twentieth centuries it was the Jews. Today Islam and globalization fill French hearts with trepidation, the latest perceived threats to the cult of the nation and the secular republic.

It's tempting to spend a day or a week or an entire lifetime here enjoying the first 4,600 or so years of the history of Paris, starting with the Neolithic canoes and ancient Roman ruins displayed in a former greenhouse. From them you move down the centuries to the Belle Époque, with time stopping somewhere around Art Déco: Other museums deal with the recent past. Scattered around are sculptures in low relief of kings on horseback—horny Henri IV, for instance—and 3-D models of the Ile de la Cité and other neighborhoods destroyed by Napoléon III and Baron Haussmann. There are café interiors, salons, sweeping staircases, suites of carved paneling, entire salons and their furniture, monumental carriage doors or stained-glass windows, and more, much more. Marcel Proust's bedroom is furnished with the bed he died in. An entire Art Déco ballroom painted in 1925 vies with a complete Art Nouveau jewelry shop designed by Alphonse Mucha. All of these precious objects were saved and shoehorned into the museum's rooms, an act of faith in the importance of history.

If you can tear yourself away and march past these displays, mount the stairs to the second floor, and head east, you will eventually enter the 1800s and the Age of Romanticism, the time when Paris became the world's leading city.

If the streets and buildings and shops and the other museums of the city haven't already taught you why the French suffer from neophobia—a fear of the new—and why the American boast "and he never looked back" fills them with horror, the Carnavalet will fix that. It will initiate you into the Romantic mysteries, making you a Janus, continuously glancing back before moving forward. From a practical standpoint, the Carnavalet will also fill in the visual gaps should you be lacking images of the people, places, and things that are the city's Romantic quintessence, things now gone or difficult to recognize but nonetheless there, hidden from view like the foundations of the Arsenal Library.

As in the real city outside, no chronological order or obligatory route leads you through the Carnavalet. There are no signs to follow, and modern conventions of museology do not apply here. Daunting? Not at all! It's an entertaining steeplechase of 146 rooms on three floors with 600,000 items on display in two multi-winged historic town houses wrapped around five mossy courtyards joined by staircases and passageways, one of them flying like a Chinese bridge over the Lycée Victor Hugo. In more ways than one, the museum reflects the changelessness of Paris, a city of neighborhoods and villages knitted and knocked together over time, refusing to cooperate with urban planners the way Romantic literature—or this book—refuses to provide a chronological beginning, middle, and end.

I have a favorite way backward into the sprawling nineteenth century, the fountainhead of the nostalgia and romance that fuel Paris and fill these pages. From the entrance walk east over the high school, cross the ballroom, go through the jeweler's shop, jog left, and enter the suite of narrow rooms and corridors marked dark blue on the map, numbered 136 to 128. Take them in descending order.

Hemming you in are cityscapes showing Paris a century or more ago, paintings of the Seine and Canal Saint-Martin, of villas and mansions, municipal buildings, people, parks and gardens, and a series showing the dramatic burned-out ruins of the Tuileries Palace and Hôtel de Ville following the Commune revolt of 1871. In room 130 on your left several floor-to-ceiling oil paintings showcase famous episodes from the 1870 Franco-Prussian War and the Siege of Paris. Sit on the bench in the middle of the room and face west. Most of the wall is covered by an oversize picture painted by the tag team of Jacques Guiaud and Jules Didier.

The subject is the departure of statesman Léon Gambetta by balloon from Place Saint-Pierre on Montmartre, then a dusty field, now one of the world's most venerable tourist sights. Gambetta, head of the faltering provisional, recently declared Third Republic that followed the collapse of the Second Empire, is about to risk life and limb to get out of the city to the government's temporary seat beyond Prussian lines. The big brownish balloons awaiting him look unstable, a pair of Christmas tree ornaments caught upside down in hairnets. Soldiers are hanging on to the ropes, holding the balloons down. Unprepared for the altitude or weather, the insouciant balloonists wear street clothes. One has a top hat. The Prussians will be firing rifles and artillery at them. If they are caught, they will be shot on the spot as spies.

One essential figure not shown—at least I have not found him—is Félix Nadar. These are the balloons Nadar helped the army round up, equip, and fly. On them, post office officials sent up homing pigeons freighted with the first microfilms. Each was the featherlight photographic image of hundreds of documents needed beyond enemy lines.

The birds and Gambetta made it out. Nadar and a million others—including Victor Hugo and Théophile Gautier—hunkered down in besieged Paris, somehow surviving with almost no food or fuel during the four-month Prussian siege. It was Paris' coldest fall and winter in fifty years. Following the siege came one of France's most violent revolutions, the Commune. In a single week, "Bloody Week," 17,000 Communards and hundreds of civilians and government soldiers died in house-to-house fighting. The body count has never been verified. In a repeat of 1848, thousands of corpses were thrown into the Seine, that most romantic of rivers. Its bed must be paved with skeletons.

Paris was blown apart by Prussian artillery fire. In the spring it was shelled

A Barricade during the Commune Revolt of 1871 (by Thure de Thulstrup)

and then overrun by the Versaillais soldiers sent in by reactionary elements of the Third Republic's government in Versailles. Then it was set alight by the fanatical anarchistic minority that took command of the Communards. They were attempting through violent struggle to roll back the oligarchic state swollen during the Second Empire. It had taken over from the oligarchs of the ancien régime and reign of Louis Philippe. By changing clothes and morphing with the times, big money had thrived. The Communards failed and, as Alphonse Karr said of 1848, the more things change, the more they stay the same.

In room 128, the far right wall treats you to the 1860 painting of Emperor Napoléon III signing the "annexation of the communes." This allowed Paris to incorporate outlying neighborhoods and villages. They became the modern city's outer arrondissements, including the 17th, where I once lived in rue Laugier. Looking imperial, dripping with gold at the collar, shoulders, waist, and cuffs, the odious little dictator Victor Hugo called "Napoléon the Small" holds a quill in his right hand and wears a red sash and red pants. His drooping Vandyke and prominent nose draw attention from his weak pea-size close-set eyes, the eyes of a shapeshifter and fraudster with devious intelligence. In his left hand he holds out the declaration to Haussmann, his ruthless, ambitious Prefect of the Seine, who obediently leans forward, his uniform sparkling with silver.

Haussmann is surprisingly young for a man so driven by apocalyptic urges. His cheeks and chin are free of facial hair, but a curious close-cropped beard wraps around his neck. Vanity oozes from both men. They are the twin fathers of the sanitized, rebuilt Paris, the place we

Napoléon III in all his splendor, pig eyes, mustaches, and medals

commonly think of as the City of Light. They are the destroyers of the antique and dangerous, the demolishers of the malodorous medieval quarters full of subversive plebeians, places whose magic Hugo sang in *War on the Demolition Men, The Hunchback of Notre Dame,* and *Les Misérables.* Hugo loathed Napoléon III almost as much as Napoléon III loathed Hugo. I wonder whether the dictator gloated as he crushed the exiled Hugo by crushing the cityscape the poet loved.

During the Second Empire some 25,000 buildings of centuries past, dozens of old streets, and entire neighborhoods were wiped off the map, over 300,000 families were dislodged, and the new boulevards and avenues, the new monuments, train stations, churches, and traffic roundabouts—and thousands of buildings for the burgeoning bourgeoisie—took their place. They utterly transformed Paris, on the surface of it putting the lie to Alphonse Karr. But that would be a shallow literal interpretation of Karr's complex maxim, because in the end the more things changed, the more they stayed the same.

If this was modernity as its promoters claimed, why did it not buoy the hearts of the progressives and modernists? Napoléon III's radical urban renewal scheme cloaked the real agenda of crowd control and banishment of undesirables also known as slum clearance.

"Modernity is transitory, fugitive, contingent," wrote Charles Baudelaire, "it is one half of art, the other half is the eternal and immutable."

The destruction of the seemingly eternal, immutable Paris inspired Baudelaire to dedicate "The Swan," one of his most moving, melancholy poems, to Victor Hugo:

Haussmann as "Demolition Artist" (image courtesy Brown University Library)

Haussmann pondering how to profitably evict 300,000 families

(...)
Gone is old Paris. No human heart
changes half as fast as a city's face
(...)
Where a poultry market once stood
one cold morning I saw
a swan escaped from its cage,
its webbed feet clumsy on the cobbles,
its white feathers dragging through dusty uneven ruts,
its beak pecking pointlessly in the gutters ...

Paris may change (...) but my melancholy
remains—new buildings, old
neighborhoods turn into allegories
and memories are heavier than stone (...)

One objective correlative heavier than stone sits in the middle of the same room at the Carnavalet Museum: the gaudy crib of the imperial prince who never reigned, the son of Napoléon III and Empress Eugénie. His early death during the infancy of the Third Republic brought to an end a Napoleonic dynasty poised to steal power again.

A wide stone staircase leads down to rooms filled with the portraits of the great Romantics, a rogues' gallery less homogeneous than that of Félix Nadar but equally engrossing. Before descending, pause to look at the vast painted panoramas hanging in the stairwell, panoramas that clearly inspired Nadar to his balloon exploits. Painted from above as if the artist had been in the basket of a balloon—one is shown—they depict Paris in 1852 and '53 before Napoléon III's remake. There rises Notre Dame with its tall new spire, and there is the Pont des Arts, the famous footbridge now covered in padlocks. Below the painter's standpoint are the quays of the Seine, with the cluttered Marais stretching east from city hall to the distant Bastille column. The Marais and Ile Saint-Louis were and are among the few Paris neighborhoods to have escaped "Haussmannization." Might that be why they are so enchanting and sought after today, just possibly Paris' most beloved, most romantic quartiers?

In the stairwell and the eight rooms that follow, you can unwittingly succumb to what clinical psychologists call Stendhal's syndrome, an overload of culture, beauty, and history that pitches sensitive souls into an abyss of emotion. There is no painting of Stendhal at the Carnavalet—it hangs in the Château de Versailles not far from Léonie d'Aunet.

As you walk northeast across the museum you encounter the stunning actress Rachel, looking like a Siamese cat. She briefly shared her favors with Victor Hugo and was immortalized by

Saved in extremis: Hôtel de Sens (by J. Gavin)

Nadar. Nearby is Delphine Gay de Girardin, the socialite, novelist and lover of many, including Hugo; and the literary muse Ernesta Grisi, lifelong companion of Théophile Gautier and mother of beautiful Judith Gautier, one of Victor's last passions.

You will also see familiar faces glimpsed at the Arsenal Library's literary salon. Among them is Alfred de Musset, shown young, looking more like a girl than a man, yet destined to be a lady-killer of Olympic proportions; and Eugène Delacroix, dour, severe and dark as ever. Near Delacroix looking out at you is delicate, fawn-like Alice Ozy, the celebrated demimondaine, yet another of Hugo's conquests; and there is soulful Marie d'Agoult, Franz Liszt's lady friend alias Daniel Stern the novelist, book in hand. Leaping from the wall beside her is d'Agoult's beau—Liszt was very beau—in the famous portrait by Henri Lehmann. The pianist's intensity is almost unbearable, with his pale face and thick dark thrown-back hair a blend of owl and vampire.

But do not overlook the unhappy, unloved Gérard de Nerval, lopsided of face and eye. He is one of the keys to understanding Romanticism then and romance now, a man animated by joyful melancholy. A lovely small urban landscape shows the Château des Brouillards, where Nerval lived, a place still standing on the upper slopes of Montmartre.

Not least in my personal *carnet intime* of favorite artworks is the picture of Madame Hamelin, the gorgeous curly-haired voluptuous *grande horizontale* who introduced Victor Hugo to Léonie d'Aunet—but only after sharing her bed with him.

In the final room of the nineteenth century, before you arrive at the reconverted greenhouse stuffed with antiquities, older portraits hang on the walls. They create a bridge from the Empire to Romanticism. The delicately ravishing young Madame de Récamier is shown reclining as she should be, for she is famous for having slept with every pair of pants that entered her room, including Chateaubriand's, and at least one famous skirt, that of Madame de Staël. The mannish de Staël was the bane of Napoléon I, the breathtakingly literate woman who may have been the first to use the term *romantisme*.

As a last salute, raise your eyes to the portrait of Emperor Napoléon I "the Great," the pint-size Corsican whose military prowess turned the old European order on its head and unwittingly transformed France into the heartland of Romanticism. Near him hangs Talleyrand, no introduction needed. Beyond being one of the great political chameleons of all time, Talleyrand is also thought to be the secret biological father of Eugène Delacroix. Look at the painter again as you head across the ground floor: The resemblance is astonishing.

As you leave the Carnavalet Museum—if you can find your way out—make one more stop. Seek out the portraits and caricatures of Balzac. There is one, a dusky, unflattering oil painting in a round frame that shows the novelist young and vigorous and dressed as always in black. Another portrait was painted after the only known daguerreotype taken of Balzac: He feared losing his soul to the camera. It depicts him already plump and disheveled. Several caricatures salted around the Romantic period rooms capture him better.

Balzac, Dumas, and Hugo appear as beggars in one of them, pleading for admission to the French Academy. The most famous caricature of all shows Émile Zola saluting a bust of Balzac, who salutes back. The feisty Zola of *The Belly of Paris* and *J'accuse* was Balzac's spiritual heir, though his emphatic, agitprop approach to writing might not have pleased his master.

15

BALZAC'S MARAIS

Honoré de Balzac may have been born in the provinces, the child of ambitious, narcissistic, coldhearted parvenus. But he spent his formative years studying in dreary boarding schools and at the Lycée Charlemagne in the Marais, or eking out a living under the leaky roof of a building at 9 rue de Lesdiguières a few blocks from Place de la Bastille.

For a year or more after I moved into my new office I spent many minutes of pleasant reverie waiting for the elevator gazing down, wondering who lived or worked in Balzac's room. Which dormer was it, the one to the right, closer to rue Saint-Antoine? Young ladies came and went in the rooms in rapid succession, heightening the mystery. After years of dormancy, my interest in Balzac revived. One day at my usual bookseller's stall on the Seine near the Pont Marie I spied and snapped up a vintage biography of the writer. It stank of dust and mold and had orange-yellow, flaky pages still uncut. I rushed back to my office, sliced open the cover, and began cutting more pages. But the book disintegrated, Balzac's life sifting between my fingers.

Then by accident I came across an entry in an authoritative history of Paris' streets. It put an end to my speculation, stating categorically that the numbering of rue de Lesdiguières was changed around the turn of the twentieth century. Balzac's building had been farther south, closer to the Seine, and was demolished to make way for the wide, straight Boulevard Henri IV linking the riverbank to the Bastille.

It was as if a bucket of cold Seine water had been thrown on me. I shriveled and turned my back to the window as I waited for the elevator, saddened as I often am by the violence of real estate developers, who periodically destroy parts of old Paris in the name of progress, sanitation, or modernity, a Romantic Age tradition very much alive today.

As I made my way the other day toward the Ile Saint-Louis for an evening constitutional, I passed the former premises of a school Balzac had attended, one block east of Place des Vosges on rue des Tournelles near the city's biggest synagogue. On the leafy quay near Boulevard Henri IV and the Arsenal Library I could not help remembering what Bruno Blasselle, the director of the library, had said when I mentioned my unwelcome discovery about the disappearance of Balzac's garret.

"Sometimes," he remarked, "it is better not to know."

He'd spoken softly, sadly, but with an ambiguous smile. What did he mean, "It's better not to know"? Did he mean knowledge was the source of unhappiness or disappointment? Perhaps he meant my quest would end in tears, that pulling the curtains open and revealing the Wizard of Romanticism, the Wizard of Paris, might destroy the magic and shatter life-sustaining myths.

Clearly he was being facetious. Ignorance is by definition never blissful, not in this culture where being smart is sexy, where *intellectual* is a job title and philosophers run government ministries, make movies, and write bestselling books. On the scale of disapprobation, only blind faith is lower than ignorance or that bane of Frenchmen, optimism—the maddeningly positive world view no thoughtful Parisian can abide. Blind religious faith is the preserve of a minority of believers now on the margins of this militantly secular, skeptical society that reveres the gods of pitiless reason and dark pessimism. They are heroic gods because they are mental constructs, the abstract foundations of Existentialism, and they are entirely man-made, like a civilization or a city. Knowledge destroys bliss and engenders melancholy, but in Paris, melancholy has long been prized. It is a sign of intelligence and thoughtfulness, and lies at the roots of Romanticism and romance.

As I walked toward the Ile Saint-Louis I smiled with satisfaction. The old-fashioned streetlamps cast their patented fuzzy antique halos, a nostalgic, romantic mood carefully engineered by Paris' master lighting designers to evoke the days of old. This was not bright, optimistic light; it was the objective correlative of feeling blue, a permanent *heure bleue,* as the French call the gloaming or twilight.

No, I reflected as I often do when I walk at nightfall, looking into the shops and restaurants and upper-floor apartments lit like stage sets, nothing in Paris is left to chance. Ignorance does not bring bliss, not in France.

The more I thought about ignorance, bliss, and melancholy, the more my mind circled from Balzac to the Arsenal Library and then back to an unusual study of the French I first read in 2013. It made waves everywhere in the world except, naturally, in Paris, where it was met with a shrug. A French scientific researcher named Claudia Senik coined the phrase "French idiosyncratic unhappiness." It is what I've long thought of as Balzac-Baudelaire syndrome.

Like many Frenchmen, both Balzac and Charles Baudelaire feared not the pursuit but the fulfillment of happiness: Tragedy was sure to follow. "It was too good to be true," wrote Gautier of Balzac's mistrust of anything that was going well. But as others have noted, the epithet applies equally to the tormented Baudelaire, the poet of dark, putrescent flowers.

In its essence, the Senik study suggests the French are happiest when unhappy. The reasons are many, too many to fit in a single book. As Senik told Maureen Dowd of *The New York Times,* "Our happiness function is a little deficient. It's really in the French genome."

At my office I reread the study, nodding and exclaiming as I highlighted text and made notes. According to Senik, immigrants to France—including this author—do not share the unhappiness of native French. Hence the unhappiness problem is idiosyncratic and specific to the natives, like so many things that do not defy generalization—au contraire, that *require* generalization. Psychological and cultural factors outweigh economic ones—in the study, "well-being" was gauged "beyond GDP." Clearly the French idiosyncratic malady has little to do with economic recessions or chronic high unemployment or the mass immigration of the last two decades from North Africa and Eastern Europe that has riled so many nationalists.

"The low level of life satisfaction of the French is not a recent phenomenon," Senik notes. "It has been there for as long as statistical series are available."

I suspect it has been around a lot longer than statistical series. It was

certainly tangible when I first spent time in Paris in the mid-1970s, and today it prickles the skin of the sensitive like strong acid rain.

"It is a very different Paris from the old days," wrote the greenhorn
Ernest Hemingway in "Parisian Boorishness," a piece that appeared in *The
Toronto Star Weekly* on April 15, 1922, "when the French people enjoyed a world
reputation for pleasant gentleness, affability, and instinctive kind attention."

When might those "old days" have been? Not the days of Flaubert, Balzac, Baudelaire, or Hugo. Perhaps they never were.

Defying even the worst projections of the most skillful pessimists, France
typically ranks lower than Iraq or Afghanistan in terms of expectations. Mental illness, depression, and the use of antidepressants are "exceptionally high"
by European standards. Suicide is as common in real life as it is in the pages
of Balzac.

Government statistics and those in many similar studies show divorce
rates above 50 percent. Young people, particularly women, are smoking
more than ever. Binge drinking, hard drug use, and disorderly behavior in
public are also on the rise.

This is not a cause for alarm. It seemed to me as I thought about the
study to mean simply that the French are unhappy by the standards of other
nations and perhaps even their own and that this idiosyncratic unhappiness
is permanent and a source of secret joy and fulfillment. Sardonic unhappiness doesn't keep Parisians from being romantic or seeking love, for instance, and their curmudgeonly stewardship of one of the world's most
appealing cities must surely be part of the magic of this perplexing place.

"I can scarcely conceive of a type of beauty," wrote Baudelaire, "in which
there is no Melancholy."

Balzac is even better: "Your melancholy was a charm, your unhappiness
an attraction," he rhapsodized.

Every French man, woman, and child memorizes Guillaume Apollinaire's
"Le Pont Mirabeau," singing *"La joie venait toujours après la peine"*—joy always
followed pain.

Hello, unhappiness! No wonder Françoise Sagan's *Bonjour Tristesse* is a
modern classic, and bestselling novelist Amélie Nothomb's recently published *La Nostalgie heureuse*—"happy nostalgia"—is a study of melancholy. One
of the most popular summer programs on France's most popular radio station, France-Inter, is Remède à la mélancolie—"A Cure for Melancholy."

Many pages would be needed to list the novels, plays, movies, TV dramas, radio programs, and newspaper or blog posts themed around happy unhappiness, the direct descendant of Sturm und Drang.

Short of adding vitamin D and selective serotonin reuptake inhibitors to the drinking water or performing genetic therapy, the zeitgeist is unlikely to change. Should it?

The French have no monopoly on noir melancholy: It is the ambrosia of creative genius everywhere, particularly poetic genius. Melancholy and nostalgia go hand in glove. But few other cultures are so deeply, passionately entrenched in darkness and negativity, few so adore the flowers of evil—however "evil" is construed. Is it reaching too far to evoke the ancient Gallic worship of Dis, I wonder, the god of negativity, death, and darkness, or to recall that these pre-Roman forebears of today's Parisians measured time by night, not day?

You don't have to look back two thousand years to be convinced. Religion and myth were among the casualties of the relatively recent—by French standards—Age of Enlightenment, an age that gave birth to the cult of Reason with a capital R that fueled the Revolution of 1789, also uppercase, and became in the 1800s and in the so-called modern age the yin to Romanticism's yang, the quintessence of midcentury Existentialism, also a product of Paris, inspired by Danish philosopher Søren Kierkegaard, a thoroughgoing melancholic Romantic adopted by educated Frenchmen and -women.

The essence, the kernel of Romanticism and its offspring is a longing for the lost certainties of faith and divine right, on the one hand, and the heroism of reason without God, king, or certainty on the other. A belief in the "heroism of the modern age," as Baudelaire called it, the heroism of the individual, is the prime ingredient not just in Romanticism. Opposing forces of a similar kind are everywhere and in constant, embattled balance in the dualistic French psyche, where hero worship has replaced religion. Contemporary society embodies them in its brutal, confrontational, punitive educational system, which requires children to compete against themselves and each other from preschool up, and in the nation's irreconcilable, opposing political parties, who reflect the fractures of centuries past. The divisive Tea Party dedicated to obstructionism is new to the United States, but its equivalent has always existed in France.

The Age of Ideology is dead, you say? Perhaps elsewhere it is. French factions run the gamut from the neofascist Front National to the laissez-faire center right via the Socialists to the rebranded hard-line Communists and left-wing extremists who rally under the Front de Gauche banner. The Greens and a host of splinter parties delight in slipping themselves under the fingernails of the nation. A two-party system based on compromise and cooperation is falling apart in America because of radical extremists on the right, and could never work in France for the simple reason that the range of opinions is too wide and the passion for violent disagreement too strong. A system with umbrella parties would flip itself inside out and blow away within days if it ever could be created.

Remember the "French paradox"? It used to mean the natives' immoderate eating of foie gras and drinking of red wine, culinary habits leading to long life, slender bodies, sexual prowess, and perfect health. It's a myth: The real French paradox is mental, not physical. Clear-eyed about the beliefs and myths of other civilizations, many here seem purblind about their own. What some call the American dream, the French call the American myth. Yet outsiders can perceive without great effort that the French secular trinity of liberty, equality, and fraternity is at least as dreamy and mythical and bankrupt as the putatively delusional, pathetically optimistic American myth.

In truth, most French in the mainstream make a conscious decision to live by their unattainable ideals, knowing perfectly well they are unattainable. They cherish their secular trinity at a deep, operating-system level as the lesser of evils. Despite the inevitable banter and cynicism exhibited during conversation as a sign of sophistication, when spoken in French by the French, these three words are more than a hollow slogan, the same way the American dream—in its countless incarnations—is not a hollow myth to many Americans, who prefer to believe in its attainability and remain optimistic no matter what the challenge.

As I neared the Pont Marie and scented the Seine's churning waters I realized there was a chain leading me forward from Balzac's vanished garret across the stone sidewalks of the city and backward to the heart of the Romantic agony—to one of the key secrets of Paris' romantic identity.

I was not thinking of "agony" in the writings of the Marquis de Sade or Mario Praz, but rather of the collective French mental inner sanctum, a temple founded on the principle of paradox. Simply stated, the principle is that without all this necessary complexity, ambiguity, and apparent contradiction, the layer cake of Paris so many people find appetizing would not exist today.

Had Paris been inherited by a pragmatic, optimistic, change-is-possible, yes-you-can, forward-looking nation that worshiped sunshine and good health and bleached teeth, what elements of the moldering old impractical, unprofitable, dark, smelly but enchanting past would have survived?

The thought of Balzac floated to the surface like the detritus passing in the Seine. It was in the hard-driven Marais of pre-gentrification days and on the gloomy, damp Ile Saint-Louis that dozens of Balzac's characters lived. Here in real life the author had some of his most significant encounters not only with Victor Hugo or Charles Nodier at the Arsenal, but also with Gautier and the brilliant, bizarre outlier Baudelaire.

Together Balzac and Gautier spent mind-expanding time with Charles Baudelaire in one particular mansion still standing at number 29 quai d'Anjou, on the north side of the Ile Saint-Louis. There, behind a small dormer set in the slate roof, Baudelaire lived out his wildest, most intellectually and artistically fertile years. That mansion is the Hôtel de Lauzun. In Balzac and Baudelaire's day the mansion went by the name Hôtel Pimodan and was the headquarters of the Club des Haschichins, a "medico-scientific" circle whose hash-smoking and hash-eating habitués were members of Paris' artistic and literary avant-garde. They included Dumas, Delacroix, Gérard de Nerval, Daumier, Alphonse Karr, Tony Johannot the painter, Flaubert, James Pradier the sculptor, and many others. An *escalier dérobé* linked the clubrooms with Baudelaire's and others' apartments on the top floor. Like Baudelaire's grave and his creepy cenotaph at the cemetery of Montparnasse, the mansion, for some, is a secular pilgrimage site today.

Why? Because no other French writer, artist, or intellectual—not Balzac, Hugo, or Proust, not Sartre, Genet, or Camus, Foucault or Baudrillard, not to mention Verlaine and Rimbaud, Claudel or Mallarmé—has so impressed his personality on the Parisian psyche as Charles Baudelaire. Remember his motto: "I can scarcely conceive of a type of beauty in which there is no Melancholy."

PART THREE

Baudelaire's Island

16

JOIE DE TRISTESSE, OR
THE ROMANCE OF UNHAPPINESS

For the eye-candy and canned-laughter generation that grew up as I did in 1960s and '70s America with the "tale of a fateful trip that started from a tropic port aboard a tiny ship," the cultural gap between *Gilligan's Island* and the insular aerie of Charles Baudelaire may seem unbridgeable. It isn't.

In his idiosyncratic way Baudelaire was a castaway. He too set out to explore the tropics, taking ship to Calcutta, forced out of Paris by his step-father. Secretly he was glad to escape the loveless life of his wrecked family and its suffocating, bourgeois world. Miserable during his travels, he was also eager to return, to be rescued and cared for. He wound up instead on an island in the Seine, a slum in his day, a black hole millions of miles away from Place Vendôme and his rich, sainted mother's cool embrace. Later he exiled himself to an imaginary outpost, a bizarre garden folly on a meta-phorical archipelago, a Kamchatka Peninsula of the mind. It was dubbed Baudelaire's Folly by Adèle Hugo's adoring friend, the ubiquitous literary critic Sainte-Beuve.

In his hyper-intellectual complexity Baudelaire combined the essential traits of a whole cast of sitcom and soap opera characters. At one and the same time he was naïve, world-weary, professorial, arrogant, willfully, play-fully contradictory and histrionic—without overacting, because he hated

The Aupick-Baudelaire tomb and tokens, Montparnasse Cemetery

exaggeration. He was also a dandy and rich like the millionaire Thurston Howell III.

Today an unsympathetic critic on the right side of the political spectrum, finding Baudelaire perverse and immoral, as critics did in his own day, might be tempted to describe him as a trustafarian mamma's boy with attitude.

Nothing comes from nowhere. Art springs from art, not from life. Money and opportunity operate in much the same way. Baudelaire had many advantages. His elderly father was prosperous and erudite and died when Charles was a child, leaving a fortune behind. His young widowed mother remarried a career military man, an ambitious, cold-blooded, disciplinarian lieutenant colonel named Jacques Aupick who for some time had known her intimately. The dashing reactionary rose swiftly in the ranks to field marshal, minister plenipotentiary, ambassador, and senator, surviving multiple changes of regime in the style of Talleyrand, Léopold Hugo, and other ductile opportunists.

Aupick was famous in his day for his cruelty in quashing rebellions and his ruthless imposition of colonial rule. Some considered him a hero. For Baudelaire, Aupick incarnated all that was violent, ugly, brutish, repressive, and loathsome in French society from the days of Napoléon I to Napoléon III, a human blight from the First to Second Empire. Worse still, Aupick stole the affection of Baudelaire's mother, Caroline, an unforgivable act.

Tragically, Baudelaire predeceased his beloved mother and is buried at Montparnasse in the vertical Aupick family tomb, sandwiched for eternity between her and his nemesis, an ending worthy of Edgar Allan Poe.

By the time he moved to the Ile Saint-Louis in the early 1840s, Baudelaire at the age of twenty-one had already written many of the poems in what later became his masterpiece, *The Flowers of Evil*. He had traveled; had quarreled definitively with his stepfather; had lived an impeccably debauched bohemian life, changing address dozens of times; had contracted the venereal diseases that would eventually kill him; had befriended the equally riotous Félix Nadar, Henri Murger, Balzac, and other artists; and had frittered away most of his considerable inheritance. He spent the rest of his short but productive life—dying in 1867 at the age of forty-six—pleading for funds from the administrator of his trust, his perpetually conflicted mother, and a select group of friends.

A big spender with a bad business sense, Baudelaire was, contrary to common belief, a workhorse, with astonishing stamina. When he wasn't repeatedly rewriting his poetry, prose poems, essays, and articles, he was busy translating the complete works of Edgar Allan Poe, all the while dabbling with dangerous substances, drinking to excess, and trying to satisfy his insatiable lady friends, Jeanne Duval in particular.

Meet Jeanne, the celebrated Black Venus, the trustafarian's wild child and dominatrix for over twenty years, a mighty Aphrodite with a powerful contralto voice. Some thought she had Cajun roots but was Caucasian; others that she was from Haiti or Santo Domingo and had nut-brown skin and practiced voodoo. Yet others said she came from the Antilles and was a lesbian who slept with men only to earn a living. Some who knew her and had brought her to their rooms in the Hôtel Pimodan swore she was black African or mulatto—Théodore de Banville and Nadar, for instance. A small-time actress and dancer when not renting out her body, a muscular body that mesmerized and enslaved Baudelaire, she was the diametrical opposite physically and temperamentally of ghostly Mimi, that other shared passion of the artistic avant-garde. Jeanne had a mop of kinky hair and was tall and willowy, a voluptuous sorceress, "a grass snake in motion" her black eyes "as big as saucers," said Nadar.

Félix Nadar was too close a friend of the poet's and too concerned about hurting his own wife's feelings even after Baudelaire and Jeanne Duval died to admit outright that the Black Venus had also been his mistress. But his familiarity with her right down to her strong, peculiar scent was too intimate to be innocent. He acknowledged he'd known her before he met Baudelaire. She was blessed, Nadar noted in his memoir, *Baudelaire intime*, with a startling physical presence and an overdeveloped bosom that made her lithe frame look, he said, like a branch bent by a superabundance of fruit.

Jeanne went by different names—possibly none of them real. No one knew where she was born, who her parents were, or how old she was. Later on, no one seemed to know when she died, where, or of what, though syphilis is usually cited as the cause. Whoever she was and whatever the color of her skin, she had Baudelaire's number, taught him the pleasures of pain, and ruled his passions, inspiring some of his most astonishing, disconcerting poems. Among other appearances in *The Flowers of Evil*, she was the passive

observer in "The Carcass," a memento mori in verse reminding readers that
we are all dead bodies waiting to happen:

> *My love, do you remember the thing we saw*
> *That fine, fair, summer morning?*
> *The thing at the bend in the trail, a rotting carcass*
> *On a gravel-strewn bed*
> *Its legs raised in the air like a lusting woman*
> *Burning and bursting with poisons*
> *Showing off shamelessly, casually*
> *Its belly, swollen with gases.*
> *The bright sun shone down on this putridness,*
> *As if to roast it right*
> *And repay mother Nature a hundred times over*
> *For the elements she'd combined;*
> *And Heaven was watching that sublime stiff*
> *Blossoming like a flower.*

Blossoming like a flower of corruption, a flower of evil, no doubt. When
this poem was published Nadar dubbed Baudelaire "The Prince of Rotting
Carcasses," a moniker the poet did not appreciate. It may well have given
rise to the school of *littérature faisandée*—meaning, literally, well hung or gamy,
as with pheasants and wild game left to gently decompose and tenderize—
the hallmark of sickly, depraved, post-Romantic decadence.

Jeanne was also the "mother of memories, mother of mistresses" in "The
Balcony":

> *The nights ignited by the fire's fierce fashions,*
> *The shadows of the unveiled Invisible,*
> *How sweet thy breast, thy heart and all its passions!*
> *We have often said strange things imperishable,*
> *On the nights ignited by the fire's fierce fashions.*

Those nights and those passions smelled of sulfur and they scintillated
infernally, as Arthur Symons' classic 1900 translation suggests with its unforgettable line "Scents and heats of Hell's Hallucinations."

It has been said Baudelaire was a follower of Satan obsessed with Edgar Allan Poe—a curious role model for a young aristocratic Parisian—and that his life came to resemble the lives of the American author and his tormented characters. According to one of Baudelaire's many sympathetic biographers, Charles Asselineau, the poet studied Poe's detailed description of how he created the feeling of fright in "The Raven." Baudelaire then applied Poe's principles of frisson to his own writing, perfecting the process when he lived in the damp, ghost-infested Hôtel Pimodan. Glance up at its façade and you'll see it looks disconcertingly like the mansion in that other American classic *The House of the Seven Gables* by Nathaniel Hawthorne.

"Baudelaire identified himself with his model," wrote Asselineau, "to such a degree that he embraced Poe's friends and hated his enemies as if they were living people."

Could the profoundly American Poe have imagined that his manias and his love of the grotesque and arabesque would wind up distilled into the work of the most sublimely Parisian, the most read, quoted, and revered of French poets?

17

SEX, DRUGS,
AND STRIKING POSES

The first time we met Baudelaire was toward the middle of the year 1849 at the Hôtel Pimodan," wrote Gautier in his biography of the rebel, a rebel with a cause: the worship of art above all else. Baudelaire dedicated *The Flowers of Evil* to Gautier, the "exquisite poet," the red-vested renegade from the Battle of Hernani.

Gautier also lived for a time in the famous mansion in "a strange apartment that communicated with Baudelaire's via a private staircase hidden in the thickness of the wall, and which was haunted by the spirits of beautiful women loved long since by Lauzun."

Paris has never been lacking in secret staircases or spirits or beautiful women, as Gautier well knew. It seems fitting Baudelaire should choose to reside where the impecunious ladies' man the Duc de Lauzun had lived in the late 1600s. The duke stubbornly brought home his forbidden prize, the indomitable, staggeringly rich Anne Marie Louise d'Orléans, Duchess of Montpensier, better known as La Grande Mademoiselle. After many difficulties and late in life she became Lauzun's lover, though not his wife. The difficulties were engineered, as is often the case, by her family, but the barricades to marriage were erected by Louis XIV himself. He was also passionate about his kissing cousin. Like a plutocratic version of the relationship between Abélard and Héloïse or Romeo and Juliet, the liaison of Lauzun and La Grande Mademoiselle was a favorite romantic tale from the days before Romanticism.

That is one reason the dilapidated Hôtel Pimodan was the perfect aerie for Baudelaire to roost in. He was deeply, irretrievably romantic despite his futuristic literary innovations and his frequent use of the word *modern*.

Baudelaire had no title but like the Duc de Lauzun was aristocratic to the core, a nobleman in the wider sense of the word *noble*. His bearing and measured arrogance are other reasons he's a role model today, the ideal heroic modernist. Young, secular, postmodern Frenchmen and -women spray graffiti on the quays of the island and leave notes and tokens atop his tomb at Montparnasse Cemetery, invoking his intercession in their existential, sexual, and professional troubles.

Gautier's descriptions of Baudelaire's looks and clothing tell much about the man, his times and our own, and suggest multiple readings of Baudelaire's true character and sexuality.

"He was striking," Gautier observes. "He had closely cropped hair of a rich black color. It fell over a forehead of extraordinary whiteness, giving his head the appearance of a Saracen helmet. His eyes, the color of Spanish tobacco, suggested great depth and spirituality, and had a penetrating quality which was, perhaps, a little too insistent. His teeth were white and perfect, his mouth visible under a light, silky moustache screening its contours. The mobile curves, voluptuous and ironical as the lips in a face painted by Leonardo da Vinci, the nose, fine and delicate, somewhat curved, with quivering nostrils, seemed ever to be scenting vague perfumes. A large dimple accentuated the chin, like the finishing touch of a sculptor's chisel on a statue. The cheeks, carefully shaved, with ruddy cheekbones, and the neck, of almost feminine elegance and whiteness, showed plainly because the collar of his shirt was turned down with a Madras cravat."

Voluptuous and ironical, a face painted by Leonardo, *of almost feminine elegance . . .* Was Baudelaire androgynous? One of Nadar's more unusual theories is that Baudelaire was in fact sexless, a virgin, "The Virgin Poet." That is the subtitle of Nadar's memoir, *Baudelaire intime: le poète vierge.* Nadar had known Baudelaire as well as anyone could, and he believed the sex stories were a sham, that Baudelaire had never known women biblically and had only loved his mistresses in other ways. Nadar did not specify which ways, but pain and suffering are often mentioned. Baudelaire's true passionate love for as long as he lived was his mother.

Shocking? This is less unlikely than it seems. Victor Hugo had been a militant virgin poet before marrying Adèle; Balzac and Flaubert claimed to practice chastity to heighten their powers (but neither was remotely a virgin). All three worshiped their mothers—in fact, Flaubert's life was ruled by his. Baudelaire worshiped his *maman*, too. More: When young he was also erotically in love with her. "There was in my childhood," he wrote her, "a period of passionate love for you."

He was feminine without being effeminate, fastidious till the end about his manicured hands and their cleanliness; he washed them often and wore gloves—light pink gloves, Nadar reports—much of the time. But many men and women of his day were fastidious and wore gloves. Baudelaire was an aesthete, a quiet, cool observer, not the type to hug anyone, man or woman, or show emotion. A virgin, Baudelaire? The proto–rock star worshiped like a secular god by young Frenchmen and -women?

"There is no question, strangeness in all things remains the dominating characteristic of Baudelaire," Nadar explained. "Like many others who continue doggedly to dig through the complexities and contradictions of his soul, to scour his brain, we are trying to decipher the undecipherable."

Baudelaire, the proto-decadent, became the spiritual master of J. K. Huysmans and Proust, not to mention generations of fellow poets and philosophers. His was a twilight Romanticism, the crepuscule that illuminates the Ile Saint-Louis today with a studied nineteenth-century glow, a damp, bruised orange light smelling of morbidity. The scent of decay made Baudelaire's nostrils flare with pleasure.

Even Baudelaire's celebrated brand of dandyism was hard to interpret. Was it vanity or provocation or both? "He wore an overcoat of shining black cloth, nut-colored pants, white stockings, and patent leather shoes," Gautier tells us. "Everything was fastidiously correct with a stamp of almost English simplicity intentionally adopted to distinguish him from the artistic types with the soft felt hats, the velvet waistcoats, red jackets, and thick, disheveled beards." Here Gautier was poking fun at himself. "Nothing was too new or overdone about him. Charles Baudelaire indulged in dandyism to an extent, but he would do anything to avoid looking like he was wearing his 'Sunday best,' a mode of dress so dear and important to the Philistine but so disagreeable to the true gentleman."

Having outgrown Poe in later life, Baudelaire became militantly clean-shaven. He found mustaches "the remnant of an old-fashioned picturesque-ness both childish and bourgeois to retain." Shorn of "superfluous down," Gautier remarks with his usual friendly wink, Baudelaire's fine head "re-called that of Laurence Sterne, a resemblance highlighted by his habit of leaning his temple against his first finger, which is, as everyone knows, the pose the English humorist strikes in the portraits placed at the beginning of his books."

Critically for his spiritual heirs, Baudelaire cultivated this meaningful anti-philistine pose, the one Rodin, also an island regular for many years, later modified, making more masculine and forceful for *The Thinker*. It's a pose you see many young Frenchmen—and Frenchwomen these days—studiously striking at cafés and on park benches as they blow and bat at smoke or mutter into cell phones and poke at tiny screens. The word *poseur* isn't German, Italian, or English, and no translation is needed. The roots of this word lead to Baudelaire.

The way contemporary poseurs speak in ellipses and convolutions also deliciously recalls *le poète maudit*. "His courtesy was often excessive to the point of affectation," the faithful Gautier observed. "He measured his phrases, using only the most carefully selected terms, and pronounced certain words in a particular manner, as though he wished to underline them and give them a mysterious signification. Italics and capital letters seemed to be marked in his voice."

Of course the Baudelaire pose and the poet's mannered speech are fre-quently encountered not only in real life in Paris but also on stage or screen. They are the requisite, distinguishing features in countless slow, idiosyn-cratic French films unfettered by anything as vulgar as plot and driven instead by the melancholy plucking of lint from navels.

Strolling along the quai d'Anjou, I halted my constitutional one eve-ning, hopping up and sitting atop the mossy parapet, staring up through the overhanging poplar leaves at the gilded ironwork, the dolphin-shaped downspout and steep slate roof of the mansion pierced by glinting half-moon eyes.

The Hôtel de Lauzun was under restoration for nearly two years, from 2011 through 2013. Only construction workers and engineers were allowed to enter, and by the time the remodel was finished, almost nothing was left of the "original" décor, which had already been "restored" or changed several times in the 1800s. Fortunately I had the luck to visit the mansion's high-ceilinged gilded rooms twice, once nearly twenty-five years ago and again a decade after that. During my second visit, lingering, then retracing my steps as the group of visitors moved forward, I climbed a narrow service staircase to the top floor and began trying the doors, feeling my way to the poet's rooms above the carriage entrance, at the east end of the building's riverside wing.

A bohemian party boy and dandy himself when young, Charles Asselineau was a regular in those rooms and reported in his biography that Baudelaire's narrow three-chamber apartment was papered in red and black on both walls and ceiling. In the main room was an alcove, a chimneypiece, a couch piled with books, and two original oils by Émile Deroy, one of them a now-famous portrait of the poet at the time he lived in the mansion. The wild-eyed Nadar saw the portrait being painted. Nadar adds three telling details about the room. The floor was covered wall-to-wall with a thick carpet; the carpet was sprinkled daily by the scent-obsessed Baudelaire using the kind of nose-tickling cheap perfume Jeanne Duval wore; and, a red flag, the real object of veneration in the room was the miniature of Baudelaire's beautiful young mother, Caroline.

But the curious detail that has long fascinated me most in descriptions of Baudelaire's dark, fusty rooms regards the half-moon dormer and the view. Baudelaire had gone out of his way to mask the lower and middle panes of the only window overlooking the Seine. Just the upper panes were left clear so that the poet might raise his eyes and "see only the sky."

Nadar was one of the last to see Baudelaire alive in the sanatorium just off today's Avenue Victor Hugo where he died. Nadar recounts how the poet, struck by terminal syphilis, was no longer able to speak normally, though his mind remained active. They pantomimed a dialogue about religion and death and immortality. Standing at the window of his room while gazing at the changing Paris sky, Baudelaire shook his fists and muttering, cursed God. Nadar, a freethinker, said, "Then you do believe?" Baudelaire motioned to the immense and beautiful firmament, waving and struggling to speak. "Look up," Nadar understood him to be saying. "How could God not exist?"

As I stood at Baudelaire's window meditating and looked down at the river, a tour boat cruised by, its PA system blaring a short version of the tale of Lauzun and Baudelaire in French and then English. A car honked insistently. "How did you get up here?" an official-sounding voice demanded, startling me. "This floor is not open to the public."

Red-faced, I spun around and said I'd been looking for the bathrooms— it was an emergency—and had gotten lost. Before the skeptical employee could challenge me, I strode past him and down the *escalier dérobé*, rejoining the group in the second-floor salon of the west wing, the famous one where the Club des Haschichins met.

There, and in other rooms in the riverside east wing, an earnest guide went on in French about how Baudelaire had drawn inspiration from the wall and ceiling décor for his poems, and how the hallucinatory effect of the hashish and opium distorted and expanded his vision. Gautier, ever lusty and mirthful, had occupied a room next to Baudelaire's for a time and been with him on several occasions at "fantasia sessions." He noted how, in his own experience, "the nymphs, the goddesses, the gracious apparitions, burlesque or terrible, come out of the pictures, the tapestries, from the statues displaying their mythological nudity in the niches, or from the grimacing china figures on the shelves." Alas, those movable elements of the décor are no longer in the building, and Baudelaire's rooms have been entirely reconfigured, but the ceiling frescoes still give visitors to the mansion a tantalizing neck ache.

It was shortly after the scaffolding came down and before the Institute for Advanced Studies of Paris moved into the Hôtel de Lauzun at the end of 2013 that I noticed the carriage door of the mansion had been left open. I stole inside, and as a team of workers came out, I slipped through the tall iron gateway at the end of the drive into the courtyard. Within seconds the building supervisor was standing next to me. I smiled and played dumb and exaggerated my accent and pummeled him with questions about Lauzun and Baudelaire. He ushered me out politely but couldn't help showing me he knew more than I could ever know about the history of the place.

Fixing me through thick glasses he told me his father had been in charge of the building before him and that he'd lived in an apartment inside the Hôtel de Lauzun for forty-three years. Clearly he was obsessed by the duke and the poet, and knowledgeable in an idiosyncratic way. Warming to our encounter, he showed me the secret staircase and pointed out the ground-floor rooms of the southern wing, in the courtyard, where a carpenter had had a workshop in the days of Baudelaire.

"That's where Baudelaire had his bed made," he said. "You know about the bed?" I shook my head, playing dumb. "It was made in the shape of a coffin, you know that," he added gleefully. "He slept in a coffin bed, like Sarah Bernhardt, but she imitated him. It was up here," he went on, point-ing and waving enthusiastically, "that he tried to commit suicide." He paused for effect and smiled wickedly. "Of course it was an act. He cut himself up to get his mother's attention."

Lines from Baudelaire's "Spleen" sprang to mind: "his regal bed is a cof-fin drowned in care, / and ladies of the court, for whom all kings are fair, / seek a smile from that young skeleton."

Did Baudelaire really sleep in a coffin-shaped bed? There was Gautier's unforgettable description of Baudelaire's poetic imagery of coffins, beds, and death: "He describes the chill ennui of a dead person who has exchanged his bed of luxury for the coffin, who dreams in his solitude, starting at each drop of icy rain that filters through his coffin-lid . . . We see the room of the coward gallant . . . the ironical specter of suicide comes, for Death itself cannot quench the fires of lust."

Baudelaire's morbidity was notorious, but I had to wonder if the affable guardian of the mansion was pulling my leg. Sarah Bernhardt's coffin bed is a confirmed fact, however, and her morbid inclinations were recorded by many.

Legends and tall tales obscure the life and death of the *poète maudit*—a man accursed, damned, and forsaken by society and God. Gautier outlived Baudelaire by five years and set out to debunk one myth about his feline, elegant friend—the myth that he was a hophead, a drug addict. Report-edly Baudelaire tried opium and hash only a few times as an experiment but was repelled, as was Gautier after ten "sessions." Neither man could stand the notion that a poet might need artificial stimulants to perform. "He compared the ecstasy that it produced to that of a maniac," Gautier wrote, "for whom painted cloth and coarse ersatz decorations replaced real furniture and a garden full of living flowers. He came but rarely and then only as a spectator to the séances at the Hôtel Pimodan."

But when does a spectator become a voyeur?

Following Gautier's logic, Baudelaire's celebrated essay "Artificial Paradises" is a denunciation, the opposite of the demonic initiatory pamphlet that some—usually those who haven't read it—style it to this day. How many hipster movies and hard rock songs has the edgy title inspired? Many, it is clear, some of them very recent. Apparently the long-haired, gangly Jim Morrison didn't get the true message. By coincidence Morrison sang of voodoo and the City of Night, transposing Paris to Los Angeles. Morrison died of an overdose in a nightclub and was later discovered in his bathtub in the Marais, in the narrow old rue Beautreillis directly across the street from the rooms where the contralto-voiced voodoo priestess Jeanne Duval once lived, bankrolled by Baudelaire.

These were the rooms where Baudelaire kept the Black Venus late in their relationship, and made love with her in a most original and diabolical fashion—as a virgin, if Nadar was correct. Jeanne's four-hundred-year-old smog-etched, ocher-stone building to this day bears a carved keystone showing a woman's head. Squint a little and the head looks like the one in pictures of Jeanne Duval. Stranger still if you believe in such things, Morrison's tomb, usually peppered with trash and bottles and often sprayed with Dionysian graffiti, is only a few minutes' walk from Nadar's similarly cult grave at Père-Lachaise Cemetery.

Potbellied, hyperactive, and irrepressibly curious Balzac was another of the famous visitors to the island mansion. Despite his girth, he did not waddle. You have to imagine him striding along the quay, making sure he wasn't being pursued by debt collectors, tapping the sidewalk with his famous lethal walking stick, then ducking into the wide carriage door of the Hôtel Pimodan. Balzac was even less inclined than Baudelaire to take drugs, though he was a notorious coffee addict with a specially designed pot that brewed all day, and he certainly enjoyed his wine. With amused reverence Baudelaire wrote about Balzac's first time at the Club des Haschichins.

"Balzac undoubtedly thought there is no greater shame or keener suffering than the abdication of the will," Baudelaire remembered with a scratch of his quill. A slave of the Black Venus, if anyone knew what abdication meant it was Baudelaire. "I saw Balzac once at a meeting of the club when he was contemplating the prodigious effects of hashish," Baudelaire continued. "He listened and questioned people closely with entertaining vivacity. Those who knew him would guess he was bound to be interested. The idea shocked him in spite of himself. Someone presented him with the *dawamesk*," he continues, referring to the potent mixture of hash, ground pistachios, butter, and honey the club members consumed, under medical supervision. "He examined it, smelled it, and gave it back without touching or tasting it. The struggle between his almost infantile curiosity and his repugnance for the abdication of his will betrayed itself in his expressive face. His love of dignity prevailed. In effect, it is difficult to imagine the theorist of the 'will,' the spiritual twin of his character Louis Lambert, consenting to lose even a particle of this precious substance."

The "substance" wasn't the hash. It was Balzac's self-control, his indomitable will.

Gautier was there, too, lounging on the couches of the Club des Haschichins that night, staring at the frescoes and baubles, and confirmed Baudelaire's report. "Only, we would add this telling detail, that in giving back the spoonful of hashish offered to him, the only thing Balzac said was that the attempt [to use it for mind-altering purposes] would be useless, and that hashish, he was sure, would have no effect on his brain. That was possible. This powerful brain where willpower was enthroned and fortified by practice, a brain saturated with caffeine and the subtle aroma of moka, and never obscured even when he drank several bottles of light Vouvray wine, would perhaps have been capable of resisting the temporary high of Indian hemp."

So Balzac played tough. After the incident he claimed in his own writings that he had tried the drug, that it had wrestled with him briefly but seemed innocuous and was nothing to be feared—not in his case. The hash had no lasting effect, he boasted; he had overwhelmed it with his power of concentration.

It's not hard to imagine Balzac's expression as he thought and wrote this white lie after the mythic event. With his thick lips pursed and his neck stiff, he would have thrown his long hair back and dashed off the words before pacing back and forth with a satisfied smile, clutching the lapels of his signature outfit, a long, flowing dark robe. He would have struck a heroic, defiant pose like the one shown in the monumental bronze portrait of him by Rodin, the unmistakable statue now standing on Boulevard Raspail in Paris' Montparnasse district and at the Musée Rodin at Meudon, not to mention in the Smithsonian, the Met, MOMA, and other institutions worldwide.

Balzac by Rodin, Boulevard Raspail

I've often imagined Balzac, Gautier, and Baudelaire—three inveterate walkers—striding around the Ile Saint-Louis together, Three Musketeers in Romantic garb, accompanying the saucy, tall, scantily dressed Jeanne Duval from a fantasia session at the Hôtel de Lauzun back to her perfumed aerie a few blocks west and south across the island. She lived at 6 rue de la Femme-sans-Teste, called rue Regrattier today. As Hugo did with Juliette, Baudelaire housed his muse nearby, either on the island or, later, in rue Beautreillis across the river.

Her modest Ile Saint-Louis address was particularly convenient to Baudelaire, since he too lived for a time on the south side of the island in another historic building. Full of memories heavier than stone, it still stands on the corner of quiet rue Poulletier and leafy quai de Béthune and is impossible to miss, a second perfect Baudelaire address. As is true of the vintage building Jeanne Duval lived in on rue Beautreillis, the street door here on the quay is crowned by a carved keystone of a woman's head. But this time the head has creepy bat wings and harpy claws sprouting from it instead of arms and hands. The nightmare harpy doesn't look a thing like Jeanne. Not a thing.

Whoever the model for the keystone really was, the twisted love affair of mutual possession that united Baudelaire and Jeanne Duval and the frisson-inducing building he brought her to inspired another late Romantic, the journalist and novelist Gaston Leroux. His name doesn't ring a bell? Leroux is the author of one of the bestselling murder mysteries of the early twentieth century, *La Poupée Sanglante*—called *The Kiss That Killed* in English. It features a poet voyeur who climbs a ladder to peer out of his narrow sky-light at a beautiful maiden who lives next door in the celebrated Hôtel de Hesselin, a maiden who's caught up in a louche love affair and scientific experiment, some Frankenstein-style body remaking, a vampire, a mass murder with butchery, and some of the most wonderfully evocative descriptions of the crumbling, grimy Ile Saint-Louis in all its decadence that I've encountered.

Leroux's better-known book is *The Phantom of the Opera*, a work that leapt off the silver screen and, in the guise of Lon Chaney, wrapped itself around

Harpy keystone over the door to Baudelaire's former abode

my impressionable adolescent mind, sank in its sharp claws, and drew me to Paris. It was a hell of a sequel to *The Red Balloon*. Strangely Leroux, the Edgar Allan Poe of France, was born almost precisely nine months after Baudelaire died. Did both believe in the transmigration of souls?

Lon Chaney starring in The Phantom of the Opera

18

ISLANDS IN THE DREAM

From the lovelorn Lauzun via the dandies Baudelaire and Balzac to the self-adoring Rodin, the good ship Ile Saint-Louis and its crew of romantic voyagers steamed into the twentieth century with bespectacled, plump Gaston Leroux and his operatic phantoms at the helm. It soon became a symbol of expat Americana, the watery home of Bill Bird's Three Mountains Press and Ford Madox Ford's *Transatlantic Review*. Both were headquartered in the same building at number 29 quai d'Anjou.

In the 1920s and '30s a movable ghetto of expats, many of them self-styled modernists who were clearly Romantics, including Ernest Hemingway, revolved around these twin literary beacons. They hung out at the cheap river-boatman's restaurant a few doors down from them called Le Rendez-vous des Mariniers.

I stood now in front of what had been the Rendez-vous and pondered as a motorcade of vintage Citroën 2CVs rolled by, driven by garrulous guides wearing berets, Edith Piaf crooning from the radio through the open sunroof. A posse of casually dressed twenty-first-century tourists lapping ice cream cones jostled past, blissful and possibly ignorant of the island's literary history. At the Rendez-vous and in similar dives, the island's resident foreign millionaires of the Roaring Twenties and the Great Depression could slum in safety in a winy atmosphere. Harry and Caresse Crosby, Nancy Cunard, and Helena Rubinstein also had their private salons in mansions dotted on quai d'Orléans, rue le Regrattier—two doors south of Jeanne Duval's place—and quai de Béthune across from Baudelaire, respectively.

Rubinstein, the latecomer, a refugee from the rigors of the 1929 crash, distinguished herself by having the Hôtel de Hesselin pulled down and replaced by a sleek Art Nouveau town house. The 1930s building still sticks out like the proverbial nouveau riche carbuncle among authentic pearls. The historic mansion she destroyed happens to have been where Gaston Leroux set *The Kiss That Killed* a decade or so earlier. Instead of *La machine à assassiner* (*The Killing Machine*), the sequel to this book should have been titled "the makeup millionaire who massacred a landmark."

I've often wondered as I wander around the island's tony perimeter whether Hemingway's French was good enough to allow him to read Baudelaire, Balzac, or Leroux in the original and whether he realized the hash smokers' club was only a few doors down the quay from the long, steep, malodorous staircase leading from the sidewalk to the riverside. This is where he liked to work, a quiet urban patio the copyeditor-journalist-novelist from Illinois favored in fine weather.

In those early days when Ernest and Hadley were lyrically "very poor and very happy," Hemingway would put on his tennis shoes and, like his fictional hero Jake Barnes, trot downhill on the balls of his feet, ever the athlete, leaving behind his cold, cramped apartment in the Latin Quarter and his shivering wife and child so he could get down to work with the boys. He would bounce across a temporary wooden bridge from the Left Bank to the island and traverse it swiftly, throwing punches, treading the same worn cobbles Baudelaire and Jeanne Duval walked daily decades before him.

Since Hemingway was never anything like poor—he actually had a good yearly stipend from his paper, and Hadley had a trust fund—and since his first marriage was fraught from the start and fell apart after his joyless, guilty adulterous affair with Pauline Pfeiffer, one conclusion might be he wasn't happy at all, and certainly was not for long. That perpetual, recidivist unhappiness dressed up as joie de vivre, the four Hemingway marriages, and the incurable melancholy and nostalgia of Hemingway's pathetic later years, may have been what yoked him to Paris. Fleeting joy eluded him but kindled fond memories, memories heavier than stone.

Had Hemingway followed the example of Victor Hugo and kept the same wife while changing mistresses or simply added mistresses to the roster, he would have saved time, energy, and money, and who knows, maybe found *true* happiness. Hemingway lavished resources on philandering and getting separated, divorced, and remarried. It must have cut into his stock of creativity and his precious earnings. Clearly lust and love were hard to distinguish in his mind; one must have had to justify the other, with marriage sanctifying the dark passages between.

This seems especially odd since Hemingway was so like Hugo in so many ways. Perhaps he subconsciously followed in Hugo's footsteps but faltered where the Frenchman skipped ahead. Both were obsessive about money; both wrote standing up, facing walls; both were serial womanizers; both experienced an essential moment in the church of Saint-Sulpice, where Hugo got married and Hemingway prayed for sexual potency with Pfeiffer; both came from solid middle-class families racked by depression and suicide; both had a fascination with the ocean; and both wrote novels about old men and the sea. Both were also fearless, self-sacrificing, heroic, and talented, which compensated for their narcissism. Both wore beards, resembling each other, and in old age they were striking, distinguished, and desirable properties. Lastly, both lived within hailing distance of Saint-Sulpice and, had they been alive at the same time, of each other. What might they have said? Perhaps a conversation actually occurred between the living American and the deceased Frenchman during a visit to the crypt of the Panthéon.

Whatever Hemingway really felt and experienced and thought in Paris when he lived in the Latin Quarter and worked on the Ile Saint-Louis, the city was certainly more interesting than the washed-out one featuring in the pages of *The Sun Also Rises* or *A Moveable Feast*. It was as hard and real then as it is today, as hard and real as New York, Los Angeles, or Chicago in the twenties and thirties, cities described with clear-eyed courage by many American writers with their own brand of nostalgia and romance.

It's odd that a man like Hemingway who risked his life in brutal wars, boxed, hunted, fished, and caroused with the best of them would choose to tint the gritty realities of Paris, preferring fantasyland. His newspaper articles from the 1920s were more honest, revealing much about the process of "nostalgification." The City of Light was certainly darker and more inter-esting than an amusement park for the misnamed Lost Generation. Doesn't every generation start out lost and stumble forward, even with GPS? A century before Hemingway, the Romantics did.

"During the wars of the Empire while husbands and brothers were in Germany, anxious mothers gave birth to an ardent, pale, and neurotic generation," wrote Alfred de Musset in 1836. "Behind them a past de-stroyed, still writhing on its ruins with the remnants of centuries of absolut-ism, before them the dawn of an immense horizon, the first gleams of the future, and between these two worlds—like the ocean separating the Old World from the New—something vague and floating, a troubled sea filled with wreckage, traversed from time to time by some distant sail or ship trailing thick clouds of smoke: the present . . . only the present remained, the spirit of the time, angel of the dawn that's neither night nor day."

All that was left for the Lost Generations of Musset and other Roman-tics, the forebears of modernist revival rebels, was the bottle, the hookah, and the whorehouse, followed by the sanatorium, the madhouse, and the morgue.

Paris' dark influence on Hemingway was clearly inescapable. It may have been systemic and fatal, though genetics and family history also played a part: The Hemingway clan has suffered for generations from melancholic depression sometimes accompanied by suicidal tendencies. Hemingway ended his life like a true Parisian heroic modernist—like Gérard de Nerval and Isidore Ducasse and others including Baudelaire and Balzac and de Musset. Those who didn't kill themselves with weapons, nooses, or drugs worked until they dropped dead prematurely. Hemingway drank himself to oblivion and then blew his brains out dreaming of Paris. That's the dark angle few of his hagiographers evoke, perhaps because it seems an act of irreverence to a literary god who worshiped a peculiar sanitized sepia vi-sion of Paris, a god as great in America as Hugo, Balzac, and Baudelaire are in France.

The differences in the styles of worship of these literary icons reflect national characteristics. They underscore why the American romance with Paris is complex and paradoxical, rooted in myth and willful self-deception. The distinguishing difference, it seems to me, is the enduring French ca-pacity to glory in the imperfections and weaknesses of genius wherever they occur, and to speak or write with pride about adultery, homosexuality, drug addiction, alcoholism, and suicide as parts of life and possibly essential to the creative process of many artists, whether they're literary gods or not. For the French, talent excuses much, genius excuses all, and prudishness is inexcusable. Parisians in particular like their heroes and their game *bien fais-andé*, their cheeses ripe and unpasteurized, and if the biographers of Henri IV are right, their bedmates au naturel.

Another difference in these nations' points of view is directly related to the city of Paris. The French seem cognizant of the seamy, scabrous, dangerous, desperate, and wild sides of the City of Light, the sides exposed by Balzac, Hugo, Baudelaire, Zola, de Musset, and others, the world of Gaston Leroux and his dark thrillers set in the opera house or on the Ile Saint-Louis. Today that edgy Paris is found primarily though not exclusively outside the beltway. Many French heroes in everyday life struggled and some still struggle to keep the City of Light real, to keep its historic core from becoming the kind of denatured theme park for Lost Generations other contemporary lovers of the city promote, complete with Disneyland-style elephant trains for tired tourists and vintage cars driven by guides wearing berets.

If Hemingway really did have profound epiphanies in Paris, sexual or otherwise, or come to grips with the gritty and fascinating reality of the place beyond the expat ghetto, those illuminations are not visible in his words. "*A Moveable Feast* serves the purpose of a double nostalgia," wrote Christopher Hitchens in a review in *The Atlantic* when the novel was reissued in 2009, "our own as we contemplate a Left Bank that has since become a banal tourist enclave in a Paris where the tough and plebeian districts are gone, to be replaced by seething Muslim *banlieue*s all around the periphery; and Hemingway's at the end of his distraught days, as he saw again the 'City of Light' with his remaining life still ahead of him rather than so far behind."

Hitchens got part of it right. To some the appeal of Hemingway's cult memoir clearly is the nostalgia, the picture it paints of an ersatz city of dreams. But I would pitch a screwball at his other claims. The outskirts are mostly white and secular, and only a fraction of French Muslims are seething, sometimes for good reason. A century ago the *banlieue* replaced the inner-city working-class neighborhoods of the Faubourg Saint-Antoine and

Prototypical tourist mobs (by André Castaigne)

Ménilmontant as repositories of frustrations and aspirations. But the "tough and plebeian districts" still exist; they're just off visitors' radar screens. To say the Latin Quarter is touristy is a tautology. Like Montmartre, it's the very definition of touristy. Parts have lost their soul to commerce. So have other neighborhoods.

But Paris was thoroughly touristy before Hemingway's and Hitchens' day. The literature of the last century and a half groans with crabby expletives about hideous hordes and the damage they wreak. The sun also rises, but there is nothing new under the Paris sun. The nostalgia for a mythical yesteryear à la Hemingway or Hitchens is as old as the world, and here to stay. So is the phobia of Islam and latent racism, each as undeniable as it is troubling.

PART FOUR

The Cult of Les Grands Hommes
(et Les Femmes)
or How the Panthéon of Gods
Came to Earth in Paris' Latin Quarter

Gothic Romantic architecture, the quintessence of romance

19

THE ARCHITECTURE OF
ROMANCE

There is a spot on the quai d'Orléans on the sunny south side of the Ile Saint-Louis near the mansions where Harry and Caresse Crosby and Nancy Cunard lived, a scenic parapet to sit on at a fork in the Seine at its widest. From it, rising above the poplars, you see in one glance the flying buttresses of Notre Dame on the Ile de la Cité and high upon the Left Bank—crowning a hill of higgledy-piggledy tin, tile, and slate roofs—the clumsy faux Bramante dome topping the Panthéon.

The twofer view has romance and Victor Hugo written all over it: He was officially the first and is still the most illustrious "great man" to be entombed in the secular Panthéon when it reopened in 1885. The towers of Notre Dame's façade, instead, form the famous giant H for Hugo. The missing V is abstract, standing for *Victor* and *victory*. It was V.H. who ultimately saved the cathedral, a "poem in stone," from ruin.

That uncanny giant H is not really why Hugo turned Sainte-Beuve into Quasimodo and Adèle into Esmeralda and battled to have the cathedral restored, as some detractors claimed. But it certainly provided a comical hook to hang the novelist's caricatured ego on.

Both temples were conceived as churches. But they are opposites in most ways. They are the twins of Romanticism: ecclesiastical, pagan, secular, symbolic, yin and yang.

From this Seine-side perch, what you see most clearly about Notre Dame

The façade of Notre Dame Cathedral

are the cathedral's buttresses, a herd of rearing stone stallions. The equine ensemble leaps in superimposed tiers supporting walls made light by tall stained-glass windows reaching almost to the eaves of the steep, fretted roof. It is topped by an enormously tall ironwork spire— ambiguously inspirational to those with carnal romance and not religion in mind.

As is so often the case in Paris, the flesh outperforms or melds with the human spirit and perhaps the Holy Spirit as well, because the medieval Gothic cathedral was brutalized during the French Revolution, then buried alive by fantastical, irreligious "restorations" carried out in the mid-1800s by Eugène Viollet-le-Duc. He was a progressive, an eclectic, antiacademic, anticlerical, revolutionary architect of extraordinary and at times outlandish verve. He resuscitated Notre Dame, creating a saintly Frankenstein of limestone cross-dressed as Our Lady.

Viollet-le-Duc did not so much restore but rather completed the building or rebuilding of scores of churches, monuments, and citadels in France. John Ruskin, who fancied himself a purist, denounced this approach as irresponsible and irreversible destruction. By today's standards, Ruskin was right. But for Viollet-le-Duc, artifice was all. His re-creations are a big part of the magic of Paris today—the gargoyles, spires, grotesques, caryatids, and strixes, those ghouls peering down from balconies, towers, turrets, and massive stone walls. They are the quintessence of the Romantic imagination, entirely false yet so appropriate, so quintessentially Paris that if they were removed, even the purists might weep.

These elements of Viollet-le-Duc's faux medieval stonework correspond

*The Vampire, above by Charles Meryon, and The
Hunchback of Notre Dame, right, by Luc-Olivier
Merson*

Ile de la Cité, the downstream tip, Paris' most romantic spot? (by J. Gavin)

to the equally elaborate novelistic technique Victor Hugo employed in *The Hunchback of Notre Dame* and elsewhere.

The illustrious master of words was not satisfied writing an accurate historical novel, though like Viollet-le-Duc he believed a degree of verisimilitude was important to the narrative and he researched his works thoroughly. What was absolutely indispensable for both was capturing the essence of the thing, the message or hidden spark that would bring to life buildings or pages of ink squirming with wily, loathsome, desperate, half-crazed people and dirty, dangerous, dilapidated places. Many unforgettable scenes in Hugo's novel were set here, on the Ile de la Cité, but like 95 percent of the island's medieval layout, its twoscore places of worship, the Romanesque heritage and half-timbered remnants of yore, the backdrop for *The Hunchback of Notre Dame* is no longer, wiped clean by Napoléon III and Baron Haussmann.

The peculiarly Parisian Gothic Revival that Hugo and Viollet-le-Duc spearheaded, the supposedly "native style" of France, incarnated this idiosyncratic French philosophy of artifice and wanton fiction. Opposing factions of planners and architects have wrangled about it ever since.

From the Ile Saint-Louis, stroll across the banal 1960s footbridge linking the islands, push through the swinging iron gates, and enter the garden behind Notre Dame. If you can navigate your way around the scrum of snapshooters in front of the Virgin-and-spire fountain, head from there south under the clipped lindens and pause on the paved park road above the Seine's narrowest stretch. If you look up at the life-size bronze sculptures ranged along the roof of the cathedral where the transept and nave meet, under the spire you'll notice one figure facing in the opposite direction of the others. He's staring up. That figure is a self-portrait of Viollet-le-Duc, a tongue-in-cheek reference to Bernini's *Four Rivers* fountain in Piazza Navona in Rome.

You may not be able to make out the features of the sculpture without binoculars, but you've probably already seen Viollet-le-Duc in Nadar's famous photo of him as a distinguished, slim elderly gentleman with a bushy white beard and a hairless pate. While Viollet-le-Duc was ten years younger than Hugo, his orbit intersected with the poet's at many junctures. They shared friends and rivals from Sainte-Beuve to Stendhal and the enigmatic Prosper Mérimée. Both Viollet-le-Duc and Hugo were on the same side of

Viollet-le-Duc as Apostle (photo credit: Harmonia Amanda)

the barricades in 1830 and 1848. Their paths diverged after Louis Napoléon Bonaparte's bloody coup d'état in 1851. Hugo resisted and went into exile until 1870, continuing the Battle of Hernani against Napoléon III from Jersey and Guernsey. Viollet-le-Duc stayed and thrived at the Second Empire court with Prosper Mérimée.

A regular at the Arsenal Library, Mérimée moved on from writing stories, notably one that became the opera *Carmen*, and fantastic tales to become the inspector general of historic monuments for King Louis Philippe. Thus Mérimée serendipitously became quirky Viollet-le-Duc's even quirkier boss. Both befriended Eugénie de Montijo. When she married Napoléon III and became Empress Eugénie, Mérimée and Viollet-le-Duc were able to influence the volatile emperor and perhaps prevented some of his worst excesses.

A curious remnant of Romanticism is the fact that faux Gothic trumps all other styles to this day. Polls and plebiscites are clear. Many in Paris assume the Eiffel Tower and Louvre are the city's most visited sites and are surprised to discover half-mile lines to enter Notre Dame or climb its towers. The venerable, many-times-restored cathedral is over 850 years old, yet beats all comers: 13.5 million people visit it annually, nearly twice as many as the Eiffel Tower and twenty times the Panthéon's take. Whatever purists make of Viollet-le-Duc's fanciful restorations and however many natives or residents gripe about the difficulty of using Notre Dame for spiritually oriented reflection and prayer, the building works.

Artifice, blissful ignorance, and self-deception are key. Does anyone know or care the sculptures are copies, most of the stones in the cathedral are new, the stained glass was largely redone, and the Gothic church of all those years ago looked remarkably less Gothic? Probably not. The magic of the site emanates from intangible, hidden sources, from notions, hopes, dreams, beliefs, misconceptions, and, who knows, perhaps from the ancient foundations and crypt. The site has been holy since antiquity. The palimpsest of civilization vibrates for the sensitive. Gird your loins, wander in, if you can during off-hours in deep winter, and be engulfed. The light seeping through the stained glass dances with the dust motes, and the sound of organ music and prayers covers shuffling feet, chatter, and clicking shutters or ringing cell phones. The chill is not wholly from the damp and cold. Even freethinkers can be moved.

20

THE ANTI-ROMANTICS

From the Haussmannized blandness of Ile de la Cité, hopscotch up to the Panthéon starting, preferably, behind Notre Dame and crossing the short span of Pont de l'Archevêché. You'll participate in Paris' now celebrated, unplanned contemporary art-installation-cum-romantic-happening, an orgy of thousands of mating padlocks and combination locks attached to the bridge. This is the bête noire of public officials. There is an upside: The romantic scarification of trees on the Seine has abated. The locks also glint alluringly in the sun or moonlight and glow strangely at dawn and dusk and when the streetlamps ping to life. Many locks are now beribboned, like luggage, in a vain effort to make them distinctive.

Performing before them, enlaced amorous couples and newlyweds from Asia, America, and Africa (and a few stray optimists from France) pose for photographs, each clicking closed a lock, spinning the tumbler or tossing the key into the Seine. I have heard these neo-Romantics invoke the gods or angels of eternal love and devotion. Others ask with sardonic delight how long it will be before the municipal authorities cut off all the locks and grates. Will the divorce lawyers of coming decades issue bolt cutters or demand the combinations in settlements? "Love in chains is not love," one young Frenchman tagged the bridge, but few paid attention; the graffiti was in French.

Beware the silent tourist train gliding by as you double back west on the Left Bank down curving alleys laid out in the days of the Roman Empire. Then amble into the Square Viviani, a pocket-size park with a fine view of

Locks on the Pont des Arts

Notre Dame. In the corner of the park near the Romanesque church grows Paris' oldest living tree. It is a locust tree dug up in the New World, shipped back to the Old, and planted in 1602. Henri IV was king, the Pilgrims had not sailed, and the Declaration of Independence of the United States was 174 years in the future. The tottering "witness tree" has been propped up by a cement crutch for over half a century. It is the object of veneration by those who, like me, admire resilience and tenacity. The city has grown outward around the tree, a spider's web or snail shell now over ten times as

populous as it was in 1602. I get dizzy thinking of the thousands who have sat in its shade, contemplating Notre Dame or the mysteries of life and the possible meanings of eternity.

The bulging unspectacular hodgepodge church of Saint-Julien-le-Pauvre abuts the tree. Fittingly, the visible parts of Saint Julien are about nine hundred years old. The unseen foundations and subterranean chambers go back to the sixth century or earlier.

A hundred yards west of the tree and church, another sixth-century sanctum, Saint-Séverin,

squats on the far side of the modern crossroads. This was where two Roman highways met. In the ninth century one of them became the main north-south pilgrimage route to the shrine of Saint James the Greater in Spain, better known as El Camino de Santiago. Like all of Paris' sanctums from late antiquity, Saint-Séverin was rebuilt in the Middle Ages, then again in the Renaissance before being added to and "restored" by Viollet-le-Duc or his associates and heirs. The bell tolling soulfully from the six-hundred-year-old belfry is the oldest in the city, cast in a foundry in 1412, a rare escapee from war requisitioning and the French Revolution.

Saint-Séverin before Viollet-le-Duc's gargoyles were added (by J. Gavin)

What is it about the tangle of unpredictable narrowness surrounding Saint-Julien and Saint-Séverin? Is it the lack of symmetry, the random ratio of the height of the sawtoothed buildings, each different, to the width of the streets and alleyways? What makes this and other parts of the Latin Quarter human, frail, friendly, and likable?

My guess is the magic does not emanate from the wall-to-wall faux Greek taverns headquartered here, where dinner plates are tossed to the floor after a meal, or the taverns' neighbors, the mildewy jazz clubs that once hosted greats like John Coltrane. Is it the faux French provincial bistros, the Turkish kebab and North African couscous joints? I suspect the romantic atmosphere is not the result of the airborne lamb fat and the fritter fryers brimming with toxic-smelling grease, either, the souvenir stands, the unwelcoming cafés, and the third-rate hotels whose carpets are stiff with filth. What is it, then?

It might be that everything in the Latin Quarter is made to the measure of man—and woman. The proportions are human, the widths and heights instantly comprehensible. The shapes of the cityscape, the curves in the streets and buildings, the unevenness, the different textures and materials—stone, brick, wood, tin, tile—are organic and more than merely pleasing to the eye. They are comforting. They feel natural, like a woodland or forest grown over centuries, selectively cut, grown again and again, interspersed with clearings and meadows. There is no straightness, no symmetry. Perhaps most important of all, there are no dead, blind walls. Every inch is alive and occupied, accessible, with windows and doors and displays to tempt and entertain. This is the opposite of the corporate street, the imposing monolith of the big-box store and shopping mall, the skyscraper, the grid of modernist efficiency. It is humble, vernacular, independent, chaotic, and unpredictable—and thoroughly Parisian.

Once you've crossed the straight, broad rue du Petit Pont and plunged into the alleyways, raise your eyes again to Saint-Séverin's façade: The sublime spectacle of gargoyle spouts, spires, and other ornaments awaits. They are not flamboyant Gothic, as some guidebooks falsely advertise, but fanciful Romantic inventions brought to you thanks to the incorrigible Viollet-le-Duc, Prosper Mérimée, Victor Hugo, and others down the last two centuries. These are the people who re-created or fought to preserve old Paris from Napoléon III and then, in the 1960s and '70s, from his fellow modernizer Georges Pompidou, a banker-turned-politician bent on transforming Paris into New York or Chicago.

Both Napoléon III and Pompidou failed for a simple reason: You can modernize Paris but not Parisians.

Behind Saint-Séverin stand the remains of Paris' last charnel house, a vaulted ossuary once overflowing with bones. Rarely open, it is now the main architectural feature in a handsome garden where the pious pray and others peck or picnic.

One street west, rue de la Harpe marks a boundary. A few dozen sixteenth- and seventeenth-century buildings still stand. Gone are the others; gone too are the medieval byways, including the kinked section of rue de la Harpe that climbed toward the Panthéon and Luxembourg Garden. On it once stood the teetering house where Félix Nadar shared an artist's studio with the other bohemians starring in *La Bohème*, the real-life place where Mimi posed and Murger wrote his famous *Sketches from Bohe-mian Life*.

The alleys and streets here once ran atop the ruins of the ancient Roman bathhouse at Cluny, still the oldest preserved site in the city. Cluny is the quintessence of romance and Romanticism. Gothic or Renaissance gables and vast salons with massive timbers and mammoth fireplaces, spiraling or sweeping stone staircases, mullioned windows, stained glass, hidden passageways: Such was the abbot of Cluny's Paris hideaway. It is shoehorned into the hot, warm, and cold rooms of the third-century Roman bath complex where Emperor Julian the Apostate was crowned in 360 AD. The magical hodgepodge was saved in extremis in the 1840s and turned into the National Museum of the Middle Ages. It was too important to be wrecked even by the supreme wrecker, Napoléon III.

I like to visit these islands of antiquity at dawn when the vampires and owls sleep, before the tourist traps beckon, before the buses disgorge the flashing hordes, before the air is thick with trans fats and hucksters' cries.

Hotel de Cluny saved, not improved (by Thomas Shotter Boys)

You too may begin to feel the power of what's random and ancient yet alive, and understand how romance survives in hostile urban environments like hope or faith or moss and four-hundred-year-old locust trees, spawning new generations of sensitive dreamers passionate about historic preservation.

As in the Marais, Paris' bobo paradise, in the hard-driven Latin Quarter's back courts and on upper floors, students from the Sorbonne or the School of Medicine, professors, artists, mimes, housekeepers, small-business owners, and other embattled longtime residents from pre-gentrification days live behind double glazing armed with earplugs. Some join the Bacchanalia; some share cupboard-size rooms and cold-water taps and strive for excellence in and out of the mainstream. Romanticism lives on.

There are moments, albeit rarely, when I wander these and other remnant streets around Saint-Séverin and nearby Saint-Germain-des-Prés, when the words of William Blake play in my head. They reformulate themselves to fit the worlds of Baudelaire, Nadar, and Jim Morrison, and the Paris of today. "Tiger, tiger, burning bright," they tease, "in the cities of the night, what immortal hand or eye could frame thy fearful symmetry?"

Symmetry and regularity is what the "modern" Paris of the anti-Romantics Napoléon III and Haussmann are all about and why their remade city appeals to a certain kind of visitor.

Symmetry and regularity suggest light, openness, cleanliness and safety, streamlined modernity, military precision, predictability—the opposite of the perceived oppressiveness and chiaroscuro obsolescence of the old Paris the Napoléon-Haussmann duo trashed. Everyone is entitled to a preference in architecture and urban planning. Remember Victor Hugo's rejection of the classical notions of symmetry, order, and proportion: "The beautiful has but one type, the ugly has a thousand?" Ugly is beautiful; beautiful is boring, stultifying, and authentically ugly.

Here is a game I sometimes invite friends and guests to play after I take them for a stroll. Imagine a mental list of your favorite Paris sights, the places that whisper or sing or shout "Paris" to you. Recite it and I'll tell you the when and who, what and where. Alternatively you can look up the entries with Google if that's more convenient. There's no need to think in chronological order or sort by neighborhood.

Does your list include the Eiffel Tower, for instance? That's after Napoléon III and Haussmann. The Sainte-Chapelle? That's from way before—

rebuilt and "improved" by Viollet-le-Duc et al with the addition of that impressive outsize spire. Notre Dame? Ditto. The Louvre? Sacré-Coeur? The Luxembourg Garden? The Jardin des Plantes? The Panthéon? Saint-Sulpice? Les Invalides? The Champs-Élysées? The Conciergerie? The Place Dauphine? The Grands Boulevards? The Arc de Triomphe? The catacombs? The mansions on the Ile Saint-Louis? The Cluny Museum or Hôtel de Sens? The mansions and streets and squares of the Marais, or the Place des Vosges? The Canal Saint-Martin? The Seine and its banks? The Pont Neuf? The Grand Palais and Petit Palais? The Pont des Arts? Trocadéro?

Keep going.

The Faubourg Saint-Honoré, Place Vendôme, Place de la Concorde, the Madeleine, and Tuileries? The Palais Royal, the Rodin Museum, cafés, glass-roofed passageways and shopping galleries, department stores, the Gare de Lyon, the Gare d'Orsay? The rue de Rivoli? Go on.

Notice anything? Each of these originated before or came after the seismic remake. Few of them have anything to do with Haussmann and Napoléon III, beyond often reckless remodeling, extension, or expansion marked by the dead hand of autocrats. Haussmann was no architect or city planner. He was a policeman, a prefect, the pig-iron hand empowered by the emperor to crush opponents of the master plan for Paris. The plan was Napoléon III's; he lived with a giant map of the city in his office. It had red lines for boulevards connecting blue dots for monuments and was an exercise in transforming a snail shell or spider's web into a series of starbursts. That map looks astonishingly like a battle plan or perhaps the map of a French royal hunting forest devised for blood sports, for armed men on horses and packs of dogs out to kill.

What's curious about the world's love of Paris is that hardly anyone loves the symmetrical Paris of the Second Empire, though they're convinced they do.

Let's go back to that list. The Grands Boulevards are surely of his conception? you ask. I'm afraid not. The ring of boulevards everyone prefers was built by order of Louis XIV in the late 1600s atop the fourteenth-century ramparts of Charles V. Not that the Sun King wanted to gift his subjects with a leafy promenade. His real objective was to demolish the city walls so the rebellious aristocrats who'd already tried to assassinate him during the Fronde rebellion would never be able to defend Paris again.

*An authentically Grand Boulevard—no Haussmann,
please (by André Castaigne)*

Bellicosity can evolve seren-dipitously into poetry, as Balzac knew. "Every capital has its poem in the cityscape, where it expresses and sums itself up, where it is particularly true to itself," he exclaimed about these reconverted ramparts in *À Paris!*, his love song to the city written a decade before Haussmann's arrival. "The Boulevards today are to Paris what the Grand Canal is to Venice . . . the Corso to Rome."

Those original Louis XIV boulevards were and remain the antithesis of the Second Empire. They're comparatively narrow, short, lined by uneven, unsymmetrical buildings of many ages and many heights, with sidewalks that rise and fall. Even someone as archly anti-revolutionary and bourgeois as chronicler Edmond de Goncourt could note dismally that he felt estranged in the post-Haussmann city by changes like the "new boulevards without a curve, without plays of perspective, implacable straightaways that don't feel they're from Balzac's world, that make one think of some American Babylon of the future."

There's a scientific reason for this that goes beyond questions of taste. Haussmann-type symmetry works on paper when seen from on high by the eyes of artillery designers, real estate speculators, architects, and city planners. But the Renaissance tricks of perspective that work so well in royal hunting forests or the gardens designed by Le Nôtre—the Tuileries, for instance—don't translate into psychically satisfying cityscapes. Those tricks make distant buildings and objects appear big and allow differing topographical features and street levels to appear to open up as a viewer moves toward and through them.

To feel this with your mind and body, walk through the Tuileries to Concorde and up the Champs-Élysées. It works. There is a slope, there are trees, and there are buildings of different heights and alignments.

Compare this with Napoléon III's new city, where the standardized length and width and flatness of the axes—most of them treeless and lined by monotonous boxes of the same size and height and all of them strictly aligned—create dead ends. Each apparently endless perspective narrows and closes down on itself. Each cannon-shot boulevard appears to be a cul-de-sac.

Rue de Rivoli? The long, handsome, arcaded section of it starting at Place de la Concorde was built by Napoléon I and was extended during the Restoration and under Louis Philippe. Its eastern end toward the Place de la Bastille was ordered by Haussmann and is the perfect American Babylon. It's universally unpopular—noisy, traffic-clogged, oppressive in its sameness.

What about the sidewalk cafés? Surely they're a Second Empire feature? They got going in the 1600s and reached their apogee in the first half of the nineteenth century.

The glass-roofed shopping galleries such as the Passage des Panoramas were built from the 1790s through 1840s.

The department stores starting with Bon Marché arose in 1850 before

Rue de Rivoli arcades, the upside of the street, signed Napoléon I (not his nephew)

Café culture then and now: The waiters' uniforms and atmosphere are unchanged

Napoléon dubbed himself emperor or hired Haussmann. The ones built during their tenure had nothing to do with the fiat of a dictator but rather with private initiative in the time of Louis Philippe.

How many people come to Paris to enjoy the Boulevard de Sébastopol, Place du Châtelet, and the straightaways around the train stations on the Right Bank, or the Place Saint-Michel and its comic-book fountain, the boulevards inside the beltway, or the Prefecture of Police and the Hôtel-Dieu on the Ile de la Cité? A few do, maybe. After all, some people flock to Paris preferring the Centre Pompidou to the Louvre or the Musée d'Orsay, so it's conceivable someone might prefer the Boulevard Haussmann or Pompidou's 1970s beltway, for that matter, to the alleys of the Latin Quarter and Saint-Germain, or the Luxembourg and the sycamore-lined boulevards built by the Sun King. True, much of the Louvre was remodeled and extended by Hector Lefuel during the Second Empire. But his heavy-handed academic, anachronistic work is generally what people like least about the Louvre's gloomy exterior.

I have no objection to the comfortable, blocky Haussmann-era apartment houses per se. They remind me of hatboxes, wedding cakes, and old steamships. Now that they are antiques and in some neighborhoods decrepit and less symmetrical due to the passage of time or the wrecker's ball or the shells of Big Bertha in World War I, I feel almost protective of them. If they were to be demolished en masse by a new Pompidou, God knows what would replace them. The pre-Haussmann city is gone. Why not preserve what's left and what's good—intelligently?

Almost all Paris' magical Second Empire green spaces—including the handsome garden boulevard Avenue Foch, linking the Arc de Triomphe and Bois de Boulogne—were the work of the unsung apolitical Jean-Charles Adolphe Alphand, director of public works. Alphand was responsible for Paris' charming neighborhood parks scattered everywhere, and the highly romantic Buttes-Chaumont and Montsouris, plus the remake of the Bois de Vincennes and Bois de Boulogne edging town (they predate Haussmann). He carried on creating Paris' street-level identity after the Second Empire crumbled.

There are some successful large-scale projects from the Second Empire, to be sure. They include the crazily overblown Opera House. Another architectural winner from that anti-Romantic time is the Boulevard Saint-Germain: It destroyed much, but in its curving, tree-lined elegance, is a successful addition to the city. The curves and trees are the key, but so is the fact that the project took decades to complete and the buildings are not uniform. There are of course the sewers—extended and improved by Haussmann's engineers, particularly Eugène Belgrand. Some visitors enjoy delving into them. I would pay not to experience again that bizarre spectacle of sewage and stench.

Another arguably quintessential feature of the cityscape came along in the mid-nineteenth century in the form of Paris' street furniture—the vernacular accoutrements from benches and lampposts for gas lamps to tree girdles, advertising pillars, blue enamel street signs, and drinking fountains. Alphand played a role in creating or redesigning many of these elements, while others originated during the Restoration of 1815–1830 or the reign of Louis Philippe, a king whose notions of urban renewal were progressive, incremental, energetic, and profit-driven without being totalitarian and militaristic.

It was Louis Philippe's prefect of the Seine, Claude-Philibert Barthelot, Count of Rambuteau, who famously said, "Give Parisians water, air, and shade!"

He should have added "light," because he, building on what his

Restoration-era predecessors had begun, deserves far more credit than Napoléon III or Haussmann for transforming Paris into a "city of light." But that
is part of the Paris myth: that the Second Empire somehow brought civilization, comfort, modernity, and enlightenment to a filthy, dark, benighted
outpost threatened by radical socialists. The opposite is true: The Second
Empire wrecked and bankrupted Paris and set France back a quarter century.

Louis Philippe's and Rambuteau's plans were a model for many across
the globe, including Napoléon III and Haussmann. Having subtracted the
idealism, the anti-Romantics took them to radical extremes. With its tabula
rasa approach, the Second Empire provided ammunition for the Gilded Age
visionaries of the American Babylon and the Italian Futurists who aspired
to demolish Venice, not to mention other later role models such as Stalin,
Hitler, Mussolini, and Ceaușescu. The effects of the Napoleonic mind-set
are lasting, visible in the ongoing "modernization" of China. Spider's webs,
snail shells, and other organic-shaped cities everywhere are still being turned
into twenty-first-century firing ranges and abacus grid blocks filled with
high-rises. The ongoing effort to rehabilitate Napoléon III and his prefect
reflects the spirit of our times.

Other favorite features that make Paris' streets magical today from the
imaginative Métro stops to the bottle-green newspaper kiosks are not Second Empire but rather date to the Belle Époque or the early 1900s to '30s.
Strangely, this was a period when social democracy was the guiding para-
digm, the neo-Romantic Decadents or Surrealists were in vogue, and Art
Nouveau or Art Déco flourished. Social justice turns out to be a powerful
motor of romance and preservation then and now.

Symmetry is the ultimate measure of beauty, you say? Perhaps in a face,
as behavioral scientists assure us, though personally I prefer a Picasso portrait to the models in *Vogue* and would nearly always pick higgledy-piggledy
Parisian vernacular over a symmetrical Haussmann apartment house or a
linear, soulless masterwork by Le Corbusier. The humorless Swiss modernist actually came up with a plan to flatten the historic Marais and replace it
with symmetrical, uniform three-hundred-foot skyscrapers. Why so many
contemporary French star architects are bent on transforming Paris, as Le
Corbusier was, into another Chicago, Manhattan, or Shanghai would be a
mystery if the economic rewards and self-aggrandizement were not so glar-
ingly obvious.

21

THE ACADEMY OF
THE DEAD

Now pick a street, any street, the narrower and older and more asymmetrical the better, and climb from the alleyways of the Latin Quarter south up the Montagne Sainte-Geneviève to the Panthéon and its pre-Haussmann neoclassical straightness, dead walls, and sterilizing sunlight. You can't get lost. Navigate by sight: From street corners you'll see the two-hundred-foot hovering dome of what long was Paris' tallest and least liked monument until the Eiffel Tower and then the Montparnasse Tower came along.

Parisians soon learned to love Eiffel's lacy ladder of vertical bridges. The brownish hulking glassy skyscraper at Montparnasse instead provides a useful negative model. In the 1970s it made the clumsy, poorly designed, badly built Panthéon, a mastodon trampling a hilltop, seem lightweight and likable in comparison. Perhaps if Montparnasse lasts, it too will be adopted and hailed as a masterpiece of French architecture. Its planners came from Chicago, but so what? The Panthéon came from Italy and it is exquisitely French and universally recognized as a work of genius by those uniquely qualified to say so.

Nowadays when you near the monument you'll see steel girders and platforms, networks of scaffolding, trusses and tarps. They were put in place to prevent the Panthéon from filling the neighborhood with rubble. It threatened to collapse and crush the symbolic spirit of the French Republic.

The Panthéon's drum beats the march of the nation

Leaking at the joints and riven throughout with rusting metal, the dome, hidden buttresses, and substructures could no longer hold, like Yeats' poetic center of cosmic gravity.

Yet compared with twelfth-century Notre Dame, the Panthéon is new. It was conceived by Louis XV's architect Jacques-Germain Soufflot, dedicated to Sainte Geneviève, the longtime patron saint of Paris, and built between 1764 and 1790. This was not a propitious time for Catholics or royals. Before it could be completed, the windows had to be filled with stone to prevent sagging, and that was only the beginning of the Panthéon's woes.

The history of the monument some call the "Académie Française of the dead" has parallels with the roller-coaster ride of modern France. The church's role isn't a happy one. Luckless Sainte Geneviève was driven out by the Virgin Mary as the city's patron after Louis XIV was born in 1638, and her original shrine, an abbey, was later flattened. Since Sainte Geneviève still rated worship, she was promised a very large and new one as long as she agreed to cure the next king, Louis XV, of a sudden illness he contracted during the Siege of Metz in 1744. She did. After a mere twenty-year delay, the grateful monarch raised a bejeweled finger and commanded that work commence on the new Royal Church. But it was not to be. The job took decades to complete, Louis XV died, Soufflot died and was laid to rest in his work site, Louis XVI came and was ousted and beheaded, and the saint's powers waned during the atheistic Revolution of 1789. In 1791 the temple of divine right was designated the seat of the cult of the secular republic, the new "Temple of the Nation."

As teeters the Panthéon, so teeters France. Once again the nation is balanced on the edge of an abysmal identity crisis worse than its cyclical economic crises. Meanwhile swarms of "experts" wrangle over the temple's future while others less expert but harder working—most of them imported African laborers—prop up the great drum that beats out the march of French time.

The Christian cross inside the Panthéon and the inscription outside on the tympanum—"A Thankful Homeland to Its Great Men"—have been hoisted and pulled down many times, like flags signaling a round robin of monarchy, republicanism, or the communistic Commune. The stable bedrock is a single massive tomb in the crypt. No need to guess—it belongs to Victor Hugo. Ironically the bard of Gothic wound up encased in an archaic Greco-Roman sarcophagus in a neoclassical pile, a graceless, leaden hodgepodge of the magical Pantheon in Rome, the exquisite Tempietto by Bramante, also in Rome, and other handsome temples in Paestum and elsewhere, all Italian. Like so many French artists and architects, Soufflot trained in the Eternal City and did his Grand Tour of the Italian peninsula.

Whether you like the neoclassical style or not—Hugo did not, noting that "Soufflot's Sainte-Geneviève is certainly the best stone Savoy cake ever baked"—it fits the site from a certain historical perspective. The ancient Roman forum of Lutetia Parisiorum, the city that produced Paris, lies in front of the building, spilling like a river of melted memories under rue Soufflot all the way to Boulevard Saint-Michel. The builders of the Panthéon unearthed ancient Roman Lutetia as they mowed down the medieval city and erected the temple, square, and symmetrical neoclassical administrative buildings around it. Over the last centuries the Roman forum has been excavated, mapped, and covered. The only visible trace of it is a wall in an underground parking lot. What might Alphonse Karr have said? Through destruction, reconstruction, the wheel turns, Paris abides.

Beyond Hugo and the Panthéon's distinguished secondary figures—

Dumas and Zola foremost—the sight's other attractions are the mesmerizing view from the dome, more intimate than from the Eiffel Tower or Montparnasse, and the even more mesmerizing pendulum in the nave. Foucault's famous movable, nomadic pendulum has been several times a guest in these precincts. Like so much in Paris, it's a replica, a copy, something mobile yet permanent. That doesn't alter its wondrousness. I remember watching it being reinstalled in 1995 after an absence of decades. I circle by every few years to watch its swing and meditate on its divining significance.

I returned recently to find the same toothy guard as always lurking amid the towering Corinthian columns outside. He informed me with the same wicked glee that the panoramic terrace was still closed. As before, he barked at reluctant customers, saying there was plenty to see, Foucault's pendulum and over seventy of the tombs of France's great and good, "including women now," he added like a barker. Women—this was a novelty.

The vastness of the chill void, the height of the nave, and the aerial dome's celestial lantern are dramatic enough to suck air from the lungs. Was that a pigeon winging through shafts of light or the Holy Ghost? That a freethinker could wonder is an indication of the awe the interior is capable of inspiring. Its spell is not pleasant but rather affecting, in the style of a war memorial or abandoned industrial plant, a paean to yawning gigantism. How can current government plans succeed in transforming the site from "haunted to inhabited," from bloodless institutionalized propaganda machine to humane lighthouse of goodness? It is a daunting task made harder by the building's forbidding architecture: above all, in my view, by its tall blank walls, walls with no openings, no windows or doors, no way in or out.

Plumb line under the dome, Foucault's pendulum dangles from a wire two hundred feet long. Back and forth it swung in the clammy chiaroscuro, demonstrating as it did in 1851 the rotation of the Earth, marking the seconds, the minutes, the hours, and the days. Back and forth it shuttled. Back and forth my eyes followed, my head beginning to spin. It was not the pendulum moving forward, I knew, but I, we the people gathered on the perimeter, the Panthéon itself, the city of Paris, the Earth, moving around the plumb bob.

Mesmerized, I understood something: The bob was Paris marking eternal returns as everything spun around it. Paris was as eternal as Rome. The

Victor Hugo, hero and tomb as common currency

real Paris is of the mind, so it doesn't exist and can't age. That's what the Carnavalet and Paris' cemeteries are all about. That's what the Panthéon aspires to be: a machine for stopping time without divine intervention.

Too cold to stand still, I clambered down echoing stairs into a scrubbed yet mildewed crypt. French notions of gallantry are pervasive, but nowhere more so than in the Panthéon. Until 2015 the vaulted tombs of the great men shared their club with a single great woman, Marie Curie, a naturalized Pole. There was also the wife of another great man, the chemist and statesman Berthelot, who over a century ago refused to be separated from her. He died shortly after she did, unable to live without her. So the giant doors of the Panthéon swung open double wide. This struck me as more than romantic. It was chivalric. But the mentality of the Belle Époque could be surprisingly latitudinous and postmodern.

As I stood before the heavy stone sepulcher of Victor Hugo, tears welled in my eyes, and, as in Notre Dame or Saint-Séverin or on that snowy morning in 1986, my head stuck through a rooftop, I wondered if it was the cold or something more. It was more. The more I have learned about Hugo, the more nonplussed I am, the more I wish he could be resuscitated and lead the country and the world. I stopped myself. That was nonsensical. He already does lead France—from behind. The Panthéon is a transmitter broadcasting Hugo's ideals on the collective memory band. Memory is heavier than stone but lighter than air.

The myth that Hugo was the first here is a myth, yet that doesn't change his ownership of the edifice. The revolutionary hero Mirabeau, another lover of women, a devious one, was the original tenant, the man the revolutionaries converted the former church to honor. He is recalled on a memorial plaque. But few other than historians associate Mirabeau with the site. Ditto Marat, the firebrand, unforgettably knifed in his bathtub by Charlotte Corday: He was the second "great man" resident here. Both were evicted as the Terror's blade chopped neck and neck. Later, droves of Napoleonic cronies were "Panthéonized" and remained in the crypt while flags of different colors ran up and down the flagpole. Who remembers them?

Hugo was different. He was the anticlerical believer, a mystic, a man with faith in man, woman, the perfectibility of the species, and God or the immortal soul, but an enemy of organized religion. "Truth, light, justice, conscience—that's God," he wrote.

Hugo had been a peer of France and representative in the July Monarchy, had resisted Napoléon III during the Second Empire, become a senator of the Third Republic, and battled against slavery and misery, fighting for the poor, the downtrodden, and women. While he lived he was the hero of democrats, socialists, and republicans. When he died in 1885, the redesig-

Hugo as keystone, Avenue Victor Hugo

Funeral of Victor Hugo: millions of mourners

nation of Sainte-Geneviève as the Panthéon kept the Third Republic from sliding back into monarchy. His death marked the triumph of social democracy, a dented model that has survived world wars and the Nazi Occupation, the Great Depression and economic dips, globalization and continuing attempts by the resurgent right and big business to savage the welfare state.

Genius is often recognized postmortem. It is impressive and indicative of those bygone times that as Hugo entered his eightieth year, three days of national celebrations began. The first day marked the fifty-first anniversary of the Battle of Hernani; in an odd juxtaposition Hugo the democrat was given the kingly gift of a Sèvres vase formerly reserved for royalty. On the twenty-sixth of February he celebrated his birthday with family and friends. The next day 600,000 people walked down Avenue d'Eylau in the 16th arrondissement, a human caterpillar inching from the Champs-Élysées and taking six hours to creep by. Though he had suffered a stroke in 1878, Hugo stood in the winter cold with his window thrown open, nodding appreciation until each marcher had passed. By then Adèle had been underground for fifteen years. Out of view stood Juliette Drouet, the mistress of the house. The following day, Avenue d'Eylau was renamed Avenue Victor Hugo, and Hugo famously received letters addressed to him "in his street."

Juliette died two years later, leaving the iron-sided poet to live another two years before succumbing to pneumonia in 1885. He was eighty-three, a ripe old age, especially in those days.

Hugo's birthday party was impressive, but his funeral and the march to the Panthéon eclipsed it, the biggest ceremony of its kind in French history. He had wanted to be buried a poor man, his pauper's coffin in a pauper's hearse. His wishes were honored. The black mariah had two simple wreaths of white roses. But it was left overnight under the Arc de Triomphe, a symbolic victory of Hugo's peace over warmongering and the Bonaparte dynasty, and a shot fired across the bows of aspiring monarchists ready to subvert the fragile Third Republic. Sorrow was buoyed by joy: Hugo had been a bon vivant, so it seemed fitting that tens of thousands of Parisians partied through the night, a Dionysian fête in his honor, according to the Nobel Prize–winning novelist Romain Rolland, who was there. Celebrations centered on the Place de la Concorde and, perhaps inevitably, the sculpture of Strasburg modeled on Juliette Drouet.

Before dawn 2 million mourners followed the hearse from the Étoile to the Panthéon, a dignified procession of black on black. Along the four-mile route, banners flapped, emblazoned with the titles of Hugo's greatest works—*Les Misérables, Les Contemplations, Les Orientales,* and others. Gas lamps were shrouded in black. They burned through the day, an eerie reminder of the poet's last words: "I see black light."

Before dying Hugo had declared in writing, "I believe in God." This was more than afterlife insurance: His faith in the immortal soul and its ability to communicate with the living had been a lifelong conviction.

As I stood before Hugo's tomb, my eyes closed, an irreverent thought occurred to me. Was Hugo sending me a message? Why, if Marcellin Berthelot could lie in the Panthéon with his wife, Sophie, back in 1907, making her the first female resident of the building, couldn't we show twenty-first-century open-mindedness and reunite Victor with Juliette and Adèle? Wasn't it time idiosyncratic French polygamy, *le ménage à trois,* was recognized as an institution?

The idea was far from outlandish. It actually fits with the current Socialist government's plans to memorialize the struggles of women's liberation. A breach was made through the firewall of male exclusivity in the fall of 2013: Readings by the Comédie-Française designed to animate the Panthéon kicked off with selections from George Sand, a militant feminist and pioneer of sexual freedom. In 2015 two French female resistance fighters from World War II were transferred to the Panthéon. Might Sand not be moved from her country seat at Nohant west of Paris and laid near her old friends, Hugo and Dumas? She was a resistance fighter of a different kind.

"I weep for a dead woman, and hail an immortal," wrote Hugo in his famous funeral oration to George Sand, which he might have addressed to himself. "Have we lost her? No. Towering figures die but do not vanish . . . they fully realize themselves. By becoming invisible in one form they become visible in another. Sublime transfiguration . . . George Sand was an idea; she is beyond the flesh, freed from it; she is dead yet she is alive . . . Others are great men; she is the great woman. In this century destined to carry to completion the French Revolution and begin the human revolution, the equality of the sexes being an integral part of the equality of mankind, a great woman was needed."

As always, Hugo was a century ahead of his times—in fact, two centuries.

In 1886 the year after Hugo was Panthéonized, Sand had a Paris street named in her memory, a tony address in the 16th arrondissement not far from the spot where Hugo died.

Before exiting the Panthéon, I saluted Dumas the outsize musketeer and the feisty Zola as well, heir of both Balzac and Hugo, and waved to Jean-Jacques Rousseau, the progenitor of French Romanticism. There remained Voltaire to hail, and Marie Curie, whose tomb did not actually glow. Having done my rounds, I detoured to find someone most others skip: botanical explorer and utopian theorist Louis-Antoine de Bougainville. This real-life former musketeer-become-admiral gave his name to the most beloved species of flowering creeper anywhere and helped win the American War of Independence at the Battle of the Chesapeake. He also coined the expression "Noble Savage" while in Tahiti. In so doing, he embedded in the French mind an inkling of natural goodness and equality, a notion that went viral. Without him, Rousseau and Chateaubriand would have had no anchor for their praise of the "uncivilized." Without this idea, could Hugo or George Sand have fought for downtrodden humanity, or Chateaubriand dream of bliss among Native Americans? How could umpteen generations everywhere have fought against inhibitions and taboos erected to uphold archaic notions of morality and civilization, and declare in their bohemian rebelliousness, "We are all Noble Savages?" That was and is the kernel of Romanticism. Murger and Nadar might have become priests instead of rebellious Romantics. Gauguin might never have painted his masterpieces of island peoples. Twentieth-century modernists would have limped gray-faced, not flown in primary colors into Futurism. And what would the Riviera look like without its bougainvillea?

Despite my best efforts to commune with other dead white men, I remained unmoved by the rest of the crypt. As happens each time I visit, the Panthéon's spell was eventually broken. I climbed back up the stairs amid a chatty tour group from a place once thought to be full of Noble Savages, the Temple of the Nation feeling again like an oversize propaganda exercise.

Rome's Pantheon, dedicated to the pagan gods nearly two thousand years ago, was saved from vandals by being consecrated a church, yet remains exquisitely ecumenical. In Paris a church was saved from revolutionaries by becoming a temple to republicanism. But it was also the prototype for the deconsecrated institutions of science, atheism, and ugly nationalism I once toured in the drab, despotic wasteland of the Soviet Union, the twisted child of Robespierre that continues to give birth to little monsters.

The cult of the French Republic was once a fine thing. Perhaps it will be once again. Plans are to inaugurate French presidents at the Panthéon, celebrate Bastille Day, hold ceremonies for new French citizens, and use the monument to rebuild nationhood. But the statist cult seems less admirable now when swaths of the population clamor for anti-immigrant policies and reactionary reinterpretations of liberty, equality, and fraternity. They clash with a spinning Earth of many hues and infinite diversity. We were entering a new phase that was actually very old, it occurred to me as I stood once again by Foucault's pendulum; a peg was about to be knocked down.

Crossing the nave, I heard a guide saying loudly that the heart of French patriot Léon Gambetta—he of the balloons and the Siege of Paris—would soon be transferred from an urn near the gift shop to a proper tomb. I remembered another, earlier visit, when a visitor had asked the shop attendant about Gambetta's urn. The attendant had explained that "a body part" was needed for "Panthéonization," so Gambetta could not have a tomb, just an urn. Clearly the cult of relics had not ended with the Revolution, the visitor had retorted, buying a coffee mug emblazoned with "Vive la République." I smiled inwardly now at the memory. Maybe one day, if the Panthéon lasts, the cult of body parts and of ugly nationalism will disappear.

Beyond the western end of rue Soufflot in the Luxembourg Garden, the Belle Époque merry-go-round spun dreamily as I walked by. Children rode ponies down dusty lanes shaded by sycamores. In shadowy glades in the romantic English Garden, flocks of pimply teens flopped on benches and fiddled with handheld devices as others devoured obsolete printed matter with their eyes while feasting on fries and junk food. Everyone smoked, even the tennis players across the way. I watched the tennis balls sail back and forth, back and forth, another plumb bob. Love, love, love, the players cried, then "Fifteen!" The men wore white socks like Baudelaire, and most of them certainly knew *Les Fleurs du Mal* by rote.

The pendulum swings, the Earth and the merry-go-rounds spin. Paris stays the same.

The Luxembourg: the chairs are now metal, but otherwise Alphonse Karr would recognize the scene (by André Castaigne)

PART FIVE

Romantic Romps in the Luxembourg Garden, Latin Quarter, and Saint Germain des Prés

22

A LEAFY PANTHÉON OF
ROMANCE

If you measured her height from heel to curly black coif or the glove size of her famously petite hands, George Sand, the Great Woman of the Age of Romanticism, would be small by the standards of our day.

Two entertaining ways of gauging her dimensions present themselves to the curious in Paris. You can peer into a curio case in a house museum in the 9th arrondissement dedicated largely to her and the life of the Romantics. Here portraits and a plaster cast of Sand's right arm and hand are displayed (next to Chopin's delicate left hand). Or you can stroll into the bosky Luxembourg Garden from the Boulevard Saint-Michel, take the first looping parallel alley, sit on a comfortable wooden bench, and gaze at the life-size white marble statue of George in her prime. I have touched her pearly white child's hands many times, discreetly, when no one is looking. I have seen the bloodred roses left for her and like to think she noses them in the night.

The statue is a handsome piece of work from the Belle Époque. Sand is shown in a seductive, melancholy pose. She almost looks pretty, though by her own estimate she was neither pretty nor ugly but the proverbial plain Jane. "I am too romantic," she wrote in her voluminous autobiography, "ever to have seen the heroine of a novel in my mirror."

Was she coy? No. Much more: This is willful deception. For instance,

she famously destroyed or conveniently lost an unflattering portrait
of her by Delacroix after having it
reproduced and "corrected" as an
engraving. (Delacroix, disgusted,
declared "[my] *passionaria* of a By-
ronic drama becomes a Vaudeville
heroine.")

Sand also famously said, "To be
a novelist you have to be novel-
esque."

She was a fabulous fabulist.

Look at her in that long flowing dress, with a shawl thrown
over her slender shoulders. Seated,
holding a book in her left hand,
her eyes large and suitably soulful,
Sand is the unlikely though formidable trailblazer who did more

George Sand, queen of the Luxembourg Garden

than any other in literature and life to prod, goad, tease, stimulate, pull,
browbeat, entice, educate, and argue France forward from hidebound pa-
triarchy toward something approaching gender enlightenment. If Frenchmen are as feminized—without necessarily being effeminate—as many
contemporaries claim, and if romance *à la française* is a game of harp-tickling
tenderness instead of a brutish wrestling match, Sand deserves at least
some of the credit.

The job is far from finished 140 years after her death. The hairshirted
forces of reaction still protest periodically by marching on the Champs-
Élysées, the political opposite of the Bastille. They struggle daily in the conservative media and in the places of worship of France to reverse the tide of
liberté, égalité, sexualité. Yet the twenty-first century looks set to be the century
of woman—at least in Paris—and Sand's militant admirers are legion. They
call themselves Sandistes and, ironically since they are mostly secular, take
her words for Gospel truth. While she's no longer a household word in the
rest of the world, George Sand is probably more popular today than ever
before in France.

The moss, lichen, and fallen leaves often mask the name and date engraved on the base of the sculpture. Get closer. Use your forefinger to trace the lettering. With an effort you can read or at least feel the words. Sand's original moniker was a mouthful and remains unmentioned: Amandine-Aurore-Lucile Dupin, Baroness Dudevant.

It's significant the sculpture was carved in 1905 by a leading artist of his day and then displayed in a prominent position in this most prominent of Paris parks. It stands near a fashionable boulevard, the last residence of Sand in Paris, on rue Gay-Lussac, equidistant from the park and the nation's temple of secularism. The Panthéon belongs to Victor Hugo and so does the Luxembourg Palace, where Senator Hugo is remembered with two busts and a meeting room. But the Luxembourg Garden is the enchanted forest, the living shrine to a pantheon of rebellious Romantics, Sand foremost among the female contingent. Perhaps coincidentally—though little is left to chance in Parisian stagecraft—directly across the path from her is a sculpture titled *Bocca della Verità*, the Mouth of Truth, inspired, needless to say, by the ancient original in Rome. Did Sand always speak the truth?

The Mask Seller, *Luxembourg Garden*

Other "mouths of truth" stand nearby: Rodin's low-relief bronze medallion inserted into the pyramidal monument to Stendhal—he of *The Red and the Black*—is precisely twenty-five paces from Sand, an admirer of his. Another forty paces away towers Gustave Flaubert, father of the modern French novel, a precursor to Proust and an inspiration to countless other writers. His unbecoming portrait-bust-memorial incorporates a bench for those who want to contemplate the creators of Madame Bovary, Julien Sorel, and Lélia in a single glance. Flaubert, who demolished received notions of romance and had no time for social democracy, nonetheless became one of Sand's greatest boosters, friends, and prolific correspondents.

Skip eighty paces south of Flaubert and you come to the bizarre bronze sculpture known as *The Mask Seller*. A nearly naked prepubescent boy holds up a bronze mask of the mature Victor Hugo—still very much alive when the monument was inaugurated in 1883. Around the base are other haunting bronze masks of Romantic greats: Léon Gambetta (the statesman-balloonist of the Siege of Paris), painter Camille Corot, dramatist Alexandre Dumas the younger, the composers Hector Berlioz and Gabriel Fauré, the sculptor Jean-Baptiste Carpeaux, the poet and critic Barbey d'Aurevilly, plus the inevitable Delacroix and Balzac, both Luxembourg regulars.

The year 1905 was a good one for Hugo and Sand, posthumously, the hopeful, tumultuous year when the separation of church and state became law again in France, after nearly a century of de facto theocracy. During the Revolution of 1789 the church had been destroyed. It was resuscitated and reunited to the state during the Empire. Progressive Revolutionary laws were rolled back by Napoléon I or the restored Bourbon kings. Even the "Citizen King" Louis Philippe turned out to be retrograde, hypocritical, and corrupt. Needless to add, Napoléon III made matters worse: His wife was a fervent reactionary Catholic. The more things change—again.

The triumph of secularism and anticlericalism during the Third Republic was among Romanticism's lasting gifts, paving the way for divorce, abrogated in 1816 and reinstated in 1884, thanks largely to Senator Victor Hugo's efforts. Church and state got divorced in 1905. Then following the Liberation in 1944, women finally got the vote. Later still, during the Fifth Republic, women gained control over their own bodies, first with birth control in 1967, then abortion. That was in 1975—exactly ninety-nine years after George Sand died.

As Sand well knew, women's bodies—their reproductive organs, breasts, faces, hands, feet, ankles, voices, dress and speech and behavior and morals and more—were a matter of public concern and comment during the Age of Romanticism, more so even than they are today, when undernourished, nicotine-fueled fashion victims still teeter off the runways of the Tuileries onto the sidewalks of the city, and countless mainstream magazine covers display emaciated or superabundant female flesh as a consumable object.

Wan, wraith-like starveling object-women in Sand's day were even more dressed up, girdled, trussed, and buttoned from wrist to elbow, paraded around under parasols to prevent working-class tans, admired, chaperoned, protected, adored, and venerated as martyrs of love spiritually superior and physically, mentally, and emotionally inferior to men. If they refused to conform, grew stout in youth, or were unlucky and unattractive or stepped out of line they were scorned, shunned, insulted, ridiculed, caricatured, shamed, loathed, detested, and marginalized. Adulteresses like Léonie Biard were jailed or secluded in convents while their male lovers like Victor Hugo walked free. Flaubert's wayward Emma Bovary was an antiheroine, reviled by millions of men and women alike, and the novel, banned and censored for a time, was widely considered immoral.

Harsh, judgmental treatment was applied with particular vigor to women of the middle and upper classes, and to the so-called demimondaines and *grandes horizontales* who serviced and sometimes married upper-class men. As a minor aristocrat, George Sand experienced the gamut of reactions—good, bad, and unusual—because she was anything but usual in her masculine femininity and unbecoming appetites.

Sand also knew public review was not entirely a gender-skewed double standard. Political correctness was as inconceivable then as hypertext or the exploration of Mars—though Jules Verne did manage to send Félix Nadar into space in *From Paris to the Moon*. Roasting was and remains the rule for both sexes in Paris. Men were subjected to ridicule for their ungainliness or ugliness or the size of their noses or foreheads or feet, their height or skin tone, the length of their hair, their failure to follow dress codes, and their bohemian or other potentially subversive type of lifestyle, their homosexuality or sexual prowess or lack of physical strength and courage. Conformity to convention was de rigueur and rigorously stifling. Rebellion was genuinely risky, more than the fashion statement it is today in France and much of the Western world.

For some, fashion and theatricality were part of the love game. Men also cultivated the cadaverous look, according to Théophile Gautier, to seduce women who thought them ethereal, vulnerable, and at death's door, therefore deserving of pity and a lark. Ailing was like going to the front, the chances of long life were slim, so carpe diem and into the sack.

But in Sand's day, men had more wiggle room than women whatever the social class and could also defend themselves by public retorts or dueling—commonplace into the early twentieth century. It was also easier for men and boys to pass unnoticed. They were not under constant scrutiny.

That's why, when you imagine the baroness in the Luxembourg Garden as a young lady—say, in mid-1830, when she left her dissolute husband the Baron Casimir Dudevant at Nohant in the Berry region and moved with her even younger lover to Paris, shacking up at 25 quai Saint-Michel—you might not have seen her dressed as she is shown in her flattering marble sculpture in the Luxembourg Garden.

A cigarette or cigar glued to her fleshy lips, her curly black hair tied up and tucked away, the future George Sand wore boys' or men's clothes from boots to hat, as she had in the countryside. She was a country girl born in 1804 in Nohant to a peculiar ménage, her father a wealthy landowner who married for love, her mother the flirtatious daughter of a Parisian seller of birds. Aurore's father died when she was very young. Her unloving mother took wing, returning to Paris and leaving her children to be brought up by Aurore's formidable paternal grandmother. After a spell in a convent in Paris, Aurore was married at barely eighteen—disastrously—to a drunken skirt chaser. She promptly produced two children, the second of them, Solange, by her first known lover Ajasson de Grandsaigne. When Sand like her mother decamped to Paris, she parked her son Maurice and little Solange and lived free—with a handsome yearly allowance, even bigger than Hadley and Ernest Hemingway's. Unlike Hemingway, she rarely cried poor.

There is little doubt Sand was manly in many ways or that some of her male lovers were feminized, effeminate, bisexual, or homosexual. But descriptions of her as a man-eating nymphomaniac lesbian and cross-dressing virago or Amazon on horseback, bow drawn, underplay several essential gender realities of her day.

Sand herself was of course an unapologetic country tomboy and fearless adventuress, but Sand's own perfectly feminine mother had often dressed in men's clothing in Paris to move about unnoticed. Other bourgeois and upper-class women did, too. They wouldn't deign to wear the uniform of a servant, maid, cook, or *grisette*, although this would have allowed them com-

parable mobility and anonymity on the streets. Cross-dressing as a boy or a
man in men's comfortable clothing and well-made shoes was the most effi-
cient and entertaining means of disguise and did not degrade the dignity of
highborn or wealthy ladies. That Aurore also enjoyed playing charades and
living an endless carnival with sexual ambiguity as the theme is unques-
tionable.

Above all, dressing as a man quenched Sand's real thirst—for freedom
and equality with men. How else could she go in and out of cafés, restaurants, and the theater unaccompanied, or smoke in public without provok-
ing a riot? She got in trouble only a few times when playing at Boy George:
a gang of anti-Romantics began to rough her up until they discovered the
truth about her gender; on another embarrassing occasion, a scarred, aging
actress tried to put the moves on her in a box at a play, thinking her a
young gigolo. Presumably that's why Sand sometimes wore a dagger on
her belt: Paris was a dangerous place.

For an habituée of the Luxembourg who wrote tens of thousands of
pages, setting dozens of novels, stories, and plays in Paris, not to mention a
multiple-volume autobiography, Sand surprisingly appears never to have
specified which sections of the park she preferred or what her rituals were.
She came often, particularly when living on Quai Saint-Michel, rue de Seine,
and quai Malaquais—each within half a mile on foot. The movements, pref-
erences, and habits of others—Balzac, Hugo, Delacroix, Murger, Nadar,
Baudelaire, and much later, Hemingway—are easier to map. But Sand, the
master or mistress of confessional living, the woman whose life was a novel
and a sermon, is silent.

Taking liberties in the style of Sand, I imagine her striding swiftly with
her shapely short legs from the Panthéon into the park, toward the alleys of
clipped sycamores or the stand of horse chestnut trees, passing the spot
where her statue now stands, then moving in a cloud of tobacco and dust
amid sculptures of the queens of France, down the shallow staircase toward
the octagonal pool, the centerpiece of the garden behind the vast rusti-
cated stone mass of the Luxembourg Palace.

Completed in the 1620s for Henri IV's imported Italian queen Marie de'
Medicis, when Sand showed up, the grounds of the Florentine-style Luxembourg were the most popular public promenade on the Left Bank. In my

imaginings, Sand rarely walks alone. By the time the baroness has crossed this enclave of timelessness, she has changed her name, address, outfit, and companion dozens of times, and has ripened from her late twenties into what today we would consider her prime.

Familiarity breeds passion: the timeless Luxembourg then and now

23

THE SAND PIT

The first man striding alongside Aurore barely able to keep up is a certain Jules Sandeau, a handsome, mild-mannered teenager seven years her junior. Like her, he's an aspiring author who will go far, but not in her company. Though their affair was short-lived, it propelled the baroness from Nohant to Paris. It also left her with a vocation, a new identity, and a distinctive bestselling brand name: J. Sand. The pair cowrote sentimental romance novels, signing J. for *Jules* and lopping off the *eau* as a disclaimer of Sandeau's sole paternity. Against all odds J. Sand's books sold.

Sand wasn't the only gentlewoman wielding quills: One in five authors in the mid-1800s was a woman, and many adopted men's names the way they wore men's clothes, for practicality and marketing. But women writers were rarely taken seriously.

The initial J morphed to a G when Aurore shed Jules Sandeau. Then the G filled out to Georges and then George with no final s, in the English style, because English literature from Shakespeare and Milton to Byron or cheap contemporary English romances was the rage. It's said that the name George pays secret homage to a teenage girl the adolescent Aurore befriended in the convent school they shared for three years, foreshadowing her Sapphic bent.

Jules and George lived together in an attic at 25 quai Saint-Michel with a killer view of Notre Dame. She was in heaven. She had come seeking "the picturesque poetic Paris of Victor Hugo, the city of the past," and had struck vintage gold. Like a character in one of their collaborative novels the real Jules Sandeau was distraught enough to threaten suicide when Sand caught him in flagrante betraying her and evicted him from their nest. As the relationship entered its final throes she moved downstream and he took refuge with a mutual friend. The friend happened to be Honoré de Balzac, then resident half a mile due south of the Luxembourg Garden in rue Cassini near Paris' astronomical observatory. The cheerfully sardonic Balzac was already a god by the early 1830s, a good friend to have unless he borrowed money from you or proposed you enter into one of his harebrained investment schemes. Luckily for Sand and Sandeau, Balzac admired both and did not hit them up for a loan.

But Balzac soon detected the fundamental difference in their views: "You seek man as he should be," Balzac told Sand over dinner one night at his luxurious if far-flung apartment. "Me, I take him as he comes."

Balzac was bluffing. He knew he rarely took people as they came, gleefully exaggerating their faults and vices, thrilling in noir. What he didn't approve of in Sand was the moralizing, didactic side of her fluid, prolific prose. This didn't affect their long and cordial friendship. It lasted until Balzac's premature death in 1850. While he produced over a hundred novels, Sand came in second with around eighty—plus her sprawling autobiography.

Balzac may well have uttered this remark the same fateful night he grabbed a candle and accompanied Sand back across the dicey stretch of road between the observatory and the safe southern gate of the Luxembourg Garden. She worried about his returning alone, an easy target on dark streets, but Balzac, a scrappy notorious night prowler, was undaunted. Muggers would either flee in terror when they saw him, he quipped, or think him a powerful nobleman and lead him home.

Ironically, while Sand dressed as a man, Balzac often put on a long dress, a shawl, a bonnet, and gloves and limped around, a mysterious lame elderly widow, to throw off the debt collectors who pursued him much of his adult life. No one accused him of being an effeminate cross-dresser.

Sand also remarked pithily that she found Balzac to have a childish and childlike core, a fantasist who lived in his own crepe-shrouded fairyland.

Within a few years of landing in Paris, Sand had penned several novels,

Marie Dorval as femme fatale (by Léon Noël)

including *Indiana* and *Valentine,* and was growing in fame and notoriety. She seamlessly melded Gothic elements in the style of the English or the dashing Prosper Mérimée with the contemporary edge of Balzac, adding a pinch of spiritual yearning à la Chateaubriand and a dash of surprising, disconcerting originality, autobiography, and transformative love and sex. The confessional sexual fantasies of *Lélia,* her first truly scandalous novel, established her reputation as a provocative artist. Sainte-Beuve was wildly enthusiastic, sought her out, and soon introduced her to his influential friends. At least two became her lovers.

Before, during, and between them, the next in line on her arm as she strolled around the Luxembourg in man's clothing was not a man. It was Marie Dorval, the stage actress with a signature sexy hoarse voice, the one who sang for the Romantics gathered at the Arsenal Library. A onetime lover of Dumas and many others—including, possibly, Victor Hugo—Dorval also loved some remarkable women. At the same time she pursued Hugo and her longtime rival Juliette Drouet. Unlike Sand, Drouet appears to have resisted Dorval's advances. Juliette failed as an actress, outdone by Dorval and others, but won the ultimate prize: Olympio. On Juliette's modest tomb in the cemetery of suburban Saint-Mandé you can still read the proud words: "The world has his thoughts, me, I had his love."

Dorval triumphed over Juliette Drouet onstage: For Hugo she incarnated Marion de Lorme, courtesan of the Place des Vosges. Having given up on Victor and Juliette as bedmates, she soon found serendipitous amorous communion with the latest artistic celebrity, George Sand. That didn't stop her from remaining the official mistress of bewitched dramatist Alfred de Vigny. He penned the perennial classics *Chatterton, Othello,* and *La Maréchale d'Ancre.*

"A. de Vigny has twin reasons to dislike me," Hugo remembered in one of his secret *carnets*. "*Primo*, that *Marion de Lorme* earned more at the box office than *La Maréchale d'Ancre*, and *Hernani* made more than *Othello*. *Secundo*, that I at times have given my arm to Madame Dorval."

Blinded by his jealous suspicions of Hugo's supposed treachery—the two men were good friends—de Vigny was blindsided by Sand's ambidextrous sexuality and came to loathe her, but would not relinquish Dorval.

As Sand and Dorval dally in the afternoon shadows of a giant purple beech tree, near the rue de Fleurus exit from the Luxembourg, the one Hugo used daily for years, do they keep watch to make sure the lumbering Olympio doesn't come tramping on their tiny feet? He lives a few blocks away in a huge house in rue Notre Dame des Champs, still officially with Adèle, and walks in the garden while writing in his head, imagining, perhaps, Esmeralda and Quasimodo or the first meeting in the Luxembourg of Marius and Cosette, future stars of *Les Misérables*. Not yet a socialist, Sand has no time for Hugo's left-leaning antipoverty plays and novels or his outsize ego—though she loves the Paris he evoked in *The Hunchback of Notre Dame*.

Do they avoid Balzac, also a mad walker-writer who has taken sides with Jules Sandeau, lending him a couch, and incarnates Sandeau and Sand in his novel *La Muse du département*?

Must they rush away when de Vigny or Sainte-Beuve and Adèle appear?

Perhaps both Sand and Dorval wear disguises, Sand a gamekeeper, prefiguring D. H. Lawrence, and Dorval a role-reversing baroness. Or maybe they come out only at dusk, like vampires. As a rule Sand works through the night and rises at four in the afternoon, and Dorval too is a nightingale.

Fetching, feminine, with wisps of light curly hair parted over a forehead almost as prominent as Victor Hugo's, with an impish, expressive face, small, fine lips, and animated blue eyes, Dorval was temperamentally and physically the opposite of Sand. Dorval understood and did not judge Sand or her broad appetites, providing an easy exit from Sand's affair with the unfaithful spurned Sandeau. Unlikely as it seems, Jules Sandeau would shine among the literary lights and one day become Dorval's lover too.

Sand's Sapphic liaison with Dorval inspired some of the most intense, sensuous pages of *Lélia*, a coded manifesto of sexual freedom and equality still devoured by the young today.

"Rest your cool hand on my shoulder burning with love and unkissed by man's lips," Sand wrote, "only your scented breath and damp hair can quench it . . . spread your intoxicating perfumes, strip your moist crown of its leaves . . . I want to live to see you again . . . leave now . . . if they see you they'll steal you from me and I'll be forced to give myself again to men . . . let me kiss your snowy neck and forehead."

Marie Dorval dreaming of George, Victor, Alfred or . . .

Sensuous without being seamy, *Lélia* is still among Sand's most popular books, a key to understanding the French psyche. In it, the author-heroine's quest for tenderness extends to the physical act of lovemaking, a reminder of Adèle Hugo's unlikely choice of the toadlike but gentle Sainte-Beuve as her lover.

Reenter Sainte-Beuve, a platonic admirer of Sand and privileged resident of the Luxembourg Garden, as matchmaker. Though busy pursuing Adèle and avoiding Victor, he found time to organize social gatherings and make introductions. He knew just the fellow for George—or so he thought.

If you walk around the sunny southern loop of the Luxembourg heading for the turn-of-the-century gingerbread gatehouse, when you pass the orchard of espaliered apples and botanical contortions, pause to glance right. Rising above the dreamy lawn and flower parterres next to the luxuriant yew tree is a stone bust of a plump, contented-looking middle-aged man. His head is round, thatched by patchy hair, his nose is shaped like a baby's boot, and a mischievous smile curls his thin lips Mona Lisa–style. A loosely tied foulard now green with moss lends an artistic air but cannot hide the

Sainte-Beuve's impish smile, in the Luxembourg Garden

double chin of the hedonist. Quasimodo? This is the author of *Volupté*?

It's an irony of fate that behind Sainte-Beuve is the Belle Époque white marble monument called *The Happy Family*—a nearly naked young couple, their child, and a kid, meaning a young goat. For many years when I passed the homewrecker Sainte-Beuve's bust I wondered why he seemed so pleased with himself; then I discovered his victory over Victor and understood. He'd charmed chilly Adèle, unseating awe-inspiring Olympio, whom he redubbed "the Cyclops." Now he would ex-

tricate Sand from weepy Sandeau and the notorious Dorval's clutches.

Like Hugo or Balzac, Sainte-Beuve knew everyone in Paris, including Prosper Mérimée. Unaware it was Sand who had courted Dorval and was enjoying the Sapphic affair, Sainte-Beuve put forward Mérimée as a

male love prospect. Sand paused long enough to give the Gothic-loving author of *Carmen* a try, but the chemistry was clearly wrong. Mérimée wound up immortalized as an unlikable character in *Lélia*, yet another male incapable of understanding or satisfying a woman needing a patient, tender touch. No literary slouch, tit for tat Mérimée portrayed the affair in *La Double*

Méprise, giving the level-headed wounded man's side, a conventional tale of unbridgeable gender difference that resonates eerily to this day.

In the heat of composition Sand read an early version of *Lélia* to the delighted Sainte-Beuve. Enmeshed in his famous affair with Adèle and intoxicated by lust, he maintained a secret apartment for his trysts in Cour du Commerce Saint-André, kitty-corner to Paris' oldest café, Le Procope. It just happened to be near both the Luxembourg and Sand's apartment. Sainte-Beuve was deeply impressed by Sand but was also aware of the flak she would inevitably catch. No ingénue, if he was taken aback by Sand's lesbianism or the sexual-performance wish list detailed in the book, he did not say so.

Sainte-Beuve cuts a dashing figure?

Denying the laws of hydraulics the narrator of *Lélia* wonders among many other things related to love and sex about the unfairness to women of the missionary position, the man always on top. She also wishes men had long, enticing hair like women. Apparently she had not yet met the long-haired Baudelaire, Gautier, or Nadar—but perhaps they were too young for her. Or were they? Feminized youthful masculinity was essential to her program. Stay tuned.

Perhaps Sainte-Beuve kept in mind Sand's yearning for a tender young long-haired acrobat when he made his second, life-changing introduction.

24

BUTTERFLY CATCHER

George, meet Alfred, Alfred de Musset. It's the spring of 1833. The sap is rising. As the newly formed couple pass beneath the perfumed tunnel of blooming horse chestnut trees near the beekeeper's shack and stop to study the old-fashioned hives of the Luxembourg, you might be forgiven for being momentarily confused. Which is Alfred, which George?

Alfred de Musset was tall and wasp-thin, blue-eyed and bird-beaked, a dandy dressing in black with golden locks so long, scented, carefully coifed, and abundant that for years he was teased and called a sissy and a girl. He possessed all the ingredients necessary to enrapture Sand—and many others. A drama queen, he loved fashion, playacting, and cross-dressing. Victor Hugo disparagingly dubbed him "Miss Byron." He worshiped his mother and was ecstatic to find a motherly older woman companion. Like Baudelaire, he was born old in spirit, a wizened veteran and a needy little boy rolled into one. A titled viscount, he came from a good if penurious family. His lack of a fortune did not prevent him from hobnobbing with more fortunate aristos and becoming Paris' most notorious teenage roué, a dissolute party boy and playboy, gambler and drinker who slept by day and caroused in whorehouses or his friends' châteaux by night.

Musset's was the acceptable form of upper-crust vampirism inspired by or mirroring Charles Nodier's metaphorical masterpiece *The Vampire*. Gothic literature was meant to be read on many levels, one reason it's still readable today.

Charming and funny and supremely talented with words and sketch-book too, the precocious Musset was quaking with delirium tremens before he hit adulthood. In this he may be the spiritual father of countless artists and writers since then, notably Baudelaire, Murger, Rimbaud and Verlaine, Modigliani, John Coltrane, Jim Morrison, and the actor-director folk-rock idol Serge Gainsbourg, who keeled over in a nimbus of nicotine and alcohol in 1991. His daughter Charlotte Gainsbourg, the movie star, now excels at incarnating Romantics. Like Gainsbourg, Baudelaire, and Rimbaud, Alfred de Musset appears to be a role model for today's Parisian bourgeois bohemians and neo-zombies. Musset said his was a century "in mourning," forever dressed in black. Existentialist bohemians the world over live in a Musset revival without even knowing it.

Somehow Musset also managed to write reams of entrancing poetry, spirited plays that are still required reading in France, and inspiring accounts of his travels in romantic lands. He would go on to write one of the century's greatest accounts of a hopeless love affair, *Confession d'un Enfant du Siècle*, inspired, it goes without saying, by his liaison with George Sand. Books about the book, Sand's retort to the book, Musset's brother's response to Sand's book, poet Louise Colet's retort to Musset's brother's book, plus movies, stage plays, countless articles and learned studies have dissected the affair to the breadth of a damp hair on a burning shoulder, as Lélia might have put it. Only the tale of Sand's later liaison with Frédéric Chopin has possibly been more retold, at least in France. Having waded across this watery literary love tangle, a Parisian *Heart of Darkness* replete with snapping crocodiles, blood-filled leaches, and giant insects, and having lived long enough to see the affair reenacted by generations of Parisian adolescents, I can only reiterate that Alphonse Karr was right as usual.

On a bench in the sun by a statue of Bacchus or in the cool, dark alley of sycamores by the Medicis Fountain, young Parisians today fill the Luxembourg Garden, perpetuating the roller coaster of passionate, all-consuming love, hatred, jealousy, rejection, betrayal, renewed passion, rejection again, renewed betrayal, and so on, ad infinitum, all of it in public in clouds of boozy smoke, like Sand and Musset. Billing and cooing and mauling each other, the quintessential Romantic couple chain-smoked and drank fine wine at a prodigious rate—1,200 francs' worth in a few months, according to Sand's accounts when she lived on quai Malaquais in the famous "blue attic," their romantic love nest overlooking the Academy of Fine Arts. That was more than many middle-class employees earned in a year.

Take a paperback copy of Musset's novelized version of their story with you, pack biographies of Musset and Sand, then add in her *Elle et Lui*, Musset frère's *Lui et Elle*, and Louise Colet's *Lui*, about her affairs with Musset and Gustave Flaubert. Pick a bench or a table at the park café and spend several weeks immersed in a deeply French yet universal tale of lust and betrayal, pausing long enough to flirt with passersby and share a bottle or three to put you in an empathetic mood.

With due respect to Sand, Alfred's is by far the more riveting version of the affair, his words beautifully crafted, the images of Romantic Age men and women leaping like suicide victims off the pages. If only it had been a novella.

"Posterity will repeat our names like those of the immortal lovers whose names are one," he wrote Sand in a letter after the final implosion, "Romeo and Juliet, Abélard and Heloïse."

Breathtaking immodesty was another hallmark of Musset. Strangely there is no statue commemorating him at the Luxembourg, perhaps because his successor Chopin is represented here so splendidly, on the opposite side of

the park from Sand. Truth be told, the sculptor of the Chopin memorial was clearly more interested in the muse of music. The composer's bronze bust perches stiffly atop a ten-foot-tall base broken Michelangelo-style by a ghostly naked ravishing muse who beckons to the ethereal hero with coiling hair, beseeching eyes, and puckered lips. It might have seemed unkind to Chopin's immortal soul, or offensive to the phantom of Musset's bruised ego, to divide the park between them.

Not to be outdone by Musset's send-off in words, Sand snipped

Chopin and Muse at the Luxembourg

off a lock of her hair, stuffed it into a skull, and had it delivered to him post-haste. Just as they are today among neo-zombies and trendy bobos, skulls were big in Sand and Musset's Gothic Revival days. The difference is Sand sent a real skull.

Steeped in canny self-righteousness, its heroine portrayed as a saint and martyr of love bound to a delusional madman, Sand's account, written much later, makes a troubling read when it isn't merely tedious. Few have so accurately charted the shoals of others' narcissism without recognizing their own. To paraphrase Balzac, she saw men and women the way they *should* be—according to her. Sand justified, corrected, redacted, and rewrote history, neatly excising her embarrassing affair with the handsome Venetian doctor Pagello—*quelle horreur, un Italien.* He saved Musset's life. She also elided her on-a-dime turnaround as she dumped Musset, embraced Pagello, and then took up with the madman Musset again, then abruptly left both dangling in Paris as she dashed to safety in Nohant. Granted, Musset's whoring and boozing was unpardonable, but her hypocrisy may have been even worse.

"George Sand catches her butterfly and domesticates it in her cage by feeding it on flowers and nectar—this is the amorous period," wrote her friend and confidant the pianist Franz Liszt when their intimacy began to fray. "Then she sticks her pin into it when it struggles—that's the farewell and it always comes from her. Afterwards she vivisects it, stuffs it, and adds it to her collection of heroes for novels."

In real life Sand went out of her way to ensure Musset would never find out she'd been sleeping with Dr. Pagello while Musset thrashed, moaned, and sweated, nearly dying of typhoid fever in the adjoining room. She failed. Musset and le Tout Paris soon found out. Her behavior did little to improve her public image, though it's clear some women secretly admired her virility: She did what a man of her day might have done—put herself and her passion first. "The lover is dead," she announced with a black feather; "long live the new lover," she proclaimed with a white one. Beyond the militant feminism and hypocritical caviar socialism she adopted in later years, it is precisely Sand's brash macho, pushy, self-serving hedonism that seems so uncannily contemporary and makes her so influential to this day.

Surely such claims are dangerous apostasy? Heavily armed Sandistes lurk in literary marshlands ready to fire at anyone who queries the cult of

George Sand, "the third sex" (by Thomas Couture)

Queen George. As is the case in the "Hugolatrian" religion, both she and Victor Hugo are not only inspirations but also industries. Sand doesn't need a Panthéon as pulpit to proselytize or, put in Hemingway's terms, to hit a homer with her readership. The slow sexual curve ball thrown by Sand crossed the decades and landed in another French woman writer's well-oiled mitt: Colette.

Colette's life mirrors Sand's right down to the cumbersome husband and coauthor, the use of a pen name, the quest for freedom in Paris, the ambidextrous sexuality, the prolific production of sensational stories, and the astonishing popularity today.

Colette then pitched the Sand gospel into the twentieth century, where Simone de Beauvoir was waiting. The ball dropped at her feet. She inspected it and dissected it like a butterfly. If Sand was described as belonging to (or perhaps initiating) the third sex, and Colette was her spiritual daughter, then Beauvoir was her stiff academic hyper-intellectual grandchild. A century after Sand, Beauvoir wrote *The Second Sex*, the celebrated manifesto of modern feminism, heralding women's freedom from "reproductive slavery" and celebrating female sexual fulfilment. Three genders were apparently part of the equation for Beauvoir, though hedonism was out of the question.

25

MERRY-GO-ROUNDS
AND TALKING HEADS

On Sand's next several swings around the Luxembourg, after vivisecting Musset but before netting Chopin, George can be seen leading a succession of colorful gallants. The horse chestnuts give way to purple paulownia blossoms; then chrysanthemums fill pots, only to disappear in December. Icicles hang from the Medicis Fountain. The carousel spins, children ride stallions of sculpted, painted wood, and the little old-fashioned sailboats once again carve the duck-dotted waters of the centerpiece pool just as they do today in spring, summer, and fall.

The years 1836 and 1837 were banner vintages—with wine, roses, and legal triumphs for the irrepressible George Sand. Aided by her latest lover, Michel de Bourges, a gifted lawyer and outspoken socialist, she won divorce proceedings while maintaining full ownership of her château, income and extensive properties, and custody of her children. This was revolutionary, an astonishing success. In 1837 she retired the lawyer, no longer needed: His socialistic sermonizing outshone her own. She then had three turbulent affairs in a matter of months. They were so passionate and so public that even her closest friends were left reeling by the merry-go-round of emotion. Each time Sand declared unparalleled, undying love, later admitting she was capable of falling in and out of amour decisively in a single day with complete, devastating sincerity. Today she might be considered unbalanced, possibly bipolar.

Pradier, heartless musketeer, on the greenhouse at the Luxembourg

But if frequency was the measure, Sand lagged far behind Victor Hugo. In his eighty-third year Toto-Olympio noted in his secret *carnet* eight separate liaisons in a period of three months shortly before he died. No one was or is shocked by this unabashed carnality, yet Sand's corresponding carnivorousness remains unsettling to many—though not to the Parisians I know.

Staring down from the tall brick walls of the greenhouse behind the Musée du Luxembourg are the stern heads of France's great and good. They are the leading artists of centuries past, among them Ingres, Millet, Rude, the ubiquitous Delacroix, and the dastardly James Pradier, sire of teenage Juliette Drouet's luckless daughter Claire.

Pradier stands out from the others. He looks like a cross between a musketeer and a Roman emperor of the decadent period, though his *nom d'art* was Phidias. As I amble by the *orangerie* and watch the citrus trees being wheeled in or out with the seasons, I sometimes wonder whether Hugo, Drouet, Flaubert, or Louise Colet would glance up at Pradier now and smile or smirk: He was the anti-Romantic romantic hyphen joining all of them. Haughty, imperious, disdainful, and vain are four words that float to mind as I admire his massive mustachioed head wrapped in hair coiled like serpents reaching to his shoulders.

"Here is a great artist, a true Greek, the most antique of all the moderns," declared an unusually effusive Gustave Flaubert, a fellow anti-Romantic who clearly found redeeming qualities in the macho, anti-progressive sculptor. This might be because it was in Pradier's atelier at 1 quai Voltaire, a block away from Sand's apartment, that Flaubert met Louise Colet, one of Pradier's many muses. It was also in this atelier that Flaubert and Colet feathered their clandestine adulterous love nest, with the lecherous sculptor's blessings. He was, added Flaubert, "a man distracted by nothing, not politics, nor socialism, and who, like a real workman, rolls up his sleeves and works morning, noon, and night determined to do what's right and driven by the love of his art."

Pradier was also driven by a mammoth ego and lust, bedding his models, then sharing them around or booting them out, as was the custom. He dressed like a swashbuckler in real life. His first famous workshop, at 3 rue de l'Abbaye, in the former abbot's luxurious sixteenth-century brick-and-stone palace abutting the apse of Saint-Germain-des-Prés was, coincidentally, a few blocks from George Sand's apartment in rue de Seine. Here Pradier held a twice-weekly salon that Sand attended. Like the Arsenal Library salon, where Pradier was also a regular, it drew artists, writers, politicians, and Paris' beau monde from the 1820s until 1838. That's when Pradier moved to quai Voltaire and an even more luxurious atelier and apartment overlooking the Seine. The poetess Louise Colet, who was married to a luckless musician and was also the mistress of Victor Cousin, a philosopher and government minister, became Pradier's occasional model and lover before moving on to the young Flaubert.

Blessed with a cast-iron will beribboned in velvet and draped lavishly in dark corkscrew curls, the coquettish Colet was Flaubert's muse and tormentor for the better part of a decade. In real life she was tough and capable of violence. When Alphonse Karr revealed Colet's affair with Cousin in a piquant article, Colet grabbed a kitchen knife and flew across town in a rage to Karr's apartment, where she stabbed him. She was visibly pregnant with the fruit of her latest adulterous affair. This time Karr did not say "the more

Alphonse Karr digging up the dirt

things change"; instead, when asked where she'd stabbed him, he quipped, "In the back." They too had been lovers.

As beautiful as she was dangerous and saucy, Colet was the lustful lady who took the beardless Flaubert—who at eleven years her junior was an innocent provincial from Normandy—for a slow, bouncy ride in a swaying carriage on the Champs-Élysées. Their passion was then transformed in the tale of Emma Bovary into that heroine's fictional joy ride around Rouen, possibly the most diabolically subtle, erotic sex scene in all literature. She also inspired Flaubert to write some of the most beautiful and brainy love letters I've ever read, possibly because like Sand and Mimi, Colet reigned as the priestess of perfidious infidelity and paradisiacal intercourse. She famously bedded the two Alfreds—de Musset and de Vigny—not to mention Victor Hugo, and was legendarily good in bed and seriously interested in her own pleasure.

"If I considered you an average woman I wouldn't tell you this," Flaubert confided to her at the summit of their passion. "I want you to be something totally different—neither friend nor mistress. Each is too restrictive, too exclusive—you don't love a friend enough, and you're too imbecilic with a mistress. It's something intermediate I seek—the merged essence of those two sentiments. What I really want is for you to be a new kind of hermaphrodite, to give all the thrills of the flesh with your body, and with your mind those of the soul."

This sounds startlingly like George Sand—though Flaubert claimed he did not read or meet Sand until de-

Louise Colet as Emma Bovary, carriage awaiting (by Alfred de Richemont)

Flaubert: prematurely mature (by Clare Victor Dwiggins)

Louise Colet/Emma Bovary ready for action
(by Alfred de Richemont)

(by Clare Victor Dwiggins)

cades later. The hermaphrodite was not only an object of intense medical study but also an obsession of mid-1800s men and some women who may have been bisexual or homosexual or lesbian but repressed their true natures much of the time. Colet was repelled by the notion of hermaphroditism and told Flaubert so in no uncertain terms.

But was the obsession with a third gender the reason why Sand, so plain and so matronly, was such a sexual prize? Flaubert came to love Sand like a second mother, addressing her in cross-gender fashion as "Chère Maître." He loved his real, widowed mother to excess, refused to leave her and settle in Paris, and thereby sacrificed Louise Colet to her, if "sacrifice" be the word. Flaubert seems not to have regretted the break; au contraire, it freed him to write without distractions. "I love my work," he admitted, "with a frenzied, perverted love."

But even his jealous mother scolded him for treating Louise Colet shabbily, his overwhelming love for literature having "desiccated his heart." This is unfair. A careful reading of their intense correspondence suggests Colet was at least half the problem. As to Flaubert's portrayal of her in the guise of Emma Bovary, that may well have been an act of reverence: Emma is the only sympathetic, redeeming, intelligent, feeling character in what is the first truly modern novel. Flaubert had mistresses after Colet but never found another sexually satisfying soul mate.

The last word in this extraordinary letter by Flaubert foreshadows the other reason Colet's liaison was headed for a crash: She wanted the artist-writer but also demanded the *man* in her bed, and like Sand, she was a committed socialist. Flaubert sought true love through intellect and soul, avoiding messy politics. He was a landowner living off income he did not earn. He excelled at turning grammar, expectations, and roles on their heads. Flaubert was the "woman" of the relationship, and as his oft-cited "Madame Bovary, *c'est moi*," suggests, he was deeply in touch with his feminine side.

"The winter is here, rain is falling, my fire is burning," he wrote Louise, setting the scene at the end, not the beginning of the letter, another typical Flaubert reversal. "The season of long hours shut indoors is upon us. Soon: silent, lamp-lit evenings watching the wood fire burn, listening to the wind. Farewell, bright moonlight shining on green grass; farewell, blue nights spangled with stars. Farewell, my darling: I kiss you with my whole soul."

Having pumped her for details he integrated into *Madame Bovary*, he blew

Does Pradier rest in peace at Père-Lachaise Cemetery?

the final goodbye kiss to Louise by tossing on that crackling fire her silk slippers—a scented fetish, like her soiled handkerchief and a lock of her hair—and her love letters.

Clearly the inflammable James Pradier was of another breed. His many talents did not extend to literature or soul seeking. Chisel in hand and also wielded metaphorically, the master chiseler, the cheapskate was indeed "distracted by nothing," not even the desperation of his first famous mistress Juliette Drouet and their illegitimate child, who were left to fend for themselves. Welfare and child support were anathema to him.

"Pradier is a miserable imbecile, a vile, beastly man," Juliette wrote Victor Hugo, "a stupid buffoon, cowardly and faithless."

The French Academy crowd undoubtedly prefer Flaubert's version. That's because like Hugo, Sand, Flaubert, and even Colet, whose poetry has not stood the test of time, James Pradier boasts a considerable following today. Many of his promoters are collectors eager to ensure his work increases in value, and his reputation remains unsullied. Pradier did, it's true, immortalize Juliette on a scale no one else attempted.

Beyond the portrait of Juliette Drouet as the City of Strasbourg in a corner of the Place de la Concorde, I have found examples of Pradier's craft scattered across Paris: on the Arc de Triomphe, in the church of Les Invalides, on the Fontaine Molière on rue de Richelieu, in museums and private collections.

Best of all for those who enjoy relics, Pradier sculpted the exquisite silver-plated bronze hand of George Sand that was exhibited in 2004 at the Musée de la Vie Romantique, proof positive that in the Age of Romanticism hands were the object of cult worship. But the closest Pradier came to truly honoring Sand—his admirer, though a polar opposite politically—is the Canova-like white marble sculpture he made of Sappho, now in the Musée d'Orsay. The same-sex poetess of antiquity, the great beacon of Lesbos, looks surprisingly like Sand when she was young, as shown at the Luxembourg Garden.

But look again and be surprised: It's not really Sand. One of Louise Colet's many nicknames was La Muse, another "hot marble," yet another Sappho, and, it turns out, in reality Colet was the sculptor's model.

26

MERGING INTO BOHEMIA

By the time Chopin comes on tap in 1838 for a record-breaking nine-year affair with the maturing George Sand, and the couple joins the other wandering Romantics in the Luxembourg Garden, a prime piece of real estate near the Medicis Palace and Odéon-Théâtre has become the rendezvous of lean and lusty Félix Nadar, permanently nostalgic Henri Murger, and the motley gang of bohemians who will later star in Puccini's opera.

The bench the bohemians favored is still here in the virtual way Balzac's garret or Sand as immortal "idea" live on in the collective imagination. The original slatted wooden seat the bohemians lounged on in the 1840s and '50s surely rotted long ago. It has been replaced by generations of replicas made expressly to preserve the nineteenth-century Romantic identity of Paris. Equally important, the garden itself is a shrine to yesteryear. Haussmann lopped off parts, moved the Medicis Fountain, but unwittingly left Nadar and Murger's meeting place intact. It's easy to find.

If you wander north seventy paces from the damp garlands of ivy bordering the Medicis Fountain, following the curving gravel path toward the Odéon exit, you'll see a statue on your right. It's a weathered bronze with a streaked turquoise patina. It appears to honor a distinguished, bearded man, perhaps in his sixties. But look again. Take a seat on this most romantic of Paris benches, preferably with a copy in hand of *Scenes of Bohemian Life*, or Nadar's memoirs, *When I Was a Student*, about his wild times in the Latin Quarter. The man portrayed in the bust has eyes like tea bags, cascading eyebrows, and a bald head, and is none other than Henri—or Henry, spelled English style, as he preferred— Murger. He's not in his sixties but rather thirty-eight years old—*old* being the operative word. Like the consumptive Chopin, Murger died before he reached forty. To put this in perspective, Murger's beloved Mimi (whose real name was Lucile Louvet), the flower girl, never celebrated her twenty-fifth birthday. Mimi was also known to perch on this bench with

Henri Murger in the Luxembourg Garden

Murger while sniffing the tiny nosegay of violets she clutched in her famously chilled, childlike hands.

Murger, Nadar, and Baudelaire's friend the poet Théodore de Banville described the real Mimi as a sickly Parisian flower born and grown in the shade, extraordinarily pale, with an aristocratic profile despite her humble origins, "sweet lips, hair the color of bleached chestnuts, and light gray-blue eyes." Suffering was writ large across her thin, consumption-racked figure. Alexandre Schanne, the musician-painter who shared an atelier with Nadar and appears in the book and Puccini's opera under the name "Schaunard," brought her further into focus by recalling her angelic look that hid "amorality and wantonness."

In Puccini's opera, librettists Giuseppe Giacosa and Luigi Illica depicted her as "a charming girl especially apt to appeal to Rodolphe, the poet and dreamer. Aged twenty-two, she was slight and graceful. Her face reminded one of some sketch of highborn beauty; its features had marvelous refinement. The hot, impetuous blood of youth coursed through her veins, giving a rosy hue to her clear complexion that had the white velvety bloom of the camellia. This frail beauty allured Rodolphe. But what wholly served to enchant him were Mimi's tiny hands, that, despite her household duties, she contrived to keep whiter even than the Goddess of Ease."

The hands again! Like feet and slippers for Flaubert. Fetishes never die.

The clearest picture of Mimi is provided by a famous Nadar portrait. It was Nadar's wild-man lifestyle and amorous exploits that inspired Murger to write his nearly-true-to-life sketches of bohemia in the first place. Look back in time and you can see Nadar rushing through the Odéon gate into the park to meet his friends. Nadar has jogged up several blocks from 45 rue Monsieur le Prince, a grubby old building topped by the malodorous garret in which he has just spent two solid months in bed, the original Bed-In. A strapping youth, Nadar was not sick or protesting, like Yoko Ono and John Lennon in Amsterdam in 1969. He simply had no clothes to wear and couldn't leave the room. It was unheated, as all garrets were (and many still are), so Nadar snuggled under the covers. He wasn't alone. His mystery woman, his Mimi or Musette, famously wore pantaloons and yellow leather boots when she left the room to attend the Opera Ball, deliciously shocking the bourgeoisie. Passionate and hungry day and night, she and Nadar feasted exclusively on oysters, day after week after month. The shells piled up everywhere, carpeting the floor. The smell was overwhelming.

Summoning all my courage, I once found myself in rue Monsieur le Prince at a propitious moment and followed a pair of deliverymen with a refrigerator through the open street door of the building where Nadar once lived. We climbed four stories to the garret. I pushed past the fridge-bearers on the third-floor landing, raced ahead, and knocked on Nadar's door, fully expecting to see a tall, slim, smiling youth in his birthday suit waiting for Mimi and her oysters. A young Frenchman threw the door open. Clearly he mistook me for a deliveryman. I entered, glanced around, and asked about the broken fridge, wondering aloud if Nadar's ghost ever showed up and if the oysters still smelled—because of the broken fridge, of course. The confused tenant and the newly arrived deliverymen stared at me. I felt temporarily insane, sniffing the air, then backing out onto the landing and rushing off. The scent of oysters and the sea was gone. The garret seemed modern and nondescript. Nadar and his lady were no longer, at least not in this building. But they live on in the works of Murger and Puccini, and in my mind.

Nadar served as a philosophical and behavioral model for the male

Putative portrait of Mimi by Nadar

characters in Murger's tale: Parts of him are in Gustave Colline, the philosopher; Marcel, the painter; Rodolphe, the poet; and Schaunard, the musician, and each is also based on at least one real person. Mimi is the subject of at least two of Nadar's most striking photographic nudes—he made very few. They show a mystery woman, an apparition thought to be Mimi or her "sister" Musette (Musetta for Puccini). Wraithlike, angelic, wanton, hauntingly bloodless, she might be a vampire arisen, or merely the sad, starving shared *gri-sette* Nadar and his friends knew and loved, a creature suspended between drudgery, prostitution, and debauchery.

There is an inconvenient detail of chronology involving the actual Mimi in Nadar's images, however. Like Murger, Nadar may well have kissed her chilly hands and pretty little mouth, but she died before he ever picked up a camera. The woman shown was not Mimi-Lucile but Musette or Mariette. These were made up names for the demimondaine Marie-Christine Roux, the lover of Nadar and longtime mistress of Murger's great friend Champfleury, also immortalized by Nadar.

Thanks to Puccini, Mimi is better known than her creator Henri Murger. But he is still a household name in Paris and may well be the French gentleman for whom the expression "burning the candle at both ends" was coined. One of the few authentically impoverished underclass Romantics whose name lives on, he was the gifted son of concierges and began working as a scribe when he was only thirteen years old. He worked till the day he died of purpura, poor nutrition, exposure, overindulgence, alcoholism, substance abuse, and undistilled fatigue. By twenty he had distinguished himself, and in his thirties was welcomed into the empyrean of art, a friend not only of Nadar, Banville, and Champfleury but also of Baudelaire and Renoir, Gérard de Nerval and Théophile Gautier. It's startling given Murger's socialist views that even Louis Napoléon Bonaparte, not yet a dictator in 1849, came to the opening night of *Scènes de la vie de bohème*, the stage play that pre-dated Puccini's masterpiece by half a century. Then again, Karl Marx, who had seen bohemian Paris in its heyday and hated it, called the future Napoléon III a "princely lumpen bohemian."

Breaking with classic tradition, the highly romantic play and book aren't divided into beginning, middle, and end. Murger idolized Hugo. Chronology and a logical plot were considered reactionary by the Romantic avant-garde, just as they would be by postmodern writers. *Scènes de la vie de bohème* combines eighteen short autobiographical sketches that were first serialized in the magazine *Corsaire-Satan*, then transformed for stage, then reworked into what might be called a postmodern "novel" of short stories. Each shows an episode of life, love, betrayal, striving, or death among the bohemians Murger not only knew but led. The best-loved episodes—thanks to Puccini—star Rodolphe and Mimi, though Musette is nearly as important and is named 180 times in the book's pages. I counted them. Like the male characters in *Scènes de la vie de bohème*, Mimi and Musette are composites of the women the author loved. "Mimi" in fact was Murger's standard endearment, the nickname he gave to many young ladies.

Murger was an artist at life, not a great writer or playwright. But who can forget the throwaway line about Séraphine, her pretty

Henri Murger by Nadar

face blushing with "the dawn of voluptuousness . . . a veritable instrument of pleasure, a true Stradivarius of love I'd happily play an air with."

Séraphine was not Mimi, however, and Rodolphe—Murger's fictional doppelgänger—didn't love her. At the mere sound of "Lucile," Mimi's name in the book and in real life, the heartbroken Rodolphe forgets his Stradivarius and slinks off to his chilly garret. In his cold bed the pillow on Mimi's side is still indented and scented by her luxuriant animal perfume.

"And with delirious drunkenness Rodolphe plunged his head into the pillows still impregnated with the perfume of his lover's hair," Murger wrote with the verisimilitude of autobiography. "From the back of the alcove he seemed to see the ghost of the wondrous nights he'd spent with his young mistress."

"Ghost" is apt, given Mimi-Lucile's early departure from the tuberculosis ward of a Paris hospital east of the Latin Quarter. Tragically she was loaded into a wagonload of cadavers as he tried frantically to find her. She wound up in a paupers' common grave.

"Alas, thought Rodolphe, what's better, to face betrayal because you believed, or never believe because you always feared betrayal?"

Murger knew it was better to believe and seek the redemption of love, however temporary. He preached blissful or perhaps even willful ignorance. Yet he was also clear-eyed about his own sexual and emotional egoism and that of his fellow bohemians, who picked up and discarded *grisettes* like old shoes—or silk slippers. When Mimi died, he grieved less for her than for the death of his own youth. "One has creditors when young, just as one has mistresses," Murger wrote later in *The Water Drinkers* at the height of his fame in 1855, "because it's necessary to live, and it's necessary to love, but the creditors do not prevent one from becoming a respectable man, just as the mistresses do not prevent one from being an excellent husband."

Balzac and Hugo couldn't have said it better. The line would be hard to add to the French national anthem but could be carved on the Panthéon, preferably updated to reflect a unisex, androgynous world where the genders of lovers and partners are immaterial to the national penchant.

27

THE WATER DRINKERS

Before Mimi betrays Rodolophe for the last time, before the last bouquet of violets fades, before she lets drop her lifeless *gelida manina*—the freezing little hand Puccini rhapsodized—for the last time, follow her scent with Rodolphe-Murger and the spirited happy-go-lucky band from the bench at the Luxembourg Garden. Baudelaire the young dandy has just walked up from the Odéon-Théâtre wearing his patented pink kid gloves and polished black boots. He's very concerned about keeping clean. Jovial Nadar teases him about his fastidiousness and keeps his eye on Mimi and Musette. Arm in arm with Champfleury, Banville, and Schanne and half a dozen others, they head by twos and threes down rue de Médicis, then broad, tony rue Tournon. They pass the landmark buildings where Casanova, John Paul Jones, Léon Gambetta, and Balzac lived, continue down rue de Seine one block, turn left at the Parisian mecca of contemporary pastry Gérard Mulot, navigate around the bustling, recently restored Marché Saint-Germain, and skip onward two short blocks along rue Guisarde to the equally narrow medieval rue des Canettes. At the leisurely pace Mimi, Musette, and Murger prefer, it's a fifteen-minute stroll through some of Paris' most desirable vintage real estate, every inch a palimpsest of living history.

In the dark recesses of the street's best address, number 18, a familiar figure is poking around the reading room of a bookstore, his lips pursed and chin thrust forward. It's Balzac, come to make sure his latest books are prominently displayed and available for rent. Readers rarely buy books; rather they pay to sit quietly in the store and devour them. Balzac is known to some as "the prince of Bohemia" (also the title of one of his novels) because he described the world of artists and the lower depths so masterfully without belonging to it himself. So did George Sand, the aristocrat who was bohemian not in her income but in her ways and writings. Well, well, isn't Sand the slender young man with Balzac? They're too busy and too important now to acknowledge the band of unknown bohemians on the road to fame, fortune, and the morgue.

Outside in the street Nadar doffs his troubadour hat and curtsies. Then he makes a quacking sound, beats his gangling arms, and points up. On the mezzanine level of the carved limestone façade, a low-relief rococo sculpture shows three ducklings in a pond. The carving honors the street's endearing name.

Another fifty yards west at number 5 rue des Canettes is the Hôtel Merciol, one step up from a flophouse. There, on the top floor, lives Rodolphe-Murger, and there Mimi-Lucile rests her perfumed head on his pillow and gives him her bloodless hand, her warm but weak wayward heart.

"Spacious window, from which one sees an expanse of snow-clad roofs," the libretto of *La Bohème* reads, setting the scene. "On left a fireplace, a table, a small cupboard, a little bookcase, four chairs, an easel, a bed, a few books, many packs of cards, two candlesticks. Door in the middle, another on left."

The stage directions seem to refer to the atelier where in real life Nadar and Schanne lived and painted, played music, entertained, and slept—rarely alone. But it might well be a description of Murger's real room in rue des Canettes or a blend of both.

Did Puccini ever visit Murger's apartment? I can't help wondering. Did he sneak in and scale the three coiling flights of steps, tiptoeing up to the attic rooms now so comfortably appointed, heated, and soundproofed? Or am I the only one to be so foolish, the only one who prefers to believe? I believe that on many levels the tale of Murger's bohemians is true, is universal and timeless, and is close to the bone, to the rib cages encasing the hearts and tubercular lungs of luckless Mimi and Rodolphe and a million others like them then and now.

"Vision entrancing," Rodolphe sings to Mimi by his window, "illumined by rays of pure moonlight, your charms enhancing, my dreams be ever dreams so heavenly and bright, fired by adoration, of your sweet fascination, I claim this kiss of love."

Granted it sounds better in Italian.

If I stand in this time-warp street at dawn, when the party crowd is gone and the shops aren't yet open, if I wait long enough to let the characters take hold of me, I get choked up. Rodolphe's memorable line plays in my head: "Life's fairest flower is love!"

Shakespeare, Hugo, Musset, and other lovers have written or thought this universal hope in their own words. A double-pneumonia fever of memory sometimes seizes me, a fleeting quest to capture a moment of magic suspended in the stream of time, attached to eternity by a name or a place or an image or a smell, a public time, and a time in one's own life. In my case, the time is my youth in San Francisco when I was a summertime usher at the opera house, or those early years in my maid's room in rue Laugier, and the first time my wife and I saw *La Bohème* together at the Opéra de la Bastille.

It may well be maudlin to be entranced by Murger and Puccini or believe in the transformative power of love. Gautier reminds us, apropos of Murger, that few things are more pathetic than a white-haired bohemian. Murger himself saw the institution of bohemia as a critical stage in the life of an artist, not an end in itself. I recalled now, standing in front of his one-time attic, his famous last wishes. Thirty years ago they had helped ease me out of my own garret: "No music, no noise, no bohemia!"

When Murger died, the son of impoverished concierges was a Chevalier of the Legion of Honor. Among the thousands attending his state funeral at Montmartre Cemetery were many surviving bohemians plus the literary arbiter Sainte-Beuve and Jules Sandeau, both stars of the French Academy and neither one a sentimentalist.

The wickedly genial Flaubert was caustic about sentiment and bohemia, and his feelings about Murger were clear. Why else would he have named Emma Bovary's cynical, faux romantic lover "Rodolphe"? Flaubert hated the Latin Quarter and all it represented. A student of law, he'd lived in a shabby room south of the Panthéon, miserable and cold and homesick for Normandy. He certainly wouldn't have belonged to Murger's modest company. They stood for artistic passion and sacrifice, but also unwashed poverty, and they clamored for utopian social justice and women's rights.

Even more damning than the rascal Rodolphe of *Madame Bovary*, Flaubert's other sweeping masterpiece *Sentimental Education* evokes those hateful student days and paints multiple portraits of sardonic, opportunistic self-styled republicans, socialists, and bohemians of the Murger stamp. They are every bit as loathsome and untrustworthy as the bourgeois parvenus and petty aristocrats who inhabit this singularly antiheroic, anti-Romantic book. It's a coming-of-age story about

Emma Bovary and the rascal Rodolphe (by Clare Victor Dwiggins)

sexual initiation, adultery, dueling, double-dealing, and treachery, and a thousand other things, and is one of my all-time favorites of French literature. Despite his studious detachment, however, Flaubert fills the novel with a paradoxical idealism, an abiding belief in art and love. He was a Romantic against his will, like so many Frenchmen and -women today.

Strange: Paris is a city of heirlooms labeled with commemorative plaques. Yet no plaque marks the handsome if humble building in rue des Canettes where Henri Murger and Mimi lived. It is at least three hundred years old, a place where so much happened and so many lives were changed in the Romantic era and are perhaps being changed in the present, too. Few appear to know that Murger's garret in the former Hôtel Merciol is still here,

Baudelaire in the Luxembourg Garden among Flowers of Evil

or that outwardly the building looks the same as in the 1840s, with its many-paned windows and a façade of plaster with curious raised sections resembling picture frames. Plaster pilasters frame the entrance door. Above are the gabled dormers where Murger lived. Today the ground floor is rented out to unremarkable shops. But in Murger's day it was the headquarters of the Société des Buveurs d'Eau, whose members were theoretically too poor to drink wine but wisely wouldn't swallow water—hence the irony in the name, the Society of Water Drinkers. There was one exception: Félix Nadar.

It was with these heavy-drinking bohemians that Gaspard Félix Tournachon, the wildest of the wild, became Félix Nadar. Other members of the society had irreverent or nonsense nicknames and spoke in Gothic-sounding pig Latin. Nadar had the peculiar habit of adding *dar* to words. His friends nicknamed him Tournadar or Nadarchon, and he shortened them to Nadar. As had happened with George Sand, the pseudonym became a brand and he stuck with it.

Nadar may have worn outsize earrings and crazily colorful troubadour outfits; he may have been followed by the French police and considered "a dangerous activist spreading subversive doctrines among the young." But he rarely, if ever, drank alcohol, not for puritanical or health motives. Effusive, narcissistic, and hyperactive, he didn't need wine to be drunk on life. In an age when Paris' drinking water was unsafe, consuming it was an act of courage or foolhardiness. When not sipping corrosive, tar-like coffee, everyone swilled wine, beer, and gin. Alcohol was both drink and food, and wine was man's best friend. When Mimi enters in the first act of Puccini's opera, she faints from cold and hunger and is revived not with water but a glass of wine, the bohemian's lifeblood. Their trinity was wine, love, and song.

"It's time to get drunk," wrote Baudelaire, an honorary member of the Society of Water Drinkers, "time to shed the martyr's shackles of Time, time to be seamlessly sloshed, on wine, on poetry, on virtue, as you prefer."

Baudelaire also noted elsewhere with typical, cheery aplomb that Death—"sleep's oblivion"—awaits us all, a balm, but in the meantime there was wine, "divine child of the Sun."

Nadar was a founding member of the society, but whether Baudelaire was really a regular at the society's gatherings or knew Mimi and Musette is unsure. Baudelaire, Nadar, and Murger worked for the same magazines, but their social circles didn't necessarily overlap. It's certain that Baudelaire and Nadar spent time with Murger and the bohemian crowd at the real watering hole of the bohemians, their public living room, painting atelier, and more, Café Momus.

28

MOMUS IS THE WORD

"Momus, Momus, Momus!" sing Colline, Marcel, and Schaunard, the swashbuckling trio of Puccini's *La Bohème.* "Gently and soft to supper let us go."

Add in Rodolphe and the trio becomes The Four Musketeers, as inseparable a band in fiction as on stage and in real life. Marching together from the Latin Quarter or Saint-Germain, they would cross the Seine on the Pont des Arts and besiege the Café Momus every day. Sometimes, as in Act Two of *La Bohème,* Mimi would join them. The café was warmer and brighter than the unheated attics and studios where Mimi the sickly plant spent sunless days.

Murger's attic in rue des Canettes stands near the corner of busy rue du Four. Crossing this thoroughfare the other day I walked up rue des Ciseaux, one of the short, narrow medieval streets typical of the neighborhood. Would the bohemians veer left and around the façade of the church of Saint-Germain-des-Prés or go the other way around? If left, they would have entered a warren of alleyways swept away by Haussmann.

A modern walker crosses the Boulevard Saint-Germain and passes Les Deux Magots, the famous café where latter-day Romantics, modernists, and existentialists like Apollinaire, Hemingway, Picasso, Janet Flanner, Simon de Beauvoir, and Sartre nursed drinks and chain-smoked for days at a time. Set in amber like much of Paris, Les Deux Magots is an exquisite tourist trap where an espresso sets you back seven bucks, a glass of wine twice

No padlocks: in the foreground the Pont des Arts sketched by J. M. Whistler

that. Upscale nostalgia has a price. I like to peek in at the brass railings, the dark woodwork and old-fashioned banquettes, and the black-and-white photos hanging above the tables the greats claimed as their own. Here Picasso met his paramour the photographer Dora Maar, and Hemingway hung out with Flanner, the *New Yorker*'s correspondent but also a refugee seeking sexual freedom and European culture. Sartre and Beauvoir received their lovers and acolytes here, often separately, but sometimes in a prelude to intimate threesomes.

At the end of rue de l'Abbaye, the footloose Romantics would pass the first atelier of James Pradier, at number 3 on the ground floor of the tall, sprawling brick-and-stone mansion from the 1500s. With outstretched arms practically touching the sides of an alleyway, rue de l'Échaudé, they would rejoin rue de Seine and stride north to the river, ducking under a passageway to the Institut de France and across the quay to the city's best-loved footbridge then and now, the Pont des Arts.

The route is familiar to art lovers for its concentration of galleries and for the School of Fine Arts on rue Bonaparte, a factory of contemporary unwitting Romantics. In the 1970s I stayed in the Latin Quarter and Saint-

Pont des Art: new forms of bondage and servitude or romance?

Germain several times, and in the 1980s often lunched or dined at historic Le Petit Saint-Benoit a hundred yards northwest of Les Deux Magots. I still make this run at least once a week for the atmosphere, the humble beauty of the weathered buildings, and the many hallowed sites—for instance, the apartment at 25 rue de Seine where George Sand lived with Sandeau in 1831, and the place where Baudelaire lived, next door at number 27, in 1855. Few know Baudelaire was also a resident of rue de Seine, and there is no plaque to tell you so. The reason is simple: Baudelaire moved over fifty times; the

Just possibly the most romantic spot in Paris: Pont des Arts

municipality would go bankrupt marking his haunts. Two blocks away at 17–19, rue Visconti, the narrowest alley in the neighborhood, Balzac ran his ruinous printing establishment in the late 1820s. Delacroix took over in the mid-1830s.

A short staircase leads from the quai de Conti to the Pont des Arts, the city's other celebrated continuous contemporary art happening. There were no beribboned, graffiti-sprayed padlocks attached to the bridge's railings and grates in the days when Murger and Mimi and their friends walked over this footbridge. No one threw keys in the Seine, and photographers were few. Blissful ignorance about the Pont des Arts is not possible for me because I have been an eyewitness to its evolution for too long. Today's bridge is not the same bridge people crossed in the Romantic Age. I crossed that bridge many times in the 1970s before it was wrecked by barges and a passing riverboat. It was rebuilt in 1984. It wasn't replaced by something postmodern, a steel and cement span for cars and trucks. The magic of the bridge and the spot were preserved.

There are those who claim the most romantic place in Paris is the triangular Square du Vert-Galant on the downstream tip of the Ile de la Cité, where weeping willows dangle their branches in the Seine. The giant bronze equestrian sculpture of Henri IV, "the evergreen galavanting geezer" the park is named for, rises above the square on the Pont Neuf. Picasso loved this spot, and when polled, contemporary Parisians routinely choose the park as the heart of romance. It is enchanting. But I have always preferred the Pont des Arts, even now, when it's mobbed by buskers, tour groups,

entwined couples, wedding photographers, itinerant lock sellers,
pickpockets, and police squads.
The police apparently have no
interest in the pickpockets but
are bent on preventing lovers
from attaching their locks and
throwing their keys into the
river.

The view upstream from the
footbridge takes in the inch-
worm arches of the Pont Neuf, the park Picasso and the Parisians love, plus
the towers of Saint-Germain l'Auxerrois, the Conciergerie, Sainte-Chapelle,
and Notre Dame, and the spooky Second Empire Prefecture of Police,
where Simenon's Inspector Maigret had his office. Downstream you see
the Musée d'Orsay and Grand Palais, the Grande Galerie of the Louvre, an
infinite regression of handsome bridges, and the Eiffel Tower's elegant iron
skirt.

The view was even more romantic in the Age of Romanticism, with teetering half-timbered houses on the riverbanks, municipal water pumps, floating *bateau-lavoir,* French "laundry boats," and crumbling medieval towers.
How many times did Murger and Mimi pause to embrace on this bridge as
they headed toward the Right Bank? They crossed the quay, passed the Louvre's colonnaded façade and entered the square fronting it, arriving out of
breath and thirsty. Their goal was a café in the narrow street flanking Saint-
Germain l'Auxerrois. An old stone building still standing there housed one
of the most popular, liveliest watering holes and billiard halls of the nineteenth century, Café Momus.

"Momus, Momus, Momus!" sing Puccini's bohemians as Mimi shivers in
her thin winter coat. Unlike George Sand in real life and fiction, Mimi did
not wear men's clothes and her shoes were like high-heeled slippers. In
Puccini's opera the scene takes place on Christmas Eve. Snow and ice clot
the slippery streets and there are no sidewalks yet in Paris. The lights and
warmth of the café beckon. But Mimi and Rodolphe and the others can't
get inside. Act Two of *La Bohème* begins.

"A conflux of streets; where they meet, a square, flanked by shops of all kinds . . . A vast, motley crowd; soldiers, maids, boys, girls, students, shop attendants, gendarmes, etc. It is evening. The shops are decked with tiny lamps; a huge lantern lights up the entrance to the Café Momus. The café is so crowded some of the customers are obliged to seat themselves outside."

"Surging onward—eager, breathless—moves the madding crowd," Schaunard sings, "as they frolic ever in their wild, insane endeavor."

Venison, lobster, claret, and custard are ordered and consumed, not necessarily in that order, while the opera moves inexorably toward its tragic climax.

Today, if you enter the lobby of 19 rue des Prêtres Saint-Germain l'Auxerrois you can probably order those same delicacies from room service and enjoy them in a posh if old-fashioned décor of thick curtains and carpets, chintz, marble, and mahogany. Le Relais du Louvre is a luxury boutique hotel, the happy occupant of the premises where the Café Momus was from the time of Napoléon I until the Nazi Occupation. The hotel's staff seems blissfully ignorant of the property's history and baffled or defensive when questioned. There is no plaque on the building, and without a plaque, there is no history. Yet this was Murger's hangout, where Victor Hugo, Sainte-Beuve, Alexandre Dumas, Gustave Courbet, Baudelaire, Nadar, and countless others hobnobbed, swilled, chalked pool cues, and planned the nation's future. Were Balzac and George Sand among them, perhaps in disguise? It's a tantalizing thought. Did Delacroix and Ingres read Baudelaire's critiques in *Corsaire-Satan* of the in-house bohemian painter Léopold Tabar? Did Baudelaire wander in to check whether Tabar favored color over line— the bone Delacroix and Ingres picked for decades, and others pick for them today?

29

COLOR VERSUS LINE

I f Balzac, Musset, and Nadar were eternal adolescents, the paradoxical Eugène Delacroix was eternally ancient and earnest as only a young idealist
can be. Outwardly he was reserved, polite, sometimes cordial. His journal,
kept on and off for forty-one years, and his art tell another tale of inner
torment, passion, longing, and dark genius. Sententious, judgmental, politically conservative, and quarrelsome, he was also capable of great empa-
thy and generosity. Like many polymaths he expressed himself as skillfully
with words as he did on canvas, paper, and plaster.

Hugo and Sand are well represented here, but the Luxembourg Garden
really belongs to Delacroix. It boasts not one, not two, but three portraits
memorializing the revolutionary colorist who is paradoxically remembered for his ambiguous *Liberty Leading the People*. The painting is ambiguous
because it depicts the inevitable brutality and the real price of violent rebellion, about which Delacroix was queasy. The canvas shows a proto–
Statue of Liberty landing with flag raised amid blood and bodies in a sort of
1830 Parisian version of the famous photograph of the Battle of Iwo Jima.
When I moved to Paris, the image was ubiquitous and coveted. In good
times I carried several in my wallet: The image of Delacroix's painting was
on the front of the French 100-franc note along with a portrait of the artist,
which also appeared on the back of the note with a depiction of his Place
de Furstenberg atelier, now a national house museum.

The French franc with his image is used no more, but Delacroix's name

Liberty Leading the People *and Delacroix as hard cash*

and image remain common currency in France. His work influenced Manet, Monet, Cézanne, Fantin-Latour, Signac, and Van Gogh, opening doors to Impressionism, Fauvism, and Surrealism and inspiring young artists to this day. His life is studied by all. He was also celebrated as the color-driven nemesis of Ingres, the master of line. The irony is that Delacroix's line drawings and sketches are as fine as his colorful oils and murals, perhaps finer and certainly lighter and more spontaneous. He's hailed as the leading Romantic painter, the painter of bold color, yet he abominated Romanticism and was an unabashed Luddite. He was also the opposite of a bohemian, theoretically the highborn son of a plenipotentiary Napoleonic minister. More probably his father was Talleyrand, his longtime protector. Delacroix was destined for glory.

Likewise, in reverse, Ingres the so-called Classicist applied color to his paintings, not simply to fill spaces between his masterful lines. His often sensuous, provocative, boneless, ambiguous female figures are not in the least classical. A convincing argument has been made that Ingres' colors

Self-Portrait of the Artist as a Young Man: Delacroix

and compositions were purposely shocking and mannerist, or pre-Symbolist and thoroughly modern. Yet Ingres joined forces with Victor Hugo in defense of Paris' Gothic art and architecture, and Delacroix did not. Often described as a brutish, blunt-fingered, vulgar man of humble origins, Ingres was disliked by most who knew him and had less influence than Delacroix on French painting.

The haughty, handsome, privileged Delacroix instead is everywhere. He frowns at you from a trio of prestige locations in the Luxembourg Garden: below Victor Hugo on the base of *The Mask Seller*; from the greenhouse near Pradier; and from the heights of an exorbitantly Romantic fountain, probably my favorite in Paris for its Decadent, fin-de-siècle, late Romantic kitsch.

Muse and Painter: the Delacroix memorial fountain, Luxembourg Garden

Would prickly Delacroix be proud? Surely not: The mask is a lifeless caricature, the bust on the greenhouse is at best uninspired, and the fountain, featuring Death and a luscious tearful Maiden, is so over the top, brimming with the sculptor's lust for his female model, that the reticent, prudish painter would faint if he could see it. He might approve of the patina of the bronze and the shady location under the western alley of giant sycamores, but the composition?

Imagine a short, thin, pale man with luxuriant wavy dark hair and a closely trimmed mustache, always dapper, often dressed no matter what the season in dark, heavy suits with a white shirt and wide cravat or striped foulard to protect his delicate throat. Théophile Gautier depicts Delacroix as distinguished by "a ferocious beauty, strange, exotic, almost disquieting." He was, said Baudelaire, "a curious blend of skepticism, politeness, dandyism, willpower, cleverness, despotism, and that special goodness and tenderness that accompany genius."

Up the dusty alley of mottled old plane trees he comes, flanked by a pair of even thinner, younger gentlemen. One of them is weak and wan; the other smokes a cigar. Look again: He of the cigar is a she, and she wears a dagger on her belt.

Did George Sand and Chopin actually stride around the Luxembourg with Delacroix? Absolutely: She and the pianist lived nearby, and all three were close friends, dining and vacationing together. Five of Delacroix's ateliers and six of his apartments were a five-minute walk from the garden. Maurice Sand, George's son, became Delacroix's pupil starting in 1839. Maurice would develop considerable talent and go on to illustrate his mother's bestselling books. Chopin was the living composer Delacroix—passionate about Beethoven—most admired. In 1834, Sand's publisher also gave Delacroix the unusual commission to portray her wearing men's clothing while smoking. A few years later, Delacroix painted the double portrait of Sand and Chopin that was cut in two and sold in separate lots. Chopin is now in the Louvre, Sand at the Ordrupgaard Museum in Denmark. Their destiny was irreparable separation both before and after death.

But as they walked and talked on a bright April day, visiting the Luxembourg's museum, where Delacroix's first famous painting *The Barque of Dante* hung, afterward touring the palace and park, did the reticent Delacroix tell Sand how much he admired the daring of her novel *Lélia*? He was so taken with it, we're told, that he painted several versions of the ghoulish dramatic death scene, Lélia Standing before the Corpse of her Lover in the Monk's Cavern.

Of a mind with Balzac, Delacroix did not share Sand's utopian vision of humanity, nor did he approve of the agitprop militancy of her writings. But unhappy endings were true drink to all Romantics, and for Delacroix, as for Baudelaire, melancholy was a motor of creativity. That idiosyncratic French pact of inspired sadness binding Delacroix to all the great men and women of his time is what binds him to his fellow French citizens today.

30

A DRUNKEN BOAT,
A STARVING WRITER, AND
TWO GIANT CLARINETS

Though Delacroix is a park habitué, his real sanctuary isn't the Luxembourg but a church located two short blocks northwest. Like local residents Victor Hugo and, a century later, Ernest Hemingway, the painter would exit on rue de Vaugirard, flanking the Musée du Luxembourg, then walk down the narrow, slightly sloping rue Férou, unaltered since the early 1500s.

His goal was the massive neoclassical church of Saint-Sulpice, an architectural hodgepodge that took two centuries to complete. En route he would pass a sumptuous town house at number six, the one with plaster putti moldings and garlands and a carriage entrance flanked by sphinxes. Is this where Athos lived? Why not: Alexandre Dumas named the street but never provided a number, so let's assume it was, the rue Férou being the hypotenuse of the so-called Triangle of the Three Musketeers.

Look again at those sphinxes: The indelible mark of the musketeer of Romantic modernism, Hemingway, remains. He slept here and wrote here, freshly married to his second wife, the heiress Pauline Pfeiffer. They lived luxuriously on two upper floors, though on paper for posterity he was forever cold and starving and penniless and unspeakably happy to be unhappy. He also frequented the Luxembourg Garden and museum, of course, to hunt squab with his infant son and avoid the tortures of Paris' delicacy-scented air, which suggested the purchase of foods he clearly could not afford—not, at least, in the "moveable feast" of memory.

Hemingway loved starvation, apparently, because hunger made him see clearly, and he saw clearest of all when contemplating the paintings by Cézanne then hanging in the Musée du Luxembourg. In his writings, the museum seems as if it were a million freezing, fraught miles away from the places where he lived in direst poverty. In reality his various rooms or apartments were a magical fifteen-minute walk away, and his latter-day gilded bohemia was just half a block down rue Férou.

What might Cézanne have made of Hemingway's observations? Was Hemingway perhaps a proto-cubist writer the way Cézanne was the proto-cubist forefather of Picasso and Braque's patented Cubism with a capital C? Hemingway learned to sculpt his simple sentences from Cézanne, he claimed, and Cézanne learned a great deal from Delacroix, though an untrained eye has difficulty making the connection. But it was the poet Apollinaire who coined the term Cubism, not Cézanne or Picasso or Braque. Apollinaire and Picasso were great admirers of Delacroix.

The chain of art has many links, and it twists and curls as it unites creative spirits across disciplines and centuries.

A hundred yards down the street the formerly blank stone wall that hungry Hemingway and gloomy Delacroix knew well has been transformed in recent years into the Rimbaud "Drunken Boat" poetry wall. The full text of the poet's best-known work, combining real and metaphorical travel and sexual exploration in surreal, symbolic language, is writ large in black letters on ocher limestone. Beyond the beauty of some of the oceanic imagery, the key lines, it has long seemed to me, are "Sweeter than the flesh of unripe apples to children," and "the green water . . . / washed the bluish wine stains from me / and the splashed vomit, carrying away rudder and anchor."

Rudderless, waterlogged, with sour wine and vomit in his mouth, Rimbaud, tortured by unavowable passions, is "swollen" by "sharp love," a love for men. This love focused itself on an equally tormented older family man prone to straying and drunken disorder, Paul Verlaine. Verlaine fell madly in love with the pretty-boy prodigy whose striking good looks hid layers of hardpan.

The Rimbaud "Poetry Wall" near Saint-Sulpice

One of the more prominent and less successful sculptures in the Luxembourg Garden is of a scowling Verlaine. It is located not far from Chopin and the Luxembourg museum and is remarkable for its hideousness. The bust sits atop a stele swarming with bas-reliefs of women. They are Verlaine's wife, children, and mother caught up in the maelstrom of violence, alcoholism, drug abuse, and depression as they try to rescue the famous poet from debauched Rimbaud. The notorious enfant terrible, archangel of homosexual temptation and searing sexual honesty, may have been a poetic genius and hero of gay liberation. But he also destroyed lives. Rimbaud was Baudelaire with bells tied on.

There is no monument to the dark, self-destructive Rimbaud in the park. Instead, it stands in front of the Arsenal Library, that other great Romantic shrine. When the poetry wall was inaugurated, some wondered why the rue Férou, home of macho musketeer Athos and Hemingway, had been chosen for it. What no one tells you, wrongly assuming you'll know, is that the first time the seventeen-year-old rebel Rimbaud declaimed the poem publicly in the fall of 1871, he did so in an upstairs salon in an unnamed café on Place Saint-Sulpice. Doubtless it was the Cabaret de Perrin, formerly a rendezvous of Nadar, Murger, and the Water Drinkers. No one seems to have noted the name, or if they did, that information is lost. But there is only one café on the square today. It has always had an upstairs room and has been on the same premises for over a century.

Delacroix and Chopin were already in Père-Lachaise Cemetery by 1871, Murger was with the angels at Montmartre, Sand was in Nohant preparing to push up periwinkles, Hemingway wasn't born, Proust was in his crib, but the eternal Nadar and Victor Hugo newly returned from exile may well have attended Rimbaud's reading. J. K. Huysmans, a fellow seeker with latitudinous sexual views, a latter-day admirer of Rimbaud, might also have dropped by: He was twenty-three and curious yellow. Who knows?

I like to think the unnamed café was the famous hangout where movies like *La Discrète* have been shot, and where today, on Tuesday evenings, a group of French writers and poets meet and hold literary events: Café de la Mairie. It's kitty-corner to the church. Murger, Rimbaud, Verlaine, Baudelaire, and others live on in the boozy atmosphere.

The church looms over Place Saint-Sulpice, casting a shadow much of the day across the terrace of the Café de la Mairie. It is only slightly ironic that Delacroix was an anticlassical Romantic and Hugo intensely disliked "ridiculous, pretentious, bastard" neoclassical architecture, dubbing the towers of Saint-Sulpice "two giant clarinets." They seem to be poised atop an upright piano or perhaps a toothy Greco-Incan temple. Yet this study in gracelessness is where Victor and Adèle were married, baptized their first children, and attended services in their pious early years, and where Delacroix's masterpieces of religious art are found. Did Hemingway look at the Delacroix murals before he had his celebrated sexual epiphany in the pews? Perhaps rebellious Rimbaud and enraged Verlaine met in secret under the colonnade or in the darkness of a confessional.

In Hugo's day, the first chapel on the south side was not associated with avenging "saint angels" or the work of Delacroix. The painter spent the last decade of his life laboring here, often painfully, covering the walls and ceiling of the chapel with his bizarre interpretations of Old Testament scenes, the coloring high on flesh tones, purples, and reds.

Mount the Greco-Incan temple staircase passing through the faux

Panthéon peristyle, step inside, turn right, and let your eyes adjust to the low light. Another short flight of steps leads into the side chapel of Les Saints-Anges. Look left. The glare in daytime makes viewing difficult and the dimness of night makes it nearly impossible. But it's worth the effort to concentrate. Generations of Romantics have stood here in silence, either awed or appalled. I began to appreciate the murals only after many tries. Now I am a regular.

In Delacroix's *Jacob and the Angel*, the muscular Jacob is shown wrestling an athletic winged redhead who tells him he will now be known as Israel. Decrypting the mural is a challenge. The angel is an incarnation of God, it is claimed, and the prevailing Christian interpretation is that this represents Christ's appearing, an adumbration of the era to come. It may also symbolize reason struggling against the spiritual. To irreverent eyes, the suspiciously handsome homoerotic pair seems to be dancing furiously like Rimbaud and Verlaine.

The Expulsion of Heliodorus from the Temple is Delacroix's other, even more intensely purple, ruddy, and violent mural on the opposite side of the chapel. In it, two airborne youths with scourges and a winged warrior on a splendid rearing charger prepare to whisk away or skewer the infidels led by Heliodorus, a tax collector come to loot the Jewish temple. Needless to say, Heliodorus is converted, the treasure is preserved, and according to Christian interpretation, the tale ultimately warns potential vandals to beware the inviolable nature of the Mother Church and its property.

The delicious irony is Delacroix, while not an avowed atheist, was inherently anticlerical and skeptical despite his longing to believe and his profound sense of spirituality. Art was his religion; painting and music were his gods. He seemed happiest and most productive, he noted in his journal, when the organist at Saint-Sulpice was practicing or playing for mass—and felt embittered because the priest would not allow him to work on Sunday or while services were under way.

In these murals, Italian Mannerism and French Romanticism dance fast and furious like Jacob and the Angel. For Delacroix, the underlying struggle was less about religion and more about the artist's wresting inspiration from thin air. The source of inspiration was one of the great unresolved issues he struggled with from adolescence onward. The paintings may also have been about the irrepressible life force of nature, the wrestlers mirroring the entwined trees above, or sexuality. Few artists of his period were as secretive and outwardly chaste as Delacroix was. When he died, a kindred spirit, Baudelaire, noted that "he was the most open spirit to all notions and all impressions, the most eclectic and most impartial *jouisseur* of all." That untranslatable term—*jouisseur*—merges appreciation with enjoyment and pleasure, hinting at *jouissance*, sexual climax. Was Delacroix avowing in paint the unspeakable?

What gives the chapel universal appeal to the secular art historian is the open-endedness of the artist's quest. What bring the murals to life for me are the endearing details: the spears, swords, and textiles, even the hats. Delacroix brought many of these accessories to Paris from North Africa when he was young and kept them as he moved from one studio to another, hopscotching around Paris until he wound up at Place de Furstenberg. There they remain, displayed in vitrines in what might well be one of the most romantic, lovingly preserved "places of memory" in the city.

31

DELACROIX'S LAST STAND

Romantic enclaves abound in Paris. Establishing a hit list of the top ten is a serious challenge. But I have no hesitation in placing Place de Furstenberg among them. The size of two tennis courts, the square is hemmed in by vintage buildings of differing heights and styles, some of them survivors from pre-Revolutionary days. That is when the abbot of Saint-Germain stabled horses and servants here. There's a round island in the middle of Place de Furstenberg, from which four towering paulownia trees spring. Their mauve and white flowers smell sweet in June; their broad heart-shaped leaves provide shade and clothing for naked Adams and Eves. The square exudes the kind of premodern magic even the most cynical passerby finds hard to resist. Lighting is part of the equation: The single streetlamp is of the mid-nineteenth-century many-branched-candelabra variety. It is set low so as to glow romantically, not blind. Until a few years ago several benches stood invitingly under the trees, making this a celebrated trysting spot. But the usual problems of incivility forced the city to remove them.

It's unclear whether the benches or trees were around during Delacroix's heyday here from 1857 to 1863. He probably would not have lingered on them. His delicate health, industriousness, and antisocial bent meant he was forever at work sketching, sharpening pencils, mixing colors and preparing his palette, painting or writing—unless he was in private, presumably in the arms of his longtime muse Baroness Joséphine de Forget. She was his

married cousin and mis-
tress. Like the Mona Lisa,
madam was enigmatic and
unforgettable. It's unclear
whether Delacroix's passion
for her was chaste and platonic.

Officially the Delac-
roix museum is an annex
of the Louvre. When you
enter number six on the
square, the courtyard and
its mossy cobbles are a
tantalizing foretaste. The
steep, ladder-like wooden
staircase into the house
museum is unfriendly to
those with handicaps. It
is authentic. The polished

Mephistopheles Aloft *by Eugene Delacroix*

wood banisters are the same ones the ailing painter slid his hands along.
Crowning the stairs is another iteration of the familiar Delacroix bust
mounted atop the fountain in the Luxembourg Garden.

Suitably somber, the apartment's many small rooms with pleasantly
scented, waxy parquet floors are filled with paintings and sketches by or of
Delacroix, plus memorabilia, documentation, and maps. A lithographic portrait of Joséphine de Forget shows the delicate young pug-nosed, light-eyed
creature with ringlets. Delacroix worshiped her. Despite his protestations
to the contrary, his Romantic pedigree is unassailable, starting with a fine
self-portrait as Ravenswood from Sir Walter Scott's *The Bride of Lammermoor*.
Romeo and Juliet make an appearance at the tomb of the Capulets, she
bare-breasted and swooning, wrapped in a white shroud but not yet dead.
Delacroix seems to have been taken in equal measure by Shakespeare and
Scott, Goethe, Gothic tales, and the Renaissance, a rich vein he mined for
decades.

Some of my favorite pieces are the fantastical winged *Mephistopheles Aloft*
and the dark, inky *Hamlet Sees the Ghost of His Father*, or *Macbeth and the Witches*.

Baudelaire saw in them the quintessence of the fantastic genre captured in words by Edgar Allan Poe—and by Baudelaire himself. Delacroix agreed, becoming an avid reader of Baudelaire's translations of Poe's short stories. Delacroix's passion for the fantastical elements of theater and the elation of music is reflected in many of his exquisite studies, another link to Baudelaire. Tellingly in his *Journal* he mentions many times the name and paintings or musical transports of a certain Boissard de Boisdenier. An amateur violinist, painter, and poet, Boissard was one of the hosts of the Hash Eater's Club. Delacroix attended its "fantasia sessions" without giving anything away in his memoirs or correspondence. Did he smoke and chew or just watch like Balzac?

Elsewhere in the museum you come across a sketch that at first appears to be a modernist, twentieth-century study of motion, a dizzying mass of vibrating, curving, energy-infused lines. It is one of the many initial sketches for Delacroix's *Jacob and the Angel,* and like the mural, is highly suggestive. Nothing could be farther from it than a delicate watercolor with graphite tracing, *Study of Flowers,* showing a poppy, a pansy, and an anemone. Delacroix painted it when vacationing at George Sand's property at Nohant. Producing watercolors of natural subjects was one of the pleasant occupations that drew him to Nohant on many occasions. Sand described him there working in "a state of delighted rapture in front of a yellow lily whose structure he had just understood."

The best is yet to come. A door leads from the apartment's back rooms to an outdoor staircase. Two flights of stairs bring you to the level of the painting studio and then into a magical private garden, with its medieval wellhead and shade trees. Delacroix had the studio built according to his specifications. He did not subscribe to the misery of *La Bohème* or the starving-artist theory propounded by the well-fed Hemingway. Delacroix's is a dream atelier. The tall, many-paned windows are calculated to provide balanced, constant light. Delacroix's painting palette is preserved here. It is the one he gave to Fantin-Latour as a keepsake, carefully prepared. So are his paint box and his favorite accessories—ceramic drinking jugs, a red shirt, a curious pistol holster and saber, an elaborately inlaid chest, and a rare stringed instrument, all bought in Morocco on his life-changing trip through North Africa in 1832, which was bankrolled by the French government. Some of these mementos show up in the canvases on the walls of the vast main painting room. A few you will recognize from the chapel of the Saint Angels at Saint-Sulpice.

In a tiny side room near the entrance to the atelier, a sanctum many visitors miss, hangs one of the most amusing items in the collection. It is not by Delacroix but by Félix Nadar: *Nadar's Pantheon*. This large-format print was done in several versions in the 1850s when Nadar worked as both illustrator and photographer. In this final version, a serpentine parade of 250 caricatures of authors led by bulging-browed Victor Hugo pulls up abruptly before the medallions of Romantic precursors, including Chateaubriand. In front are Balzac's dark head and the hovering face of Charles Nodier. But the real landmark is the towering white marble bust of *magna mater* George Sand, the living idol of Romanticism, posed on a fluted marble column. Visual artists were added only to final versions of *Nadar's Pantheon*, so Delacroix appears at the end of the procession. Apparently he wasn't offended: Late in life he sat for many portrait sessions in the studio of the mischievous redheaded photographer.

Nadar's Pantheon: Where's Delacroix?

PART SIX

Quai Voltaire

32

THE SEINE'S SCENE

The curtain rises on a Seine-side scene at the high noon of Romanticism. Louis XIV mansions and humble houses of indeterminate age prop one another up. quai Voltaire is a row of sculpted limestone or plaster façades marked by grime and brightened by geraniums or hibiscus destined to die come winter. Windows and shutters swing open and closed, familiar faces appearing and retreating, an animated, all-season advent calendar.

In this scene, we find our cast members simultaneously stepping from doorways or carriages, startled to encounter one another. George Sand strides along in men's garb, arms locked with the ethereal Frédéric Chopin on one side and Alfred de Musset on the other, his golden locks flying in the breeze. Giant Dumas pursues tiny Delacroix with sketchbook in hand. Warty Ingres leers lecherously at the bounteous model made to walk ahead of him. Peacock Pradier struts with red-faced Juliette Drouet, Victor Hugo gesticulating at their side. The wild-haired Balzac furtively exits an antiques shop, evoking his fictional antihero Raphaël de Valentin from *La Peau de chagrin*. Shy and slender Flaubert slinks alongside flaming Louise Colet. Marie d'Agoult, Alfred de Vigny, and Sainte-Beuve form a flying wedge, on the lookout for an angry Franz Liszt, who has been retired from Marie's boudoir. Watching them bump along the quay, bow, weave, snarl, avoid or embrace one another, are bemused Baudelaire and his Black Venus poised at an upper-floor window of the street's only hotel.

Fanciful? Absolutely. As Dumas famously quipped, "I have no vices, but plenty of fantasies, and they cost more."

Still, it is amusing to think of the quantity of creative genius shoehorned into one short stretch of quayside facing the Louvre downstream from Pont des Arts, and to imagine a simulcast collective encounter of the heroes and heroines who lived, worked, loved, and left each other on quai Voltaire.

The reality is less fanciful than it seems. Dumas lived a few blocks inland, on rue de l'Université, and was a regular on the quay. Sand's famous "blue attic" was a block upstream at 29 quai Malaquais, but she was also a regular, like Chopin, at Delacroix's studio at number 15 quai Voltaire. Boxing in Delacroix on both sides was his archenemy Ingres, who lived at number 11 on the second floor and painted at number 17 in a fancy ground-floor studio. Alfred de Musset lived with his sainted mother for a decade at number 25 (take the left stairway under the vaulted entrance). Pradier, Juliette, Flaubert, and Louise cavorted with each other and many others in reality and in fiction at number 1 quai Voltaire in another ground-floor atelier and in Pradier's luxurious upstairs flat. Marie d'Agoult, alias Daniel Stern, lived at 29 quai Voltaire and began her celebrated salon there, entertaining Sand, de Vigny, Sainte-Beuve, and scores of others. Baudelaire, who usually rose at noon but was adept at remembering the twilight of dawn, stared fixedly from his hotel room at number 19 quai Voltaire at the fog, sky, Seine, and cityscape. Here he quilled the sublime strophes of "Le Crépuscule du Matin"—Morning Twilight:

> *The mists spilled seas around each building*
> *As dying patients in the death ward*
> *In jagged coughs rattled out their lives*
> *And party-worn rakes reeled home to their wives.*
> *Dawn in a nightdress of rose and green*
> *Came shivering down the Seine's deserted scene*
> *And Paris, rubbing his old man's eyes, began*
> *Packing his tools, heading to work weary and wise.*

To add an asynchronous note, in a second-floor room on the courtyard in the building where the quay and rue de Beaune meet, Voltaire lived briefly in discomfort. He died there, gloriously to be remembered for centuries, perhaps forever. Earlier Voltaire had occupied a better room with a view of the Seine, but the din of the quay had overwhelmed him. He passed away in 1778, only yesterday in Paris. The quai Voltaire restaurant and café he frequented are still here, and quai Voltaire is just as noisy today, perhaps even noisier than in 1778.

Startlingly, most of the town houses Voltaire, Delacroix, Baudelaire, and the others knew and loved—or hated—are still standing and still sought after despite the noise. This is a testament to both the sturdiness of seventeenth-century construction and the apparent idiosyncratic Parisian reluctance to embrace radical urban change. The irregular, impractical buildings are a mottled mirror in which Paris and its people quiver and dart. The foundations and lower levels of the buildings date from before the French Revolution, the flimsier upper floors were tacked on during the Age of Romanticism, and many of the houses are crowned by glassy, ritzy modern or postmodern attics jutting above the skyline. Clearly some are owned by millionaires apparently unfettered by building codes.

Few things are more instructive or entertaining than leaning back between the old green boxes of the booksellers on the Seine-side parapet of quai Voltaire and gazing up at the buildings. They are yet another objective correlative of the ageless, multistory, many-layered Parisians I know.

Even more surprising than the seemingly indestructible buildings and quayside are the perennial businesses that occupy them, starting with the sellers of used books or antiques established here in centuries past. Life follows fiction on the quay: The names have changed, but some of the antiques dealers have occupied the same premises since Balzac conjured them. He created them from nothingness, setting two novels here, notably his 1831 *The Magic Skin* (*La Peau de chagrin*), in which an enchanted antiquarian's boutique on the quay provides an unforgettable backdrop for a fantastical tale à la E. T. A. Hoffmann.

"As he went down the steps that end the sidewalk of the bridge at the corner of the quay, his eye was caught by the rows of old books spread out for sale on the parapet, and he almost began bargaining for a few," writes Balzac of the suicidal young Raphaël de Valentin, who is ready to pitch himself into the river. Instead de Valentin enters a shop to kill time, waiting for dark. "We display only the dime-a-dozen things down here," says a salesman, "but if you'd care to look upstairs I can show you some fine mummies

The more things change . . . Balzac's antiques dealers continue to thrive (by André Castaigne)

from Cairo, various types of inlaid pottery, and a few carved ebonies—authentic Renaissance, we just received them—of exquisite beauty."

The novel's antihero follows the salesman upstairs and discovers the proverbial Aladdin's Cave. "Crocodiles, monkeys, stuffed boas grinned at the painted glass of the windows and seemed about to bite the busts, seize the lacquerwork, or spring at the chandeliers." Eventually he walks away with a magic skin, the talisman that raises him to fame and fortune, then ruins and kills him. A study of debauchery, greed, and the toxicity of wealth, *The Magic Skin* is my favorite of all Balzac's books—and eerily topical.

Visit one of the real-life heirs of Balzac's fictional shop and you'll find a similarly magical cache of fine art, oddments, and bizarre accessories—at twenty-first-century prices.

At least four specific quai Voltaire institutions are centuries old and emanate romance. The history of the Hôtel du quai Voltaire reaches back to the post-Revolutionary period and forward from Baudelaire to Wagner (he composed *Die Meistersinger* here). Pissarro, Wilde, and Sibelius were longtime residents. Joseph Heller (of *Catch-22* fame) and his family sojourned here. Many current friends and acquaintances of mine are drawn by the magnificent view.

Lured by the proximity of the Fine Arts Academy, the artist's supply and paint shop Sennelier at number 3 was founded in the days of the Impressionists. Of course the eighteenth-century café-restaurant Le Voltaire predates them all. Less famous but more approachable than Le Voltaire, Café La Frégate on the corner of rue du Bac took over the spot from Café d'Orsay, one of the city's lost landmarks. The d'Orsay was demolished recently—in 1881—along with the property whose ground floor it occupied. La Frégate is named for a frigate that was moored out front for decades in the mid-1800s. For a café pedigree, 130-plus years isn't bad, and though the current building is late nineteenth century, in a way the old Café d'Orsay and the storied property that housed it subsist. I discovered this delicious fact not long ago and it led me a merry romantic chase.

Fame, Fortune, Death: hanging by the skin of a wild ass (by Adrien Moreau)

33

D'ARTAGNAN'S CASK OF
AMONTILLADO

Twice a week I clatter downstream on foot following the Seine, crossing islands and bridges, tripping over loose cobbles and resurgent poplar roots, and prowling the quai Voltaire hoping to spot open carriage doors and enter private courtyards. I reach Café La Frégate and collapse into a comfortable chair. The coffee is Italian, better than most in this city of magical cafés with abysmal *café*. But the coffee and green tea aren't the main reason I go to La Frégate.

As it was in 1778, the quay is a racecourse around the clock. The terrace is too noisy for speech. Unless you want to smoke or be smoked, like me, you will go inside. Tilt your eyes up at the ceiling—it's surprising how few patrons think of this simple gesture. Plasterwork garlands and Belle Époque paintings are dotted with puffy clouds. Putti and unclad youths frolic in seductive if saccharine scenes done in the style of Boucher or Jean Bérain, painter of the Gallery of Apollo at the Louvre across the river. Tulip lamps shine upward. The beaten-zinc bar curves into a half-moon. There are banquettes and Seine-side views through plate glass picture windows.

In the back dining room a discreet plaque marks the spot where Henry de Montherlant always sat, a spot from which the novelist could watch the crowd in the mirrors but not be noticed. Montherlant was accused of collaborationism during the Nazi Occupation and though never convicted, became unpopular for a time. Ironically the northern section headquarters of the French Résistance were above the Café Voltaire next door to Montherlant's flat. He avoided the Voltaire and became a regular at La Frégate.

I do not know why, but for decades my life has been crisscrossed by Montherlant's shadow, from the Henry de Montherlant swimming pool I used in the 1980s until today. One day I will try again to read his novels, essays, and plays. A conflicted, contradictory, paradoxically romantic figure, he was unappealingly macho in the Hemingway mold, a psychologically scarred war veteran and aficionado of bullfights and other manly exploits. Yet his work is often a veiled confession or an apologia for his unhappy homosexuality and, it is said, incurable pedophilia. For much of his life, Montherlant resided five doors down from La Frégate. That is where he committed suicide, the final, sometimes courageous, sometimes outrageous act of many Romantics.

Often as I stare up at the risqué ceiling I can't help wondering if Montherlant was attracted by the convenient proximity of La Frégate and perhaps enjoyed the décor, food, and personnel or whether, like me, he knew the backstory, the tale of the extinct Café d'Orsay and the location's illustrious ghosts who inspired Alexandre Dumas.

Though Dumas appears never to have said so on paper, he certainly must have known or at least suspected when he came to the Café d'Orsay with Delacroix and Baudelaire that Charles Ogier de Batz de Castelmore, better known as le Comte d'Artagnan, lived here from 1659 to 1673. A plaque on the side of the building makes that clear. The rambling Hôtel de Mailly-Nesle, a mansion built in 1632, covered multiple lots on the quay extending south and west to rue du Bac. The real d'Artagnan lived on the corner where the café now stands, and the entrance to his apartments was via number 1 rue du Bac.

In the glory days of Louis XIV, when d'Artagnan was a field marshal spangled with honors and the king and queen were the godparents of his two children, did the royal family and court visit his rooms? Possibly they did. The heroic musketeer could do no wrong—except inconveniently die in 1673 at the Siege of Maastricht. Naturally the king and queen might pay him a call: The Louvre is directly across the Seine.

Fast-forwarding from d'Artagnan and Louis XIV to the mid-1700s and Louis XV, the royal eye roved widely and fell upon the five spirited daughters of the Mailly household, owners of a long strip of quai Voltaire and rue du Bac. They were ensconced in the gilded salons of the mansion on the quay, not yet named for Voltaire. Four of the Mailly daughters would soon not be maidens, thanks to the king's adulterous attentions. The first three succeeded one another as the king's official mistresses, the fourth was whisked to safety by her husband, and the fifth joined the ranks of the first three making the commute from the quay to Versailles.

When the accounts are drawn up, of the four Mailly conquests, two died mysteriously, almost certainly by poisoning. Why? Simple: court rivalry. Where was the poison mixed into their wine—the best way to disguise it? At Versailles that would have been risky. What about in the Mailly family home, perhaps not in the mansion itself but in the wine cellar under the building on the quay?

This is where the fantasy becomes interesting—and plausible and expensive.

In a strange and wonderful way the fifth, unhappy Mailly daughter, dubbed the Duchess of Châteauroux by the king, is as responsible for the creation of the Panthéon as is Sainte Geneviève. Here is how.

Besotted by her, the king took the duchess with him to the front during the Siege of Metz in 1744. He fell ill, and his high fever and convulsions were attributed by the duchess' detractors to her overtaxing sexual fervor. Her refusal to leave the king despite his poor health scandalized the nation. Louis could not confess or be absolved or pray for succor or take extreme unction until he had ceased his illegal, adulterous affair with the duchess, a thing he had no intention of doing. As he was about to die, the duchess was sent away. The king confessed, Sainte Geneviève was summoned, and he was saved. The duchess died in short order, however, killed by poisoning. The king's vow to reward Sainte Geneviève, though put on hold, was kept, and the church that became the Panthéon was built.

The key word in this part of the tale is *poisoning*.

Skipping into modern times—the 1830s—the mansion became the seat of the Count of Flavigny, the nobleman whose clever, rebellious daughter Marie, Countess d'Agoult, changed before the startled eyes of Paris society into the transgender novelist Daniel Stern. It was here, in the same gilded salons used by the king's mistresses, earlier frequented by d'Artagnan and royalty, salons used to this day by the mansion's occupants, that the celebrated literary salon of the Romantics was held, or so it is widely believed.

The plaque on the building at the corner of quai Voltaire and rue du Bac merely mentions d'Artagnan, nothing else. When I discovered the property's complex history, like Henry de Montherlant I too became a regular at La Frégate. It was perhaps five years ago that I realized the café's wine cellar spreads belowground on at least two levels.

A curving stone stairway leads from the café's ground floor one story down to the restrooms of La Frégate. One day when belowdecks I noticed a door ajar in the hallway. I peered in at a dark, rough wall but didn't dare go farther. Another time the door was ajar and a light on. I could see the staircase curving out of view. Waiting and listening, I had begun to descend when voices echoed up.

My next half-dozen attempts to get into the subbasement were thwarted by a locked door or a lack of light. I could not find the switch. I returned again with a flashlight but was frustrated when someone appeared heading for the facilities. Then there was a dishwasher, a deliveryman, and the manager. I cultivated a waiter for two years. One day he emerged from the depths carrying a dusty bottle of vintage red wine. I buttonholed him. Was it, I joked, Amontillado? Baffled, he checked the label. "It's Bordeaux," he said, locking the door and leading me upstairs.

The management changed after a number of years, and the waiters were replaced just as I was preparing to ask if they would allow me to visit the cellar. Finally I asked the affable new manager if she could help me solve a mystery, "The mystery of d'Artagnan's Amontillado, or his black cat, if you prefer Baudelaire and Poe to Dumas," I said.

By now she recognized me, an innocuous regular who left exorbitant tips. Otherwise she would have called the men with butterfly nets. Chuckling, she led me down to the locked *escalier dérobé*.

"You see," I felt I had to explain, "in centuries past when a mansion or convent or monument was demolished, often the cellars and foundations were reused. So it stands to reason that the basement of the Hôtel de Mailly-Nesle is still here."

She raised an eyebrow and said she had never heard of such a hotel.

The curving staircase cut through hewn stone and revealed a vaulted wine cellar running underneath the restaurant and quayside expressway. "Yes," I said, excited, checking the masonry and stonework. It was certainly built centuries before 1881 and had been modified and reused. "Have you ever found an old cask of Spanish wine," I asked, "or a black cat immured behind the wall, or perhaps a canister of poison?"

The manager stared at me, unable to decide whether I was actually crazy or kidding as usual. "'The Cask of Amontillado,'" I added, "by Edgar Allan Poe. Baudelaire used to come here when La Frégate was the Café d'Orsay, you see, and he translated the story by Edgar Allan Poe and 'The Black Cat' too."

But her Baudelaire and Poe were rusty, and she could not follow my logic, so I suggested the cask and cat had perhaps belonged to d'Artagnan or Dumas, who had an infinitely more lively imagination than I did; they were both regulars at this address in centuries past. Just think, I told her, the actual Three Musketeers in real life probably—probably—stood on this very spot and drank fine wines from d'Artagnan's cellar. "They probably slipped out under the quay or into rue du Bac through a secret passageway waiting to be rediscovered, perhaps by you."

After all, I reasoned, the headquarters of the Gray Musketeers—the color referred to the hides of their horses—stood behind numbers 13–17 rue du Bac, a block away. "Louis XV's four famous Mailly mistresses preceding Madame de Pompadour lived here, and at least a pair of them were poisoned, and goodness knows, perhaps the poison was mixed into their wine here, in this cellar."

"Ah," she exclaimed, pleased. "Ah, ah, now that's something I *didn't* know!"

Ever since our visit to the cellar, the manager's welcome has been especially warm. We are on a first-name basis, proof that there is nothing like history or culture or a tragic love story to win a French heart.

Later and by accident, and much to my chagrin, I discovered how little I actually knew about the properties on the quai Voltaire, or rather, how inaccurate was the information I had found in secondary sources.

In reality, the Hôtel de Mailly-Nesle had many wings. Some parts still stand, hidden behind 29 quai Voltaire. This was encouraging: I would one day gain entry to them, I thought, by posing as a deliveryman. In fact I simply asked permission and was led through a modern lobby and shown around the hidden mansion with great pleasure by a cordial employee of the Documentation Française, publishers of the country's official documents, the building's current occupants.

As promised by the history books, the gilded double doors of the Salon

Doré were opened, revealing a glittering room covered floor to ceiling with seventeenth-century decorations done in liquid gold. It was as good as anything in the Louvre—for a reason. Jean Bérain, the same painter who had done the décor of the Gallery of Apollo for Louis XIV, crossed the Seine to work his magic here. Putti, filigrees, floral motifs, faux niches, and delicate paintings of happy lovers provided the theme. No wonder this had originally been the bedroom where Louis XV made love to his Mailly mistresses.

Once they had given themselves to him, he in turn gave them new titles and transported them to Versailles. On the ceiling are four lust-inducing devices written in Italianized bastard Latin from the Renaissance, perfect for Louis and the Romantics who later took over. *Amor uniscet più Rubelli*, says one: "Love unites even the most resistant lovers." *Amor solo mi potea domare*, "Only Love could tame me," whispers another. A third assures viewers, presumably on their backs looking up, that no one can hold out against such a Victor as Amor, while the fourth device is an early example of a bondage fetish: *Catene quanto più soavi più strette*—"The tighter the chains, the sweeter they are." This struck me as applying not just to S&M practitioners but also to the droves of lovers on the Pont des Arts clutching padlocks and chains with vows of eternal linkage by Amor.

I had by this point in my quest discovered that Marie d'Agoult did not actually hold her literary salon in the Salon Doré, as is widely believed, but rather next door in the Salon Gris, a handsome, larger salon with gray walls. Yet now my guide during this serendipitous visit said she thought perhaps the piano concerts featuring Liszt and others had been held on the floor above in the Music Room. This made perfect sense. I was delighted to climb another story up and inspect the First Empire décor, with its scantily clad musician-muses painted on the doors.

Alas, misconceptions and misinformation seem destined to accumulate in layers and be scraped off sooner or later. I have learned since my visit that Marie d'Agoult and her mother lived on the ground floor in a vast, lovely garden apartment. It was there they had held the salon, in what are now dreary offices. This was where Rossini had hobnobbed with Liszt, Dumas, Sand, Balzac, and the whole Romantic gang. D'Agoult's brother eventually rented the floor above, the one with the gilded salon, but nowhere in the literature is it stated that he hosted his sister's literary and musical gatherings.

There was a further, final rub to this tale based on what I now knew: The Mailly property originally abutted a smaller, humbler building from 1635 belonging to a certain Pierre Hulot, a tradesman. It was in this simple corner house, not in the mansion, that d'Artagnan and his family had lived. That meant the cellar of La Frégate, while probably ancient and certainly the repository of the musketeer's wine, had nothing to do with the Mailly sisters. The poisoner of Louis XV's mistresses therefore could never have mixed his lethal brews in it, and the entrance to the tunnel leading from this historic corner café subbasement to the Panthéon did not start under La Frégate, as I had imagined. Rather, it ran from 29 quai Voltaire, from that delicious Salon Doré on the

Muse of music, Hôtel de Mailly-Nesle

noble floor to the hilltop sanctuary of Sainte-Geneviève, now home to Victor Hugo. Oh well. Whether Dumas knew any of this was also pure speculation and, it seemed to me as I sipped a cup of green tea, best left that way.

It was Balzac's garret all over again. Maybe the director of the Arsenal Library was right. Myths and blissful ignorance were sometimes to be preferred.

34

DELACROIX REBUFFS DUMAS

I took my hat and ran out," wrote Dumas in his memoirs. "I thought of Delacroix's *Marino Faliero*, I crossed bridges, I climbed the 117 steps to Delacroix's studio—he lived on quai Voltaire—and fell into it utterly breathless."

What had possessed Alexandre Dumas to dash in his best formal clothes from the Tuleries Palace across the Pont Royal to the quai Voltaire, then up four stories? Easy: the desire to help and please Eugène Delacroix, the living artist he respected more than any other. A fellow Romantic, Dumas adored Delacroix the way a child loves a recalcitrant horse or independent-minded dog. For Dumas, Delacroix was "feeling, imagination, fantasy"—and a distillate of proud, prickly stubbornness.

Dumas had been an assistant librarian to the Duke d'Orléans, the man who became King Louis Philippe in 1830. He was a good patron and backer. When the king casually mentioned he meant to buy a gift—a diamond ring or silver snuffbox, perhaps—for Victor Hugo to thank him for dedicating poetry to the duchess—i.e., the queen—Dumas steered Louis Philippe in another direction.

Why not give a painting instead, something personal and worthy of the king's originality, he asked, a painting from the royal collection?

The malleable monarch reflected for a moment, caught Dumas' drift, and opted for a generous twofer. "Better still," said the king, "hunt out for

Louis Philippe when young: art patron, dandy, friend of Dumas and Hugo (attributed to Elizabeth Latimer)

me among your artist friends a picture which will please Hugo, buy it, have it sent to me, I will give it him. Then two people will be pleased instead of one: the painter from whom I buy it, and the poet to whom I give it."

Cut back to Dumas, panting in his heavy velvet outfit, collapsed on a chair in Delacroix's quai Voltaire atelier. By now Dumas is rich and famous and owns three Delacroix canvases. Dumas remembers another painting that was savaged by the critics, an unsellable picture Delacroix keeps jealously in his studio but now, Dumas imagines, can sell to the king. Excitedly he shares the news. Their dialogue rings true.

"I have come to buy your *Marino Faliero.*"

"Ah!" Delacroix said, sounding more vexed than pleased.

"What! Are you not delighted?"

"Do you want to buy it for yourself?"

"If it were for me, what would the price be?"

"Whatever you want to give me: two thousand francs, fifteen hundred francs, a thousand francs."

"No, it's not for me. It's for the Duke d'Orléans. How much for him?"

"Four, five, or six thousand francs, depending on which gallery he'll hang it in."

"It's not for him."

"Who is it for?"

"It's a present."

"For whom?"

"I can't tell you. I'm only authorized to offer you six thousand francs."

"My *Marino Faliero* is not for sale."

"Why isn't it for sale? You were about to sell it to me for a thousand francs."

"To you, yes."

"To the prince for four thousand."

"To the prince, yes, but only to the prince or you."

"Why?"

"To you, because you're my friend; to the prince, because it would be an honor to have a place in the gallery of a royal patron as intelligent as he is; but to anyone else save you two, no."

"Oh! What an extraordinary notion!"

"As you like! It is my own."

And with that, the interview was over.

Luckily Dumas kept his promise to the duke and didn't reveal the name of the intended recipient of the gift: Delacroix would have been furious. He was not a fan of Victor Hugo, and the feeling was mutual. They were too similar, as Dumas understood without knowing of their shared antipathy. "Every artist has his double in some kindred contemporary," Dumas wrote. "Hugo and Delacroix have many points of contact." That may be, but they made sure the contact was not physical, studiously avoiding each other.

What was the real reason Delacroix wouldn't sell his painting? Proud and pig-headed, he feared the king's purchase would shame obtuse critics into publicly and hypocritically changing their views. He didn't want their false praise. They were the same reactionary clique that had attacked his works while praising Ingres, a classical torpedo they launched at the ship of radical Romanticism in the same way the Classicists of the Battle of Hernani had tried to destroy Hugo and modern theater.

"Delacroix was doomed to be pursued by fanatical ignoramuses," remarked Dumas, little realizing that Delacroix, though fond of the exuberant giant, felt suffocated by Dumas' personality and unsatisfied by the "superficiality and melodrama" of his plot-driven realistic novels, which nonetheless he devoured.

Dumas sought art without conventions imbued with hyper-verasimilitude, Delacroix sniped. Dumas was too literal, too concerned with mechanics and "incapable of accepting the role of feeling. . . . If Dumas had been a sculptor, he would have painted his statues and made them walk like wind-up toys, believing them to be closer to the truth."

Elsewhere Delacroix confided to the pages of his journal that Dumas was dogged and invasive. "He won't release his prey," he wrote. "I like him a great deal, but we are not made of the same stuff, we aren't questing for the same things, his public is different from mine, and clearly one of us is a serious madman."

Delacroix found Dumas crazily extravagant; Dumas found Delacroix heroically unbending. I have no doubt whose company I'd rather share for an evening.

What's extraordinary about Dumas' anecdote and Delacroix's notes is, if you changed the names, titles, and aesthetics and clicked Refresh, you could be part of the querulous Parisian art and literary scene today.

The dual irony is, Dumas as art patron bought Delacroix's work and defended it like a musketeer, all for one and one for all. He also induced the avant-garde painter to create one of the century's greatest and earliest examples of cutting-edge ephemera—a free-form action painting intended to be displayed for a single night. But that wasn't on quai Voltaire or anywhere else on the Left Bank. The great art happening of the Romantic Age took place at Dumas' small but focal apartment in the new heartland of Parisian Romanticism, the far-flung Right Bank neighborhood known as La Nouvelle Athènes—The New Athens. To this day questers go to Nouvelle Athènes to pay homage at the living shrines of the Romantic spirit.

PART SEVEN

The New Athens and Montmartre,
From the Heyday of Romanticism to
the Resurgence of Romantic Decadence
and the Birth of Modernism

35

DELACROIX'S PERMANENT
EPHEMERA

T he ball was already creating quite a stir," wrote Alexandre Dumas in his
memoirs. "I'd invited almost all the artists in Paris, and those I'd forgot-
ten wrote to remind me of their existence."

Seven hundred guests showed up for Dumas' party, a mob scene that
changed the topography of Paris romance. Dumas' fancy dress Carnival Ball of
1833 was to go down in history not as the biggest but as the wildest, most creative private party of its kind. It has yet to be topped when measured in terms
of talent, gumption, and panache packed into one floor of an apartment house.

It also helped put the neighborhood on the artistic map, where it remains two centuries later. The exclusive address for the party was tucked in
a courtyard behind 52 rue Saint-Lazare in the quietly fashionable Square
d'Orléans, to this day the most sought-after residential square in one of
Paris' sleeper neighborhoods, Nouvelle Athènes.

This wasn't just any Carnival party, and it wasn't primarily about celebrating the stunning success of Dumas' books and plays. You might call it
tit for the king's tat: Louis Philippe had failed to invite to his latest royal
festivities the main exponents of Paris' Romantic avant-garde, meaning the
Battle of Hernani crowd, including his protégé Alexandre Dumas. The
revenge was sweeter than bonbons.

"One of the first difficulties that arose," Dumas recalled, savoring the
tale, "was the smallness of my lodgings."

Dumas had a typical Paris apartment—dining room, living room, bed-room and study. That's all. He estimated four hundred guests might show up—le Tout Paris *artistique*, plus the Paris of politics, big money, and high society. Serendipitously across the landing from his third-floor lodgings a spacious four-room apartment stood vacant. The only things in it were the chimneypieces, a few mirrors, and the blue-gray wallpaper. Unaware of what Dumas was planning, the landlord agreed to let him borrow the space. Things were looking up.

How to decorate, upstage the king and the Classicists, and showcase the great Romantics? Dumas wanted something suitably melancholic and dark, a danse macabre of images with plenty of black, gray, and red—for blood—with the pièce de résistance painted by Delacroix. He put Paris' famous set designer Pierre-Luc-Charles Ciceri in charge of doing the ceilings and sup-plying pencils, brushes, paints, and charcoal for others. Ciceri stretched and mounted canvases on the walls and waited for the artists of ephemera to appear. Their paintings would be needed only for a night.

A human tornado, Dumas raced around town charming, haranguing, and recruiting fellow Romantics. No one could turn him down. In fact, every-one wanted to participate, including the usually diffident Delacroix. Hav-ing promised to come, Delacroix quickly forgot—or so it seemed. Meanwhile other celebrity artists jumped on board. The overall theme for the paint-ings was theatrical drama. Louis Boulanger chose a scene from Victor Hu-go's *Lucrèce Borgia* (the play featuring Juliette Drouet as Princess Negroni). Clément Boulanger would do a scene from *La Tour de Nesle*, Tony Johannot something from the *Sire de Giac*. His brother Alfred chose *Cinq-Mars*. The renowned lithographer J. J. Grandville, who famously immortalized the Battle of Hernani, opted for a huge panel done in striking red chalk, white chalk, and charcoal. It showed the living arts and artists posed as musicians in an orchestra of forty, "some clanging cymbals, others shaking Chinese hats, some blowing on horns and bassoons, others scraping on violins and vio-loncellos."

Yet other artists renowned in their day painted panels with theatrical scenery or window frames with life-size lions and tigers. Célestin Nanteuil did the surrounds and ornamentations, plus two door panels with medal-lions portraying everyone's Romantic heroes—namely Victor Hugo and his rival Alfred de Vigny.

Then there was the question of food and drink. How to kill two large birds in the bush—actually how to slaughter herds of wild game with one enormous stone? A few days before the ball Dumas organized a hunting party outside Paris and with a brace of pals braved the snow, bringing back nine roebucks and three hares. Ever practical in his madness, he swapped three of the roebucks for a salmon weighing fifty pounds and a fourth for a colossal galantine. Another buck went to reward the families of the hunting party. Two were left to be roasted whole and served on silver platters seemingly lifted "from Gargantua's sideboard." The wild hares would go into a giant pâté. And to wash it all down, "three hundred bottles of Bordeaux were brought up to warm to room temperature," Dumas details, "three hundred bottles of Burgundy were set cooling, and five hundred bottles of champagne were on ice." That made 1,100 bottles for a projected four hundred guests— nearly three per head, about right for a contemporary Paris party.

As the evening neared, the décor progressed, but Delacroix still hadn't shown up. His prestigious spot on the wall stood blank. Summoned by an urgent query he finally arrived, as relaxed and insouciant as his fellow artists were frantic and frazzled. Dumas led him to the white canvas on the wall and suggested he fill it with a *Crossing of the Red Sea.* "The sea has retreated, the Israelites have crossed. The Egyptians have not yet arrived."

"Then I'll take advantage of that to do something else," Delacroix quipped. "What would you like me to stick up there?"

"Oh, you know, a King Rodrigo after a battle," Dumas said, referring to Cervantes' *El Romancero Viejo.* He quoted a few lines of verse.

"Ah, that's what you want?"

"Yes."

"You won't ask me for something else when it's half finished?"

"Of course not!"

"Then here goes, for King Rodrigo!"

Without removing his close-fitting coat or turning up his sleeves or taking off his cuffs, without "putting on a blouse or cotton jacket, Delacroix began by taking his charcoal and, in three or four strokes, he had drawn the horse; in five or six, the knight; in seven or eight, the battlefield, dead, dying and fugitives included."

This was all Delacroix needed before getting down to the real business, the paint he would apply in brilliant, bloody color. "In a flash, as if someone had unveiled a canvas, you saw appear under his hand first a knight, bleeding, injured, and wounded, half dragged by his horse who was as hurt as he was, holding on by the skin of his stirrups and leaning on his long lance. Around him, in front and behind, the dead in heaps; by the riverside, the wounded trying to put their lips to the water, and leaving tracks of blood behind them. As far as the eye could see, away toward the horizon stretched the battlefield, relentless and terrible. Above it all, in a horizon made dense by the vapor of blood, a sun was setting like a red buckler in a forge. Then, finally, a blue sky which, as it melted away into the distance, became an indefinable shade of green, with rosy clouds on it like the down of an ibis. The whole thing was wonderful to see: A circle gathered around the master and each one of the artists left his work to come and clap his hands without jealousy or envy at the new Rubens who improvised both composition and execution as he went. It was finished in two or three hours."

Delacroix eclipsed himself, returning in time for the ball dressed in medieval robes as Dante. This wasn't an act of gross immodesty: One of Delacroix's most famous early pictures showed Dante crossing the Styx in a boat with Virgil. Dumas greeted him wearing a lavishly colorful Renaissance outfit copied from a 1525 print by Titian's brother, with features from the court of Francis I. Dumas' frizzy hair was styled in a pageboy around his head and, bound by a gold band, was made to hang over his shoulders. His jerkin was sea green and braided with gold, laced down the front of the shirt and fastened at the shoulder and elbows with gold lace. His breeches were made of candy-cane-striped red and white silk. On his feet he wore black velvet slippers embroidered with gold.

The mistress of the house, Dumas' then wife and mother of at least two of his children, was Mélanie Serres, alias Belle Krelsamer, "a very handsome person," Dumas remarks, "with dark hair and blue eyes." She wore a velvet dress with a starched collar and "the black felt hat with black feathers of Helena Forman, Rubens' second wife."

Henri III and other Valois Dynasty costumes were the most popular, though some guests appeared in the garb of Italian peasant women or shepherdesses as painted by Boucher, Madame Pompadour's court painter. There were harlequins, magicians, dolls, Turkish slaves, sailors, soldiers, and aristocrats from the time of Louis XIII, hundreds and hundreds of costumes, each different. Rossini came as Figaro and vied with General Lafayette as the ball's most popular man. His blond locks bouncing, Alfred de Musset, still embroiled with George Sand, appeared dressed as a weathercock and, given his penchant for playacting and drinking to excess, probably crowed (though Dumas doesn't say so). Nearly everyone showed up in costume, and those like Lafayette, too serious or staid to do so, weren't allowed in until they'd wrapped themselves in a billowing Venetian cape of rose, sky-blue, or black.

Though he took no credit for the invention, Dumas created stereo wrap-around sound by placing an orchestra at either end of the conjoined apartments and having the musicians synchronize and play the same tune. Dancers galloped the length of one apartment across the landing and hallway into the next, vaudeville tunes thundering in their ears.

Did Sand waltz dizzyingly with Marie Dorval and de Vigny trot with Juliette Drouet? Did Victor take the arm of that other famous actress he knew inside and out, Mademoiselle Mars, another of Dumas' neighbors? The possible combinations are a delight to contemplate.

How long the drink lasted was left unrecorded, but it's known the food finally appeared at three a.m. "At nine o'clock in the morning," Dumas recalled triumphantly, "with music resounding in their heads, they began a final gallop in the rue des Trois-Frères, the head of the procession reaching to the boulevard while the tail was still frisking in the courtyard of the square."

Dumas contemplated throwing another Carnival fête when he was still rich and everyone's favorite but, perhaps wisely, decided to let this one live on in memory.

Somehow it was fated that the flamboyant novelist would die derelict, in debt, alone, without a dime to his name. He managed to preserve one treasure throughout his tumultuous life, however, and leave it to his son, the playwright Alexandre Dumas, *fils*: Delacroix's painting of King Rodrigo.

What happened to the painting? For years I wondered, then traced it to the Hôtel Drouot, Paris' answer to Christie's or Sotheby's. The younger Dumas tried to auction it, but it didn't sell, so he took it home. When he died, it was auctioned again, and this time found a buyer. It wound up in the fabulous Chéramy Collection and then in 1914, when the collection was dispersed, was bought by the Kunsthalle Bremen, its home to this day.

Dumas the elder died broke, having lost his château, investments, and everything he had earned in decades of work—and play. The widest read, the most popular novelist of France ever, the man whose words inspired

Dumas by Nadar

hundreds of modern-day movies and thousands of biographies and studies and articles, the hero entombed with Victor Hugo at the Panthéon, wound up a pauper. The worth of his painting collection alone is incalculable. Among many others he had three fine canvases by Delacroix. The last time *King Rodrigo* sold in France, in 1913, it fetched 9,000 francs, a small fortune at the time. The current equivalent in purchasing power is hard to calculate. When you figure George Sand paid 3,000 francs per year to rent her vast, luxurious apartment across from Dumas' digs at 5 Square d'Orléans, you can begin to guesstimate the worth today of that sum. Three thousand francs would be something on the order of $50,000 to $70,000. Multiply 3,000 francs by 3 to arrive at 9,000, then add in inflation and revaluations of the currency, and the Delacroix canvas was already worth hundreds of thousands of dollars in Dumas' son's day. It would doubtless sell for millions now.

What happened to the other paintings? They were dispersed or disappeared. I did discover where another of them resides. I recognized it and made the connection not long ago when I was at the Victor Hugo Museum. Louis Boulanger's dramatic confrontation scene from *Lucrèce Borgia* hangs opposite Adèle Hugo, diagonally from Juliette Drouet, in the museum's main salon. The ephemeral lives on.

36

PARISIAN ACROPOLIS

The New Athens and abutting Saint-Georges neighborhoods spread up a gentle slope that starts behind the apse of Notre-Dame-de-Lorette on rue Saint-Lazare and rises along the boutique-lined rue des Martyrs and rue Blanche, petering out where the neon sleaze of Pigalle begins. This rough trapezoid in the 9th arrondissement is known by many as Lower Montmartre. Crossed at odd angles by tilting, atmospheric streets, a fair-size slice of the area was notorious and dicey until recently, a red light district incongruously dotted by grand mansions from the Romantic Age. The neighborhood's heyday was yesteryear, but the magic lingers.

Largely undeveloped until the 1820s, overnight the city-country-city qualities of Nouvelle Athènes became desirable, particularly for artists like Delacroix, writers such as Dumas and Sand, actresses Mademoiselle Mars and Marie Dorval, and musicians including Chopin and Liszt, plus political subversives of various stripes who gravitated toward a pair of secret hideouts on rue des Martyrs—secret to all but the spies of the regime.

Nouvelle Athènes was less expensive than the grand old-money areas near the Louvre or the Faubourg Saint-Germain. The air was infinitely cleaner than that of the congested Latin Quarter and other tawdry tenderloins in the old center of town. The gardens and houses were bigger and more spaced out, yet then as now, the Grands Boulevards with their cafés and theaters were only a few blocks away. Perhaps more important, there was plenty of room between the mansions to build artists' ateliers and light industry. That's why the great musical instrument makers of Paris set up here: Érard, Herz, and Pleyel, the three top French piano manufacturers, plus Sax, makers of the saxophone. Who knew the forebear of John Coltrane's tenor sax was perfected and patented in rue Saint-Georges in the 1840s, and the factory, converted into lofts, still stands. I didn't until I began exploring Nouvelle Athènes.

Back in the 1800s the countryside started on the far side of the line linking Pigalle, Blanche, and Clichy. Montmartre was a hill of windmills, orchards, vineyards, quarries, shanties, wild cabarets, and, ironically, sanatoriums like the one where Gérard de Nerval sought treatment. The ancient Roman's "Mount of Mars"—or the Mount of the Martyr, Saint Denis, if you prefer the fanciful Catholic-retrofit etymology—stood beyond the city limits and the reach of tax men. That's why the Romantics and the latter-day bohemians of the turn of the twentieth century transformed both lower and upper Montmartre into their turf. Romantic and bohemian the area continues to be, right down to the musical instrument stores on rue Victor Massé. There's even a vineyard. Only the quarries, shanties, and orchards are gone—and the sanatoriums.

Working for the Prix de Rome: A typical artist's atelier (by André Castaigne)

When I stumbled through Nouvelle Athènes for the first time in the 1980s seeking the backdrop to one of my favorite movies, *Sabrina*, I didn't find a rapturous Audrey Hepburn, staring at Sacré-Coeur framed in the French windows. But I fell in love with the neighborhood anyway. I incorporated its unsymmetrical, down-at-the-heel alleys and backcourts into my lower Montmartre circuit, one of the walks I took weekly to escape my maid's room in rue Laugier. Like the Marais, Nouvelle Athènes was deliciously unsavory. Like all of Paris' desirable districts, it is now a model of gentrification, with excellent gourmet shops, market stalls, upscale cafés and restaurants, and astronomical rents. However, on the upper edges of the neighborhood the bohemian bourgeoisie still live cheek by jowl with the porn parlors on malodorous alleyways flanking night-clubs and clandestine whorehouses. If you stay above or below the tattered belt of boulevard at the base of the hill, it's a joy to amble around, poking into cul-de-sacs and courtyards and hunting out the locales where the Romantics lived and worked, some of them marked by plaques, many others not.

There is no Louvre or d'Orsay to lure tourists here. I recommend visit-ing two of Nouvelle Athènes' underrated, blissfully uncrowded house muse-ums, both unusual, both preferred by intrepid, individual travelers.

The Musée Gustave Moreau in a neo-Renaissance town house is stuffed to the skylights with the disturbingly gaudy, gilded works of the eccentric Symbolist painter who lived here—with his sainted mother. Moreau drew or painted more than any other artist to date, including Picasso, and his influence on the generations that followed was immense.

Even better from my perspective is the Musée de la Vie Romantique. Everything including the dust dancing in the parlors in the freestanding house at the end of an enchanted garden is impregnated with contagious memories, memories evoking George Sand and Chopin, Liszt and Marie d'Agoult, and a host of worthy, now-forgotten secondary artists. Trans-planted from Germany, Ary Scheffer was the archetypal Romantic painter who lived here in the dreamy cottage and painted in the twin ateliers front-ing the garden. Also displayed on the walls or captured in the vitrines and showcases are the butterfly-essences of Scheffer's friends, the Devéria and Johannot brothers, two of each, all four of them big in their day. They are ripe for rediscovery as art historical footnotes.

My favorite approach to this Parisian Acropolis is by Métro to Place Saint-Georges, a venerable station with an archetypal *Métropolitain* sign from the 1930s. The subway tracks and tunnels underlie a handsome bull's-eye plaza ringed by imposing buildings rich in architectural detail and salacious anecdotal history. One of them is a neo-Romanesque, neo-Gothic, neo-Renaissance luxury town house encrusted with sculpted heads, angel-muses with outspread wings, garlands, putti, urns, and detailing. Turn to look up at the façade as you mount the stairs from the Métro exit on the east side of the square, in front of number 28. The building seems set to fall on your head. The quintessence of Romantic architecture, it is named for its most illustrious occupant, the Marquise de Païva. From that catchy name a bushy tale hangs.

Née Esther Lachmann in Moscow, the daughter of Polish Jewish immigrants, the gorgeous arriviste became one of Paris' more celebrated diamond-coveting courtesans of the mid-1800s. She started out tickling the erogenous ivories of Henri Herz, the piano manufacturer then segued through an orchestra of other lovers, including the Spanish Marquis de Païva. Marrying him—briefly—she kept the title while adding new diamonds and gentlemen to her collection and buying an even bigger mansion on the Champs-Élysées.

Delacroix supped and dined at her parties more than once, remarking on the "frightful luxury" and the vapid high society characters crowding her salon, decrying the "soporific pestilential" quality of the interminable evenings. One wonders why he returned. Dumas, Delacroix remarked with something like disgust, always seemed delighted in the marquise's company, perhaps because he had enjoyed a private tour of her boudoir. The celebrated novelist freely brought his mistresses with him and dispensed to the marquise his valuable advice on cooking, for he was stout by now and in middle age a famous gourmet, alternately poised on the cusp of extravagant wealth or destitution.

Delacroix was also a regular guest across the square in a much vaster, grander single-family mansion now known as the Fondation Dosne-Thiers. It is a foundation library belonging to the French Institute, the handsome compound housing the French Academy with the splendid domed baroque building on the Seine fronting the Pont des Arts. Dosne is the name of the plutocratic financier who developed the Saint-Georges neighborhood and built the original mansion. His wife became first the mistress, then the mother-in-law of one of the great rascals of the nineteenth century, Adolphe Thiers. Thiers is the second part of the hyphenated name. Doesn't ring a bell? Thiers held too many government posts to list, rising for decades, then falling precipitously, then rising again into the empyrean, becoming the first president of modern France and the Third Republic in 1871.

Adolphe Thiers was the frog-faced, diminutive, soft-spoken historian who ran the country for King Louis Philippe but unwisely connived and intrigued, abetted by the unwitting Victor Hugo, to bring Louis Napoléon Bonaparte back to France as a figurehead. Thiers hoped that he, the puppet master, would pull the strings and complete the bourgeois revolution that would create an indestructible oligarchy without aristocrats. Wily Napoléon III proved a superior strategist, making himself emperor and arresting his erstwhile promoter. Thiers had plenty of time to grind his small, sharp teeth waiting to get his revenge. A study in contradictions, Thiers was the peace-loving progressive who built the last ring of ramparts around Paris, the ramparts that cost countless millions and took a quarter of a century to imperfectly complete but kept the Prussians at bay during the Siege of 1870–71. They later gave Georges Pompidou ample room for the Paris beltway, built in the no-man's-land in the early 1970s.

Once Napoléon III was ousted and the Second Empire fell, Thiers took over again and ordered and orchestrated the massacre of the Communards, the ultimate threat to his pet project: beneficent plutocracy. Smiling wryly at politics and politicians for over half a century, he was in turns a constitutional monarchist and a reactionary republican, an anticlerical, rabble-rousing plotter, in favor of, then against the freedom of, the press and trade unions. One thing he was always was opportunistic; in other words, he was entirely modern, even contemporary, the quintessential Parisian.

The mansion on Place Saint-Georges is the perfect frame for Thiers, an architectural portrait if you will. When I sit kitty-corner to it on the terrace of my favorite local café, I hear his reedy tenor voice echoing and see the thick glasses perched on his nose, which made him appear harmless if not ridiculous. Instead of implementing the French republican slogan of liberty, equality, and fraternity he used his abundant intellect and oratorical skills to rewrite the history of his century and undermine democracy. Like Haussmann, he was a first-class revisionist, writing a self-serving autobiography to cover his tracks. The greatest parvenu of all time, a self-made millionaire, Thiers was the real-life model of Balzac's notorious Rastignac, the quintessence of corruption and cynicism who caused revolutions and financial collapse, unwittingly created a dictator, and applauded the butchering of over 20,000 men, women, and children in the space of six weeks in Paris. Furious, the Communards burned down the Dosne-Thiers mansion, but once they had been exterminated, he paid himself over 1 million francs from the treasury and had the state rebuild it, bigger and fancier, at the taxpayer's expense—and he got away with it. Clearly Rastignac-Thiers remains a model of virtuous self-interest to untold numbers of today's parvenu politicians, financiers, and entrepreneurs, the followers of Gordon Gecko who believe in the gospel of "greed is good."

All of the above would be amusing and extraordinary enough but is only one part of the spell Thiers casts on modern minds and hearts. He's a hero to the political right, a criminal to the left even now: Karl Marx dubbed him "the monstrous gnome," and any full-blooded French person on the pink side of the spectrum shakes with loathing at the sound of his name. His other, apolitical claim to fame, a source of endless mirth and admiration, is that, again like Rastignac, he took a rich, beautiful mistress and married her even more comely young daughter. Thiers continued the relationship with the mother with the full cognizance of the cuckolded father and the beaming bride, her daughter. How? With charisma, cash, and power: Thiers bought the cuckold Dosne, making him director of the Bank of France. He clearly kept his mistress and young wife happy in myriad other ways.

But it's not over yet. Enter the gates of the mansion and climb the short flight of steps. Pause to consider that Thiers reached a ripe old age, and his eighty tumultuous years were better than fiction. He outlived and outdid Balzac and his fictional doppelgänger Rastignac by adding his mistress' second daughter—that is to say, his wife's sister—to the ménage. The arrangement with the sisters continued after the cuckolded Dosne and then the mother-mistress died.

It was this multipartite ménage that induced Thiers to build the warren of back passageways leading from the family mansion to surrounding streets and to the house where he first lived with his wife—daughter number one— in rue Saint-Georges. The back garden and courtyards still exist and can be explored, though this is not encouraged. It has been my pleasure, over the decades, to await the mail carrier or the deliveryman or unsuspecting residents to gain surreptitious access into this private labyrinth of lust.

Luckily for those not inclined to play cloak-and-dagger, there is an easier option: Flanking the mansion is a small public park carved out of Thiers' vast garden, the Square Alex Biscarré. Here you can sit or stroll where Thiers did and observe the local reincarnations of Rastignac, Madame Dosne, and her daughters, not to mention Delacroix, Dumas, the Marquise de Païva, and other colorful contemporaries who have just stepped out of the pages of novels and into the twenty-first century.

Getting inside the hewn limestone mansion to see where Thiers and his ladies actually supped and slept is a challenge. The foundation running the property is selective and fond of for-profit activities, as the Dosnes and Thiers once were. Like other rarefied Paris interiors, particularly those wrapped in bureaucratic red tape, the easiest way to gain access is to wait patiently for months or years, buy a ticket, and attend a cultural event or be invited to the launch of a new consumer product. Is it worth the trouble? Certainly it is if you, like me, enjoy connecting with the past on site.

What you find once you've been ushered through the portals is a lavish Second Empire interior built at the start of the Third Republic, that famous "Empire without an Emperor" commanded by Thiers in tandem with a junta of monarchist military leaders and right-wing politicians in league with big business. The mansion is more likely to evoke frivolous scenes from Offenbach—*La Vie parisienne*, perhaps—than set pieces featuring soulful Chopin or fanciful Victor Hugo and Viollet-le-Duc, who also lived nearby.

Once you are inside the vast property, figures in oil portraits from centuries past and state-of-the-art security cameras observe your every step. You discover a wide, gently spiraling staircase, an endless series of rooms—and two charming oval salons—plus views from windows as tall as those of the Palace of Versailles. The cozily cluttered reading room of the library is where the serious work gets done. It overflows with valuable dusty books and manuscripts, and there are sliding wooden ladders, a parquet floor, an encrusted ceiling, and an elaborate fireplace with a carved marble surround. Statistics are gladly provided: This cache of culture contains 156,000 volumes, including 1,500 historic periodicals, 30,000 prints and caricatures, 1,000 drawings, and 2,357 cartons crammed with manuscripts from the Romantic Age. Other rooms, suites, and salons are spacious, palatial, and clearly rentable, used for highbrow conferences, inspiring concerts, and conclaves of masters of the universe (but also for soap or soup launches).

There is reason to wonder if Thiers ever visited the Hôtel de Mailly-Nesle on quai Voltaire and decided to do it one better. If you look up at the thirty-foot-high ceiling of this Salon Doré, it seems there is enough liquid gold on the plasterwork to replenish Fort Knox. The sparkling chandelier, if not authentically from Murano, appears nonetheless to contain the

Marquise de Païva's lost diamonds and other royal baubles perhaps given to
Thiers by King Louis Philippe. When you pause to consider that in Paris
there are hundreds, perhaps thousands of similar salons in use today by their
wealthy owners, you begin to understand why nothing fundamentally
changes in this country. Out back is the small private garden through which
the satyr-like gnome darted to and fro on his secret sorties.

Standing in the rue Saint-Georges outside, you can't help asking yourself whether Thiers was disturbed by the din of the Adolphe Sax musical
instrument factory across the street and down the block from the mansion.
Thiers' modest first house, the love nest where he resided when newly
wed to Mademoiselle Dosne number one, is even closer to the Sax factory.
It produced saxophones and trumpets, tubas, and other brass instruments
and could be heard for blocks around. It is said (though I have never been
able to confirm the fact) that the production line and the regular testing of
tubas and saxophones drove the hypersensitive Delacroix mad. He lived
and painted in two different locations in the vicinity and prowled the streets
daily for more than a decade.

Was the noise why Delacroix moved out of the sumptuous neo-Palladian
eighteenth-century building at 19 rue de La Rochefoucauld, a fabulous mansion owned by Baroness de Forget, which Delacroix shared surreptitiously
with his cousin, her daughter, Madame de Forget? Or did he simply need
more room and better light and some distance from the elder baroness, his
unofficial mother-in-law? In any case, he left behind great ancien régime
luxury and set up his house and atelier a few blocks northeast in a lavish
new studio.

Strangely, Delacroix's "new" workshop at 58 rue Notre-Dame-de-Lorette
and the Adolphe Sax factory at 50 rue Saint-Georges resemble each other.
Both are exemplary of early industrial-atelier architecture, both façades are
finished in plaster with classical or Renaissance or eclectic embellishments
and bull's-eye or taller multipaned windows meant to capture light, and both
are lively and very much in use to this day, occupied by small businesses
such as photography studios or magician's supply companies, offices, and
loft apartments.

The crabby Goncourt brothers lived directly opposite Sax in a comfortable flat in a fine building and appear not to have complained about tubas, trumpets, or saxophones. One thing is sure: Delacroix never passed

the Goncourt threshold. They despised him, calling him the "ravaged and bilious" dauber who painted, they said, "twisted epilepsies." They even chortled when he died and were gleeful when visiting the auction of his earthly possessions and artworks.

If it wasn't Sax that drove the Romantic painter mad, could it have been the Pleyel piano factory? Surely not: It was located at 9 rue Cadet, a quarter mile away, and equally distant in the opposite direction were the Herz and Érard piano factories. Unless Delacroix had bionic hearing, the disturbance must have come from elsewhere. Perhaps a noisy neighbor like the horn player who filled George Sand with homicidal thoughts, a jazz saxophonist riffing on Mr. Sax's invention before jazz was invented?

When was jazz invented and where, anyway? In New Orleans, as many experts claim, or perhaps in Paris, or as sometimes happens, simultaneously in both places? It's not impossible. I've long contemplated an alternative origin and etymology for the word *jazz*. Read George Sand or Flaubert or especially Baudelaire and others of their period and you regularly come across the verb *jaser*—to gossip, chatter, carry on, improvise music, and blather. Think about the definition of jazz not as music but as "all that jazz" talk, chatter, vapid natter, humbuggery—spontaneous verbal nonsense. Now I'm riffing.

What's a riff? The dictionary says it's an "ostinato phrase (as in jazz) typically supporting a solo improvisation." And it's also "a rapid, energetic, often improvised verbal outpouring." Improvisation. Outpouring. An instrument talking, singing, whining, crying. That's *jaser*. Can't you see Chopin and Liszt *jaser*-ing and dueling with their pianos in George Sand's fancy apartment in the Square d'Orléans a few blocks west of the factory, as they indeed did in real life, and someone brassy from the neighborhood joining in, playing one of those newfangled horns—a saxophone—fresh from Mr. Sax's workshop? Paris *was* one of the world's great cities for jazz from the beginning of jazz, and Square d'Orléans was the city's most musical address.

Did I say Square d'Orléans, as in New Orleans, named for the royal dynasty of the Duke of Orleans, Dumas' patron, the duke who became king at the height of Romanticism? If "jazz" was invented and the word coined in New Orleans, there might be a reason: The underlying culture and language was Cajun, and Cajun is a dialect of French. French was euphonic and romantic-sounding and lent itself to song back then just as it does today.

People *jaser*-ed in New Orleans in the Romantic Age with their vocal chords and their brass, and they *jaser* to this day in New Orleans and in Paris at the Square d'Orléans. More than once wandering in the square at night I have heard Coltrane on a sound system, the notes drifting into the handsome, perfect small square with its tinkling, spouting fountain and a pair of magnolia trees that might well be in New Orleans.

Either way, the saxophone is at least as naturalized a Parisian as Mr. Sax himself, born Belgian; or Chopin, half Polish; Liszt, Hungarian; Rossini, Italian; Herz, German; and countless other imports who helped transform the city into a crucible of culture. It's easy to forget that France's moment of greatest glory when it was the Caput Mundi of innovation, art, architecture, science, medicine, music, and much else was a time when it could not have been more cosmopolitan, globalized, and open to the world.

One day as I trawled the rue Saint-Georges thinking about city noises and saxophones and pianos and jazz, my mind rewound to *John Coltrane Live in Paris* and how I would listen to it in San Francisco and later on tape in my musky attic maid's room in rue Laugier. Did Coltrane know the ancestor of his sax came from this unremarkable street in the 9th arrondissement? When Coltrane passed through Paris in 1963 and again in 1965, both times he performed at the Salle Pleyel, when Pleyel still made pianos (the factory closed in 2013 after 205 years in business). It must have been quite a contrast for the American jazzman to segue from the elegant, monochromatic Pleyel auditorium, a prime venue today for classical music, to the smoky, seedy kaleidoscopic clubs of the Latin Quarter. He went to Jazzland and Le Chat Qui Pêche, in the medieval tangle behind Saint-Séverin, both venues now gone, and he probably dropped into the Caveau de la Huchette facing rue du Chat Qui Pêche. It's still around, but no longer smoky or likely to attract a contemporary Coltrane, though you never know.

Something tells me the uptight Goncourt brothers or Delacroix would not have grooved on Coltrane's vibes, but that Sand and Chopin, Liszt, Marie d'Agoult, Paganini, Rossini, Dumas, and even Victor Hugo would have *jaser*-ed and flipped for the way Coltrane turned Sax's upside-down hollow brass question mark into a conduit of the human soul. Chopin was the master of blue music: Is it pure coincidence that George Sand coined the expression "blue note," later picked up by the famous jazz label, Coltrane's label?

Chopin, first master of the blue note?

Can't you see it? Think of the kitschy, proto-Surrealist 1840 painting by Josef Danhauser, the famous one now hanging in Berlin. It shows all of the above Romantic characters—except Chopin, for reasons that will become obvious. Sand, Marie d'Agoult, Paganini, Rossini, Dumas, and Victor Hugo are rapt, listening as Liszt thunders on the piano, the bust of Beethoven and portrait of Byron looking down at them. Melting onto a red cushion on the floor, Marie d'Agoult looks like she has swooned, her head practically on the keyboard, while Liszt, possessed, stares zombielike at Beethoven hovering in the room through a Turner sunset unfolding beyond a Romanesque window. Cross-dressed, cigarette in hand, George Sand is shown halfway between cardiac arrest and orgasm. Her left foot rests on a locked leather-bound tome signifying the silence of words in the presence of Liszt's music. Her right finger points to another closed book in young Alexandre Dumas' lap. The other celebrities are spellbound, leaning on each other or, like Hugo, on the armchairs for support.

Sand loved blue note melancholy and she adored sickly Chopin for a time, but she also had a thing for healthy Liszt. Sand was the one most likely to be on the floor in a swoon, especially during a piano concert. This fact wasn't something Marie d'Agoult, mother of three of Liszt's illegitimate children, would have wanted to hear from her bosom friend. "You know I lie under the piano when he plays," Sand confided to d'Agoult provocatively. "I'm built of strong stuff and instruments are never too powerful for me. He's the only artist in the world who knows how to give soul and life to a piano."

Was Sand Liszt's human keyboard? Alfred de Musset thought so, and raged with jealousy. Liszt wrote music for Sand, and Sand transformed it into prose. "No man's heart has been found that is feminine enough to love you as you have loved them," Liszt wrote of Sand, the woman he considered a rebellious, ferocious, ardent Amazon and butterfly catcher.

It is often claimed Sand and the disconcertingly good-looking Liszt were lovers for a time. Perhaps Marie d'Agoult and Sand were, too—friends, lovers, and deadly rivals. Balzac wrote of the two novelists' claw-and-fang relationship in his novel *Béatrix*. It's also alleged that Marie's appetites not just in music but also in flesh gradually shifted from Liszt's strapping self to Chopin's ailing frame but remained unsatisfied. Chopin was either not interested in her or was simply too weak to act on her invitations. No smoking derringer has yet been found in the abundant literature on this intense many-sided friendship so typical of the Romantic Age—and preternaturally Parisian to this day.

Sand's effusive praise of Liszt surely would have aroused discomfort in the jealous, moody Chopin had she written it a few years later, when she rolled out from under Liszt's baby grand and began lying beneath the piano of the tubercular Polish genius. She met Chopin through mutual friends and pursued him relentlessly, netting and nourishing her butterfly, moving her theater of operations from the Latin Quarter to a garden pavilion in rue Pigalle and then to Square d'Orléans. Sand had already seen the enclave when she'd visited Dumas. The fame of the address was further enhanced by the presence of prima ballerina Marie Taglioni, another Romantic star worshiped to this day by the toe-shoe set.

The original main entrance to Square d'Orléans was on rue Saint-Lazare, a few blocks west of rue Saint-Georges, not at 80 rue Taitbout, as it now is. Some parts of the compound have been sealed off, remodeled, or demolished. The wing where Baudelaire lived for a short time, for example, and the art studio of the celebrated caricaturist-sculptor Jean-Pierre Dantan disappeared. Otherwise the neoclassical apartment houses with their porches and passageways and Doric and Ionic columns look remarkably unchanged. They were designed in the 1820s by the Englishman Edward Cresy in the style of Cumberland Terrace near Regent's Park in London.

Sand installed herself and her two children in a spacious apartment at number 5 facing Dumas' and Taglioni's former digs. Needing a modicum of privacy and perhaps also concerned about propriety, repose, and acoustics, the ailing Chopin rented his own mezzanine apartment at number 9 under the barrel-vaulted entrance to the main courtyard. There he could give piano lessons to society ladies, the baronesses and countesses and marquises. Many fell in love with him but failed where the resourceful Sand succeeded: Chopin's great passion was music, not carnal pleasure. It is possible that he was asexual or homosexual, as many now suggest; in any case, he had limited physical strength or sexual drive.

The Square d'Orléans certainly was a move up for Chopin, but also for Sand. She had started her career writing cheap romances in Latin Quarter attics with hidden rooms for her lovers, in case her over-lubricated husband teetered in from Nohant. Now she was the unchallenged queen of Romantic literature, arguably as famous as Victor Hugo or Balzac, and certainly more controversial.

With Liszt, Rossini, and Paganini as regulars, the Sand-Chopin residences at Square d'Orléans attracted marquee performers from across Europe not only in music but also in the theater, art, and literature. Sand transformed the square into a kind of freewheeling creative commons, a libertine-libertarian, vaguely socialistic upper-crust "phalanstery of the arts," as she styled it. The *phalanstère* was a utopian commune with architectural parameters serendipitously like those of the Square d'Orléans. Social engineer Charles Fourier had introduced this concept at about the time the square was built. Sand, like many other Romantics, was a sometime follower of Fourier. He imagined individual freedom and gender equality without the sexual promiscuity and tribal family arrangements of similar earlier communes planned by the even more radical socialist Henri de Saint-Simon. Both Fourier and Saint-Simon deeply influenced French thought and mores, and live on today in hybridized updated unofficial forms typifying the so-called French model of society.

"We have a huge salon for billiards, a pocket-sized garden where we can grow flowers and let Pistolet out to go *pipi*," wrote Sand to a friend, careful to include mention of her adored pet. Parisians were already dog obsessed. To another friend she described the square then (as it is now) as a village in the middle of Paris, with "a country feel." Curiously, what heightened the familiarity and friendliness was the Italian Carlotta Marliani, Delacroix's great friend, Marliani's Spanish husband, and their family. "Without leaving the big, light-filled, well-sanded courtyard in the evenings we dash from one neighbor's place to another as if we were in the provinces," Sand enthused.

"We even make potluck dinners and eat together chez Madame Marliani . . . it's a kind of *phalanstère* that's fun for everyone and where your individual liberty is guaranteed a lot more than it would be among the followers of Fourier."

What did sand on the cobbles have to do with the square's appeal to Sand? A good deal: The streets of Paris were routinely caked with mud and flooded with sewage. Sand scattered over surfaces acted like sawdust on the beery floor of a saloon. Sand escaped to Nohant whenever she could because hatred for her beloved Paris periodically seized her, especially in bad weather. "I'm always filled with terror as winter approaches at the prospect of going back to that dark apartment," Sand confided in her correspondence, "with the doorbell ringing itself off the hook, the endless comings and goings, the neighbors who blow horns or sing off-key while I work, that black filth you can't even cross wearing clogs, the bores who come to yawn for an hour or two at your place without asking themselves if they're bothering you, that lack of a sky and of light, in short all the things that make me curse and hate Paris."

She certainly came to curse and hate her life in Paris with the "melancholic, misanthropic" Chopin, "a cadaver" she was "chained to for nine years." Sand destroyed the letters he had written to her and burned or redacted many of her own letters to him, ensuring that certain mysteries would remain unsolved. He was then sent packing to his proximate death. It occurred in the rambling apartment of another wealthy admirer, the Scottish pianist Jane Stirling, on Place Vendôme. Chopin went to his grave at Père-Lachaise Cemetery apparently still loving the volatile macho lady novelist: When he died, a pouch was found in the back of his diary embroidered with the initials G.F. for George and Frédéric. It held a lock of her scented black mane. One hopes Chopin never found out he was not the only mounted butterfly in her collection to receive a snippet of hair.

Sand stayed on at the square after the separation from Chopin for another two years, alternately cursing and celebrating it. She is proof if ever any was needed that natives and adoptive lovers of Paris also understand the meaning of passionate hatred, the seesaw of emotions ridden by many who dip below or soar above the glittering surface of the city.

Gone are the mud and sewage of yore. But the horns and saxes, sour singing, ringing doorbells, and interminable winter darkness remain, fortified by modern life's many other metropolitan charms, from air pollution to screaming sirens and acoustic assault or sidewalk jousting with boorish natives and mummification by bureaucracy. These minor drawbacks are mitigated in today's Paris by countless thousands of glowing streetlights that transform the darkness into something magical, some 10,000 cafés and nearly as many restaurants, each a tobacco-scented refuge for modern Romantics, dozens of outdoor markets, hundreds of theaters and cinemas, concerts in matchless venues, 150 museums, and more art galleries and temporary exhibitions and festivals than a mortal could visit in a lifetime, not to mention the sublime parks and the Seine's seductive riverbanks, where, as never before since the time of Julius Caesar, you can stroll across the center of the city largely unmolested by vehicular traffic.

Lucky are we who live in this eventful century, and lucky in particular those who reside in the Square d'Orléans. It is private property but open to the public during daylight hours. Wander insouciantly in past the barrier—there's plenty of foot traffic because of the businesses headquartered inside. No one will notice you. The interlocking courtyards still draw a mix of music and performance artists, plus advertising executives, high-tech moguls, venture capitalists, and other beneficiaries of income inequality. Over the leonine purring of luxury cars and the *jaser*-ing of beautiful people on cell phones you can sometimes hear the fountain splashing. If you have hearing as good as Delacroix's, you might catch the strains of Chopin, Liszt, or the soulful Coltrane in the country air under the magnolias. Have you guessed it? Delacroix and Balzac were regulars here, of course, but so was Alphonse Karr. Everything has morphed, yet it seems eerily the same.

37

CHOPIN'S HAND

Like the Marais or Latin Quarter, Nouvelle Athènes is spangled with tablets, plaques, and busts evoking or commemorating someone or something wondrous. Anyone familiar with the lives of the Romantics finds traces of them in streets and under church porches, or in banal tourist hotels that once housed apartments or workshops. Nadar's famous photography studio at 113 rue Saint-Lazare is unrecognizable from nineteenth-century descriptions until you glance up and see the dormers Nadar relied on to light his portrait sessions. Shut your eyes and travel back to when he immortalized the great artists, performers, writers, and politicians mentioned in this book—plus hundreds of others—while entertaining his pantheon of friends.

It was in what is now a nondescript hotel that Nadar and his wife, Ernestine, awoke to footsteps and furniture being dragged, thinking they were being burgled. It was not burglars but Baudelaire in a playful mood. Irrepressible, he was determined to meet Ernestine but had never had the honor. Finding the couple asleep, he noticed a painting high on a wall and wanted a closer look. Nadar found the poet teetering on a chair atop the dining room table he had dragged across the room.

The apartment, garden, and photography studio where Baudelaire, Mimi and Sarah Bernhardt, Victor Hugo and Gautier, Viollet-le-Duc and Henri Murger posed are no longer, but trains still whistle in the Gare Saint-Lazare across the street, and the pattern of roadways hints at premodern roots.

A few hundred yards east, Juliette Drouet and Victor Hugo live on in the form of sighs of furtive pleasure audible under the porticoes of Notre-Dame-de-Lorette and the hulking church of the Trinité, where the pair often rendezvoused. Juliette roomed in rue Pigalle, then lived with Hugo—on a separate floor—at 21 rue de Clichy. Neither church is inspiring, but the curving sunken garden fronting Trinité is still the tryst of lovers and white-collars on lunch break.

Behind Notre-Dame-de-Lorette the storefronts on slanting rue des Martyrs mask hidden gardens, some tangled with dense vegetation wrapped around 1820s neoclassical ateliers. Here Théodore Géricault painted *Raft of the Medusa* and the Orientalist Horace Vernet created many of his giant historical paintings now hanging at the Louvre. Victor Hugo tripped through too many places in Nouvelle Athènes to list. One is clearly visible and overlooks the stately garden court of 41–47 rue des Martyrs, a posh horseshoe-shaped apartment complex. The crow's nest belvedere is where Victor took

The church of the Trinity, ideal for a tryst

regular siestas, rarely alone. A few blocks east, serpentine tree-lined Avenue Frochot is a private street of Romantic-era villas and mansions. Here Dumas before bankruptcy wrote feverishly in a garden nook, Théodore Chassériau painted his canvases in a vast studio, and the aging Hugo took refuge in verdant luxury chez his friend and colleague Paul Meurice.

One reason Hugo may have been pleased to live on this elegant street was memories heavier than stone, and flesh more tender than the night: At number 4 the celebrated demimondaine and artist's model Apollonie Sabatier held a famously saucy salon. Like Juliette Drouet, Apollonie appears in paintings and sculptures in many Paris collections, usually shown naked or scantily clad. For fifteen years Baudelaire, Gautier, Nerval and possibly his lobster, plus Flaubert, Hugo, and others were her subscribers.

So perhaps it is fitting that today this exclusive hideaway dead-ends into Place Pigalle, a distillate of the seamy side. Unlikely as it now appears, the once-fashionable square attracted a dizzying roll call of artists and writers. Many met and worked in the Café de la Nouvelle Athènes on Place Pigalle. Among early habitués was Thomas Couture, who lived at number 11 and painted the kitschy *Romans in the Decadence of the Empire,* now at the Musée d'Orsay. It is hard to miss this 15-by-20-foot canvas, an exercise in social commentary portraying the rot of mid-nineteenth-century Paris as a remake of the fall of Rome. The painting may well have given rise to or popularized the appellation *Decadent,* denoting the period of arts and literature often known as crepuscular or fin-de-siècle, the precursor and progenitor or fraternal twin of modernism.

Couture would certainly find inspiration in the pullulating Pigalle of today, decadent in novel ways. The historic building that once housed Café de la Nouvelle Athènes—where Degas painted *L'Absinthe,* Van Gogh saw starry lights in his head, Matisse sketched and sipped, Gérard de Nerval, Émile Zola, and Victor Hugo scribbled—was recently replaced by a postmodern supermarket selling exclusively high-end organic foods, proof that the rape of old Paris continues.

The fortunate Couture once maintained a garden atelier amid the free-standing villas on the south side of rue de la Tour des Dames, Nouvelle Athènes' most celebrated address. Even more plutocratic than Avenue Frochot, this short street bounded by rue de la Rochefoucauld and rue Blanche is where Mademoiselle Mars, the theater diva, and her neighbor the stellar courtesan Alice Ozy entertained on a scale grander than royalty. Mars once hosted 1,100 guests at a little costume ball, the fête that inspired Alexandre Dumas.

My loitering sometimes pays off. In rue de la Tour des Dames I habitually ring buzzers or wait at thresholds, slipping in when opportunity allows it, curiosity overwhelming common sense. If only I were young, I would simply spend the night in the bedroom of Mademoiselle Mars, as legions of gallants did, and as legions of under-twenty-six-year-olds do now, perhaps in blissful ignorance, at the youth hostel that opened in her former mansion in 2013.

On a recent visit, a helpful youth at the hostel's check-in desk encouraged me to admire the vaulted ballroom and its martial frescoes—Mars, a made-up name, was the actress' wink at the god of war. Then she showed me several Spartan dormitories. One overlooks the garden of the stunning half-moon-shaped mansion next door, the one owned by Alice Ozy, perhaps Victor Hugo's most astonishingly beautiful conquest. A labyrinth of alleyways and yards behind these mansions allowed guests to come and go unnoticed. In the hostel's cobbled courtyard watched over by sculpted lion's heads, Mademoiselle Mars liked to sit beneath a leafy fig. I was astonished to find the tree still thriving. It is a registered landmark, like the four-hundred-year-old locust tree by the church of Saint-Julien-le-Pauvre in the Latin Quarter and the magnificent ancien régime specimens of Lebanon cedar or sycamore mentioned by Hugo, Musset, and Sand at the Jardin des Plantes.

For me, the most atmospheric corner in Nouvelle Athènes stands behind rue Chaptal at the end of a narrow cobbled lane lined by sway-trunked shade trees. What other city boasts a museum dedicated to the life and times of the Romantics, a paean to romance? This must be the most "only in Paris" of the uniquely Parisian places I know. The headquarters of the Friends of George Sand is here—les Sandistes—so beware irreverence. One of Paris' more delightful outdoor cafés or tea salons, if you prefer, is also here, open in spring and summer.

Hollyhocks, lilacs, roses, hydrangeas, and scented shrubs of unknown name sprout from all sides, a tangled romantic thicket leaning this way and that, with grass and moss growing between the paving stones. The kind of antique curlicue ironwork chairs that once filled the Luxembourg Garden still grace the terrace here. The screams of children from the playground next door would have filled the maternal George Sand's heart with delight.

Sand did not actually live in the storybook house with off-kilter green shutters, but it now showcases her memorabilia. She was a frequent visitor, as were Chopin, Liszt, Marie d'Agoult, Delacroix, and other participants of Ary Scheffer's regular Friday-night salon.

Did George really lie beneath the baby grand and groove to the vibrations? There is reason to think so. A piano stands in a corner of one of the painting ateliers to this day. I once saw the 1843 Pleyel piano Chopin played on display here temporarily; it was a monstrously beautiful instrument with heavy sculpted legs and a harp-shaped stalactite housing the pedals. The sight of it set my backbone tingling. Had I been able to, I would have crawled underneath and lain with Sand's ghost despite the cigar and dagger.

Tall (for her day), dark, and handsome

The centuries seem to merge and blur as you glide through the rooms of the Musée de la Vie Romantique. If it has a slightly neo-Baroque feel, it might be due to the ministrations of the interior decorator Jacques Garcia. I wonder if he chose the throw rugs and the scarlet runner on the corkscrew stairway, and orchestrated the squeaking floorboards and piped-in tinkling music. Or did he limit himself to the authentic wallpaper which Sand described from her château in Nohant, the hanging of heavy drapery and the positioning of heavy furniture and heavy lamps, the selection of heavy picture frames, and the disposition of heavy art objects beneath the heavily encrusted ceilings? This wanton heaviness is irresistible. Bernini, come to remodel the Louvre in 1665, might feel as welcome in the charming

little house as Mimi or her look-alike, the pale, thin Princess Marie
d'Orléans, Ary Scheffer's preferred blueblood student. Marie's portrait as
wraith, destined to die at age twenty-five, hangs upstairs, a fine example of
Scheffer's art. She is wistful, archly Romantic, spiritual, and melancholic. It
is claimed that by teaching the three children of King Louis Philippe about
art, the earnest Scheffer sensitized the royal household to Romanticism,
paving the way for the king's friendships with Dumas, Hugo, and others,
thereby nudging revolutionary Romantic modernism into the mainstream.

Sand was not a looker. But if you doubt her credentials as a femme fatale, step into the main salon and you will be mesmerized. Perhaps the most
flattering if enigmatic portrait of her was painted by Auguste Charpentier.
It hangs against a tall mirror above the chimneypiece, its eyes observing
you wryly, unblinkingly, imperturbably, impenetrably. George's face is elon-
gated, a Coptic saint or a Modigliani before his time. The pale whiteness of
it and the blush pink of her Cupid's bow lips are offset by the big black eyes
and the mane of black hair set with rose-red and mimosa-yellow spring flowers seemingly plucked from the garden beyond the many-paned windows
of the house. Her hair shows no signs of snipped locks sent in skulls to abandoned lovers. Surprisingly, George is not wearing men's clothes: Charpentier
captured her the year she rediscovered dresses and used one like a butterfly
net to snare the reluctant Chopin.

The display cases are full of mementos that either thrill or make the flesh
creep. One of the more voodoo-like displays, it seems to me, is the plaster
cast of Chopin's left hand, laid out like a votive offering in a vitrine. Somehow I had not noticed it on visits years ago, but now each time I return,
I am transfixed. Though it seems fetishistic, I have the habit of leaning my
arm atop the vitrine and waiting for the shiver. Subtract the hair and the
kink in my broken baby finger, and my own left hand looks hauntingly iden-
tical to his. This is doubly strange because long ago I proved myself a con-
summate failure as a pianist, passionate but hyperactive and unable to sit
long enough to master a score.

Next to Chopin's hand is Sand's slender right arm attached to her revered, delicate hand, also in plaster. The casts were made on the deathbeds
of the pianist and the writer by George Sand's son-in-law, a notorious vil-
lain.

Among the most satisfying parts of the museum is the pair of painting ateliers in the garden. They're open only during temporary exhibitions. That's why it took me years to discover them. Scheffer may have been second-rate, a soft-focus Romantic colorist without the backbone of Delacroix. But his studios were the archetype, seen in every classic production of *La Bohème.* The bigger of the two ateliers is also remarkably like the one Delacroix used in Place de Furstenberg, with tall windows, easels, plaster casts, and paintings propped here and there depending on how the exhibition is mounted, plus a baby grand piano. If you're unable to visit it, you can nonetheless see what it looked like in 1851 as shown in the museum's charming painting *The Atelier of Ary Scheffer* by Arie Johannes Lamme. Surprised? Nothing has changed.

It was presumably in one of the studios that Delacroix first met and disliked Auguste Clésinger, the brutish, heavy-drinking sculptor who gambled and whored and inexplicably wound up marrying Sand's sensitive, rebellious daughter Solange. Heavily in debt, Clésinger once attempted to extract money from his mother-in-law and threatened her with death at

gunpoint. Solange's passion for this man, a permanent feature chez Ary Scheffer, is what ultimately drove Sand and Chopin apart. The gallant pianist was infatuated with Solange and misguidedly took her side in defense of love, crossing Sand. Delacroix relates how when he met Clésinger, a "scientific" palm reader happened to be present. He amused the gathering by interpreting the lines on people's hands. The wrathful Clésinger's palm was a scroll of bad omens and violence, it was said.

Like Scheffer, Clésinger

Chopin's Tomb at Père-Lachaise Cemetery sculpted by Auguste Clésinger

was a minor talent. Ironically, having ruined Chopin's relationship with Sand, he made the plaster casts of their hands. Later he carved the haunting white marble tomb of the pianist, *The Muse of Music*, now a landmark at Père-Lachaise Cemetery. It was, Delacroix thought, one of Clésinger's best efforts. Compared with his clumsy portrait of Queen Louise of Savoy in the Luxembourg Garden, or his sensuous, ghastly transmogrification of the demimondaine Apollonie Sabatier into *Woman Bitten by a Snake*, at the Musée d'Orsay, Delacroix was right. Mounds and piles of flowers and wreaths cover Chopin's tomb year-round, so it is sometimes difficult to judge Clésinger's artistry. Chopin loved flowers, and perhaps the monument is unneeded, since he is not really dead. His music is more alive today than ever before. He is the most popular, the best loved, the most listened-to composer of piano music across the globe. His melancholy music is the voice of Paris then and now.

38

A REAL BUTTE

Not long ago I queued with the bohemian bourgeois locals and bought a bag of raw cashews at the new organic supermarket on Place Pigalle, the one in the postmodern, stone-clad building that replaced the old corner property once home to Café de la Nouvelle Athènes. Crunching and munching I was assailed by murky recollections as I tried to recall wild nights in the rock clubs that were headquartered here in the 1980s and '90s. Noisy and foul, the clubs certainly had not been an improvement on the Romantics' café, but at least they had kept the building from being pulled down.

Nostalgia has never been my forte, yet it pervades the air of this soulful district and is hard to resist. Yesteryear throbs and glows. The Moulin Rouge deploys its mighty windmill-wings, reminding the world not just of the vintage cabaret itself but of *Moulin Rouge* and other movies about it, the romantic scenes filmed on its roof or on stage, the collective global fantasies associated with it, and more. Nostalgia is big business. France's longest-running nostalgic radio station with nonstop accordion music and pop tunes from the past honors the neighborhood's name: Radio Montmartre (nowadays re-baptized MFM). The most unabashedly nostalgic of them all is simply Nostalgie. These were the stations my Moroccan neighbors always had on in the 1980s in rue Laugier. Nowadays they play 24-7 in Montmartre grocery stores, cafés, and hotels that featured in or have merely tapped into the lucrative faux neo-nostalgia of the hit movie *Amélie Poulain*, soon to move from the silver screen to the stage.

In the same league as the Marais, the Latin Quarter, and Saint-Germain, every centimeter of Montmartre exudes memory, melancholy, wistful longing—or mindless mass tourism and pornographic lust.

Crunching, munching, and climbing Butte Montmartre at a ponderous, Romantic-era pace, I timed myself, curious to see how long it might take a man of middle age to reach the mysterious-sounding Château des Brouillards. You may recall seeing a painting of the eighteenth-century château

Montmartre's other Moulin, Moulin de la Galette

perched above gypsum quarries and fields, a small canvas that hangs in a corner of the Carnavalet Museum downstairs near the portraits of the Romantics. The squat, evocatively named "château of the mists" sits halfway up Paris' highest hill. Today it is hedged by higher buildings and flanked by a square dedicated to the pop singer Dalida. The château is where Gérard de Nerval may have lived for a time, perhaps with his lobster, where Victor Hugo and other distinguished gents of Nouvelle Athènes would spend evening hours in gallant company in the days of yore. They did not flock to the site to admire the misty view or visit Nerval. For many years part of the mansion was reserved for the flesh sport Toto-Olympio knew well: It was a whorehouse.

By stopping and starting, glancing up at vintage real estate and looking down at the spreading city or the pavement as the indefatigable Nerval habitually did, I clocked about fifteen minutes from Place Pigalle to the end of a cul-de-sac below the château. A staircase led to a narrow alleyway overhung by shrubs. Birds chirped. I was alone. Peering over a fence through a leafy garden at an off-white gabled mansion half hidden by trees, I realized Nerval and Hugo would happily have walked up here, but Hector Berlioz,

Chopin, Liszt, and others of their class who inhabited Montmartre or frequented its salons and whorehouses would have ridden in a carriage. The steep, badly paved streets were slippery back then, and the neighborhood was dangerous, a consequence of topography and history.

Montmartre's name derives from Mons Martis, the mount of Mars. Two thousand years before it became the cradle and epicenter of twentieth-century post-Romantic Romanticism and modern tourism, the site was holy to Mars, the wrathful pagan god, not Mademoiselle Mars the actress of Nouvelle Athènes. The name was garbled in the Middle Ages when *Mars* morphed into *martyr* to fit Christian hagiography. Saint Denis was supposedly beheaded near a sacred spring on this hillside. The spring caused the frequent mists that gave a name to the "château of the mists" across the street, where some historians claim Nerval lived.

The Château des Brouillards was recently on the market for about $10 million. Nowadays those seeking it could forgo a carriage or their own hoofs. If they wished they could take a municipal minibus or the Montmartre elephant train. Better still and infinitely more dignified, they could ride the funicular to a pocket-size park called Square Nadar on a terrace at the top of the butte near the basilica. They could then walk downhill effortlessly. The views are pleasing. En route a traveler would pass the remnants of an ancient Roman amphitheater; a monument to a freethinker martyred on the spot where a hundred years later the Commune struggle began, in 1871; Paris' second-oldest Romanesque church, hidden behind high walls; a square crowded with daubers and their easels; rows of wonky low buildings housing cafés centuries old; a nostalgia-themed museum with waxworks; the Montmartre vineyard; and the sites of the ateliers or apartments of dozens of bona fide poets, performers, painters, sculptors, writers, musicians, and thinkers who rethought and reshaped France from pre- to postmodern times.

If you modify the route by one block, you can also take in the stately institutional building from 1774 at 22 rue Norvins, the so-called Folie Sandrin sanatorium. This is where the luckless Gérard de Nerval was treated unsuccessfully for depression.

Nearly every day of his adult life Nerval wandered up and down and around the hallowed hill, Nouvelle Athènes, and the rest of Paris, apparently lost in thought, pausing to find his notebook and scribble some cryptic word, symbol, or sentence. People imagined Nerval was lazy, a perpetual flâneur. When Théophile Gautier composed Nerval's obituary, he described the "industrious laziness" of this strange genius, recalling how Nerval would return home from his wanderings and expand his words, symbols, and sentences into voluminous essays, poems, plays, stories, and novels. Like Gautier and Hugo, Nerval was one of the most popular and prolific writers of his generation—and one of the best.

Hugo famously said *"Errer est humain, flâner est parisien"*—wandering or straying is human, to *flâner* is Parisian. Nerval wasn't as pithy but may have outdone the master in scope. He once told Gautier he wished the streets of Paris were a scroll and he could write as he walked, automatically tracing a novel in an endless single line. This is Joyce's *Finnegans Wake* merged with Kerouac's *On the Road* and might have made more enjoyable reading than either.

Nerval was a modernist without knowing it, and his method was a kind of automatic writing. Though it is distasteful to say so, it seems fitting Montmartre became home to his spiritual heirs the Surrealists, and the haunt of that able showman Salvador Dalí. The headquarters of the exorbitantly commercial "museum" of Dalí's peculiar works is a few blocks from where Nerval was treated. Dalí's art has always left me chilled and perplexed. I wager that nine in ten of those who visit the "museum" leave disappointed, though they might be loath to say so.

Given the 24-7 activity in the area much of the year, it is hard to imagine a convalescent home atop Montmartre. But in Nerval's day the hillside was a semi-rural refuge, perhaps not of *luxe* but certainly of calm and voluptuousness, to paraphrase Baudelaire. It remained so until Napoléon III and Haussmann ordered the filling of its gypsum quarries with the rubble of the 25,000 or so buildings the great modernizers destroyed. Part of the landfill wound up at Montmartre, a disposal method that displaced for a second or third time some of the displaced, dispossessed who had been expropriated or evicted from inner-city slums and had wound up in camps here. This was Paris' homegrown favela. Eventually Montmartre was drawn inside the Second Empire's new city limits. Once the quarries were covered, developers began building on top and around them, a process slowed by wars, economic or constitutional crises, revolution, riot, and pitched resistance by residents.

Montmartre's shantytowns of the real-life nomadic *Misérables* pulled up stakes and moved around like a Hooverville of Depression-era America.

The Siege and Blockade of Paris: Balloons!

The last shanty was the celebrated "Maquis" flanking the Château des Brouillards. This sprawl of shacks was where the penniless Amedeo Modigliani holed up a century ago, his gun drawn and brushes ready. The gun was essential because of authentic danger. The paintings he produced in the most primitive of conditions, often in a state of inebriation, are now valued at millions of dollars. As was the case with many Hoovervilles in America, "charitable" neighbors, with a nod from the municipality, burned the "Maquis." Nowadays the site is a public park with a *boulodrome*, a dusty outdoor boules court. Locals pitch steel balls down the lanes, argue in the local argot, and listen to transistor radios tuned at least some of the time to Radio Montmartre or Nostalgie.

When Modigliani, Picasso, and others showed up here around the turn of the twentieth century, Nerval had long ago committed suicide, Hugo was in the Panthéon, and Montmartre had already lived its heroic heyday during the Siege of Paris and the Commune. The rebellion flared up here and caught fire at the site of a National Guard gun emplacement located where the sedate Square Nadar now offers panoramic benches and shade to tired pilgrims. Below the gun battery in a former quarry where Place Louise-Michel now stands, Nadar set up his fleet of postal balloons and Léon Gambetta took to the sky. Montmartre was a place of resistance, a battleground pocked with mass graves. Some were dug, with poetic justice, in the former quarries in the rubble of the houses destroyed by Emperor Napoléon III, then refilled with the massacred rabble.

The Second Empire and early Third Republic decimated the poor and the rebellious. Shortly after the blood had dried on the cobbles, the powers that be began building Sacré-Coeur, in the mid-1870s. It wasn't a spontaneous gesture of Christian love and charity. Rather the echoing, soulless basilica is a thanksgiving that the Communards were crushed. Parisians know the dark history of the white Byzantine hulk. The bizarre scaly silhouette is a symbol of reactionary obscurantism, the opposite of the Panthéon. To its boosters it stands for the righteous victory of wealth over parasitical, fanatical communism. As during the Terror, some of the Communards were not saints, but nowadays the government troops fighting them would be tried for crimes against humanity. The Communards executed 48 hostages and killed 877 soldiers in battle, while the Versaillais army massacred between 20,000 and 30,000 and sent several thousand others to die in penal colonies. The compelling yin and yang of history is what keeps the limestone monstrosity atop Montmartre from being grotesque or merely ridiculous.

Neither the politicians nor the church could kill the spirit of rebellious Romanticism that engendered the Commune, however. Muted, it lives on today in Montmartre in less violent forms. Even after Montmartre became a religious pilgrimage site and a beacon of the right, new generations of

Is Paris burning? Yes! The Commune Revolt of 1871 (Sackett & Wilhelms Litho. Co.)

bohemians, dreamers, and desperadoes migrated to the butte. Some came from the French countryside or abroad—Renoir, Pissarro, Cézanne, Monet, Sisley, Toulouse-Lautrec, Gauguin, Van Gogh showed up; then Picasso, Braque, Modigliani, Vlaminck, Derain, Steinlen, Erik Satie, Suzanne Valadon and her son Maurice Utrillo, Max Jacob, Louise Michel, Dalí, Cocteau, and Malraux.

One of the more controversial of these once-marginal characters was Adolphe-Léon Willette, the anarchist painter, long a hero but now abominated for his anti-Semitism. He habitually swaggered into the basilica shouting "long live the Devil!"

To many Parisians, Willette's dream seems to have come true.

When they weren't painting or sculpting or writing or being industriously lazy and partying at the hilltop cabarets like Au Lapin Agile, which is still in business today, or bedding and immortalizing each other like true Romantics of the Decadent age, they joined with feisty local inhabitants to fight to preserve Montmartre from destructive modernization. They created their own antibourgeois free "Republic of Montmartre" with their own currency. They won a pyrrhic victory against conformists, beatific optimists, positivists, academic artists, real estate developers, dreary right-thinkers, and other party poopers and anti-Romantics. Then some time during the Nazi Occupation or the postwar boom, things began to go wrong. The amber and aspic of the preservationists turned sour and crystallized. Nostalgia morphed into an institutionalized leaden cape. Montmartre awoke with a hangover to find the Devil had leased its soul.

39

DEVIL MAY CARE

What precisely is the trouble with scenic, airy, leafy, asymmetrically romantic, likable Montmartre? Perhaps it's not its own fault; the place is simply loved to death. Or maybe Montmartre tries too hard to be romantic, creating the kind of skin-deep studied ambience of a corporate theme resort without the regulation smiles and enforced courtesy. Artificiality and insincerity with an unmistakably tart Parisian flavor fizzes in the sugar-scented streets. The great names of yesteryear are exploited with shameless alacrity to market locales, products, and experiences. Familiar faces cover marquees and plaques, menus and labels. It is all too much—the wax dummies, the wheezing accordions, the berets and baguettes and easels and souvenirs, the half-melted pink candles on wobbly wooden tables and pink-mauve-scarlet hues of the décor and of everything else, the grapey "kiss-red" of the official Montmartre Fête l'Amour now held in tandem with the October Grape Harvest Fête, the Sacred Heart of commercial religiosity that would make Jesus weep, the streets and businesses renamed for artists, writers, and revolutionaries who struggled and starved and went to prison and would loathe and execrate the rape of their persons and memories if they could. Long ago they went elsewhere—mainly to Montparnasse—or went extinct. Montmartre is Bohemia Land Paris with a Main Street worthy of Anaheim. It is unlikely to change while the lucre lasts.

There are two ways of experiencing Montmartre: Avoid and revile the kitsch and crass or embrace them and look beyond. They are not mutually exclusive. I sometimes lapse into the first mode while aspiring to the second, reminding myself that this hill, like the neighborhood where I live, exists on several planes in parallel universes. The Château des Brouillards, "Maquis," and Square Nadar have become personal pilgrimage sites for me because of what I have learned about them. They are an unholy trinity pickled in Romantic brine. Each is enjoyable today for the atmosphere, tangible history, or panoramic view. They are antidotes to Sacré-Coeur.

Other antidotal sights survive sometimes in unexpected places. For instance, the park behind the basilica on rue du Chevalier de la Barre—a street honoring the man the theocratic ancien régime tortured, butchered, and murdered for failing to take his hat off before a religious procession. Giant old trees tower over the park's benches and playground. Locals gather, children kick soccer balls, and members of the boule club tirelessly toss their steel balls, oblivious to the hordes.

Around the corner from Place du Tertre at 1–3 rue du Mont-Cenis, a restaurant with a red awning revealingly named La Bohème is where Satie conquered Valadon (they met at Le Chat Noir), Modigliani picked fights with Picasso, and Max Jacob wrote the poetry that inspired André Malraux to seek him out and seek a life of culture. Malraux became France's first minister of culture. He helped save parts of old Paris from the wrecker's ball, including, possibly, the Marais building where my wife and I live. In the Belle Époque the place was called Café-Restaurant Bouscarat. The building is unchanged. It's still a café-restaurant. Look above the awnings and read the faded lettering, astutely preserved. The ghosts are in the air and in the plaster, that elusive sourdough starter I sensed when I first moved to Paris.

On the notorious Place du Tertre is the even older, more famous restaurant La Mère Catherine. When he had a few francs in his holey pocket Modigliani ate cheap and boozed here before World War I, determined to earn his nickname Modì, short for Modigliani but also a play on *maudit*, meaning damned or accursed. He loved being the heir of Baudelaire, *le poète vierge, le poète maudit*. Battling Picasso and Braque, sometimes with his fists, Modigliani remained a full-bore Romantic, figurative painter rejecting all the isms, from post-Impressionism, Fauvism, and especially Cubism to other varieties of early modernism. He refused to sign the Futurist Manifesto calling for the destruction of Venice presented to him by Filippo Tommaso Marinetti one night at Au Lapin Agile. About the time Hemingway arrived in Paris with Hadley, Modigliani died in Montparnasse a Romantic idealist, forebear of other great, self-destructive creators of the twentieth century.

As anyone who bothers to read the sign on the façade of La Mère Catherine knows, it is claimed the word *bistro* was coined here in 1815. Russian troops occupying Montmartre after the defeat of Napoléon at Waterloo demanded fast service, shouting *Bistro, bistro*—meaning quick, hurry up, in Russian. Or so the story goes.

To demand speed in Paris is to court disaster, especially when dealing with service industries. Amusingly, some Montmartre historians stake a rival claim, a purely Parisian one. They derive *bistro* from the slang word for the gut-wrenching drink *bistrouille*. This mix of coffee and wine, they say, was Montmartre's elixir. It put the fear of God into those who drank it: *La trouille* means fear in old Parisian argot and *bis* means twice, as in encore. So it was a doubly fearful blend.

One way or the other, Place du Tertre seems a plausible place for the bistro to have been born. The square's bistros have been the backdrop to umpteen movies. In Paris, fiction is clearly truer and more desirable than reality. This might be reason enough to preserve historic premises from becoming denatured fast-food joints, even if *bistro* once meant fast. Market forces will prevail. In 2013 the first American chain coffeehouse, the brand on every corner in every city in America, opened practically next door to La Mère Catherine. Other "bistro" franchises are on the way and surely this is for the best in this, the best of all possible romantic worlds.

I'm not sure why, but it gives me sardonic satisfaction to know carefree Place du Tertre with its cheerful artists and festive cafés and happy restaurants was where the medieval religious communities of Montmartre for centuries executed blasphemers, apostates, and common criminals. The scaffold and the block were the square's centerpiece. This was apt. Even more apt is the name Tertre. It means mound, as in the funerary mound that was here even earlier—and may still be underneath the square—during the Roman Empire. The temple to Mars stood across the way facing *La Bohème*.

Forget midnight in Paris. Stroll across Montmartre at dawn, the witching hour when tourist traps are empty and magical synchronism replaces tawdry anachronism. In the rosy light Mars watches as Modigliani dances with one of his long-necked lovers, Nadar sweeps by in his timeless balloon, and Gertrude Stein parroting a telegraph lumbers to Pablo Picasso's messy studio at the Bateau-Lavoir.

40

SLUMMING STEIN AND PICASSO'S BLUE ROSE

You don't have to subscribe to magical realism or even to like abstract painting to enjoy the Montmartre haunts of Pablo Picasso. He was the key transitional figure, starting out a starveling Romantic and ushering in his special brand of modern. Despite his invention or co-discovery of Cubism in the company of Georges Braque, he remained steeped in the Old Masters and the haunting works of Goya. "There is no abstract art," Picasso quipped. "You must always start with something. Afterward you can remove all traces of reality."

One trace of reality even Picasso couldn't remove was the memory of his early days in Paris. Newly arrived, the ambitious teenager and his fellow painter Carlos Casagemas briefly shared a top-floor atelier on rue Gabrielle, just below Nerval's sanatorium. In the style of Nerval, the depressive Casagemas killed himself, propelling the despondent Picasso into his so-called Blue Period. He moved a hundred yards downhill from their studio to leafy Place Émile-Goudeau. It's one of those rare unspoiled corners of the neighborhood with keyhole views, a grove of old horse chestnut trees, a slanting, asymmetrical square, lumpy old buildings and ateliers, and a pleasant café with a terrace where the artists of old, including Picasso, hung out a century ago. Some artists still do, apparently. Picasso rented space in the ramshackle artists' community on the square in a reconverted piano factory that looked, according to the imaginative poet Max Jacob, like a "laundry

Gertrude Stein and Picasso's portrait of her, above right

boat" on the Seine, a *bateau-lavoir*. Rebuilt after a fire that destroyed it in 1970, the Bateau-Lavoir is still filled with art ateliers.

Picasso may well have heard of George Sand famously detecting Chopin's "blue note" as he played the piano in Nouvelle Athènes. Whether Picasso did or didn't know the term, he was aware that the color blue has been the hue of spirituality, divine contemplation, and melancholy for centuries. From 1900 to 1904 Picasso's paintings created at Montmartre were figurative and blue in coloration, theme, and mood, reflecting his abiding Romanticism. Unsurprisingly they remain his most popular works among nonspecialists but also among collectors. *Boy with a Pipe* sold for over $104 million in 2004. Still figurative and Romantic, while working at the Bateau-Lavoir, Picasso gradually transitioned into the more optimistic Rose Period, with a year or more of overlapping tones and themes. Think of *Woman with a Crow* or the various *Acrobats* and *Harlequins*.

Though you might not guess it from the glowering look, walleyes and dark, muddy colors, Picasso's widely admired portrait of Gertrude Stein dates from this rosy period. Obviously a rose is not a rose and it isn't blue, either. Picasso was famous for his quickness, but the portrait of Stein took eighty sittings to complete. One wonders why. For each session Stein bustled across town from the large comfortable apartment she shared with her brother Leo in a courtyard on rue de Fleurus near the Luxembourg. This was the temple of art and experimental literature where Picasso would eventually meet Matisse, and Hemingway in 1922 would be ushered into Stein's inner circle—discovering Cézanne, Renoir, Matisse, and the thoroughly modern views of sexuality he explored in his late novels.

Stein often alighted at Place Blanche, hitched up her long dress, and climbed the hill to the malodorous Bateau-Lavoir to meet Picasso. The cramped living and working spaces of the Bateau-Lavoir were separated by hanging tarps or sheets that looked like sails or drying laundry. En route the intrepid Stein took in the salty sights and lusty sounds of the bohemians and artists and working-class Parisians she knew at one remove, a very large remove. A landowner and heiress to a San Francisco cable car fortune, she could afford to experiment with words, fill her apartment with rare antiques, and cultivate the arts.

Apparently Stein at first objected that her pet Picasso's portrait didn't look like her. He famously retorted, "You will come to resemble it," a line he reportedly paraphrased from Michelangelo. Stein was right: The portrait was too flattering. Picasso was also right: Her face and above all her expression came to look almost exactly like the asymmetrical haunting mask of flesh in the portrait, as photographs attest. Stein in 1933 in *The Autobiography of Alice B. Toklas* tells the story differently. "Everybody says that she does not look like it," she claimed Picasso said not to her but to others, "but that does not make any difference, she will." That sounds more like syncopated Stein than spontaneous Picasso. Later still, in 1938, she declared in her percussive prose, "For me, it is I, and it is the only reproduction of me which is always I, for me."

That is why when I lived above a lampshade factory the staplers reminded me of Stein.

How could the writing of this ambiguous icon of the twentieth century, an American Jewish lesbian who translated inflammatory speeches by Marshal Pétain and the anti-Semitic Vichy collaborationists have evolved from Flaubert, as she claimed? Stein said she based her celebrated *Three Lives* on Flaubert's *Three Stories*. She was too well educated not to know Flaubert's book was written above all to please his mentor and friend George Sand, the Romantic radical socialist, and that it was a quintessential work of late Romanticism. Stein may well be yet another anti-Romantic Romantic. She certainly embraced the cult of the ugly and other Romantic notions, including the devotion to art and freedom from sexual roles, reproductive slavery and family, and academic constraints.

Romanticism may have morphed into angular modernism on Montmartre—at least in the visual arts when Picasso painted *Les Demoiselles d'Avignon*—but throughout his long life Picasso the modern master remained a product of the nineteenth century, its revolutionary principles and blue-toned spirit.

41

SPIRITS SET IN STONE

As the years go by, the behavior of tourists in Paris gets curiouser and curiouser. While roller-coaster coils of pilgrims and gawkers wait to file through Sacré-Coeur, possibly the least spiritually inspiring place in town, the twelfth-century sanctum of Saint-Pierre in its shadow is often empty. I've been there too many times to count and have never seen more than a few souls in its cool, Romanesque interior. Antiquity wells up. Saint-Pierre is a palimpsest of stone with Roman and Merovingian foundations and two columns left over from the temple to Mars that once stood here. They are the strange dark lumpy ones by the entrance, columns hewn from volcanic rock in the Massif Central and hauled to Paris by slaves and teams of oxen at the height of the Roman Empire. Topping them are endearingly clumsy, evocatively sculpted Corinthian capitals from the AD 600s. That is when Saint-Pierre was first consecrated, conquering Mars and paganism by appropriation. The church was rebuilt and reconsecrated in 1147 before being reworked and repaired time and time again as the playbook requires. Somehow its vaults and original apse survived the Revolution of 1789. The morning sun slanting through modern stained-glass windows paints the stonework with a kaleidoscope of nuanced hues. Blue and pink predominate—perfect for Montmartre.

How did the church survive? After the anticlerical Revolution, in the practical-minded 1800s Saint-Pierre wound up with a telegraph tower atop its belfry.

The site is boxed in nowadays, and though it's on the hill's highest point, there is no view and therefore no tourism. If you could climb that belfry, however, the Panthéon would appear on the horizon in all its neoclassical splendor. This seems appropriate on several levels. Under the spreading shade trees in the cramped cemetery flanking the church is the forlorn tomb of Louis Bougainville, he of the Noble Savage. It's empty, and that's for the best. His mortal coil was whisked to the Temple of the Nation long ago.

The graveyard's other illustrious resident is remembered by a Paris square, street, and neighborhood, places where Romantic-era artistry have ceded to porn and prostitution: Jean-Baptiste Pigalle.

It is just possible the older, more potent, more spiritually charged Saint-Pierre and not Sacré-Coeur is what preserves Montmartre from the destructive wrath of Mars and the opprobrium of more recent deities.

Another neighborhood enclave is a menagerie of spirits set in stone: Montmartre Cemetery.

"I always preferred marble to flesh," claimed Théophile Gautier in a jocular autobiographical sketch. The author of *Amorous Death* and *The Comedy of Death* (not to mention *Giselle* or *The Mummy's Romance*) must be smiling in his grave. A splendidly kitsch stone pyre all verticality and pathos, Gautier's tomb rises over Division 3 along Avenue Cordier at this lovely, leafy cemetery, Paris' "other" great graveyard built in a former quarry in the 1820s a decade or so after Père-Lachaise.

Filter out the background hum of traffic and you can hear Gautier chuckling. Harp in hand, Calliope, the Muse of Poetry, sits atop a plinth at least six feet tall and seems to beckon passersby from atop the tomb. The lavish dimensions of the thing might be overkill given Gautier stood just over five feet

Gautier's tomb at Montmartre Cemetery

tall—but he compensated with girth and latitude. When he died, the stout, bearded old man of French letters was in spirit still the slim young rebel in a red vest dueling with the bald "kneecaps" at the Battle of Hernani.

Not given to blue notes, Gautier was a life-loving, joyful Romantic, full of chiaroscuro humor. He remains to this day among the most widely read and most readable of French nineteenth-century authors. I find him so: Who else could have created the character of a priest tormented by the nocturnal visits of a gorgeous lady vampire? He actually made the irreverent tale life-enhancing. He was also a collector of memory: Gautier's *History of Romanticism* is the word equivalent of Nadar's photography, capturing half a century of greatness, the operating system underlying modern France.

A Bacchus look-alike, on his tomb Gautier is depicted on the hero's shield of stone that Calliope leans on with her right arm. At first this seems odd: Gautier was best known as the father of modern ballet criticism and as a novelist. Why poetry? Actually he began with painting and poetry and lived a poetic life, according to Baudelaire. Gautier was "the impeccable poet," "the magician of French letters," which is why Baudelaire dedicated *The Flowers of Evil* to him.

Balzac famously prowled Père-Lachaise when he wanted to cheer himself up, so it's fitting he's buried there near Nerval, Nodier, and Delacroix. But I find Gautier's shady helter-skelter Montmartre resting place nearly as enchanting. An ironwork viaduct from 1888 flies over the cemetery, demonstrating that progress—if such it be—doesn't always destroy to roll onward. Below, in the dappled darkness, the requisite grass-grown lanes crisscross twenty-five acres of tombs, an elm and oak forest full of birdsong, bristling with a marble undergrowth of fantastical funerary monuments. There are tall stone ramparts from an imaginary château, and as at Père-Lachaise, astonishing, tomb-eating trees, the rusted iron bars and hunks of headstones protruding from thick trunks or roots. Other nations might cut down such weeds, but Parisians let them grow. This is insouciant ancestor worship. Particles of loved ones lodge in the living plants like human offspring.

Owls, cats, and death's-heads sculpted or real abound. Dilapidated sepulchers yawn, their grisly contents sometimes visible. Alexandre Dumas the elder lies in the Panthéon, but his son sleeps here beneath a stone canopy, his right big toe and nose broken off by souvenir hunters. That's not surprising. In French, *souvenir* refers to the object and the memory, a keepsake and remembrance of times past, heavy like stone yet as virtual as digital reality.

Gautier's is among my favorite tombs, but so is that of Marie Taglioni, the prima ballerina. She putatively lies not far away. I am fascinated by her modest mossy memorial, instantly recognizable from the strange tokens left on it by professional ballet dancers: toe shoes. Dozens, hundreds, thousands of them have been heaped here over the last century. Just as Gautier is the father of ballet criticism, Taglioni is the mother of Romantic, meaning modern, dance, the spiritual forebear of Isadora Duncan. The limestone lid and ground nearby are littered with decomposing pointe shoes. Only one pilgrim so far has left behind slippers made of metal.

As insiders are aware, however, there is a catch. Again, blissful ignorance is best preserved. Don't tell the ballerinas. The tomb actually belongs to Taglioni's mother. The dancer, officially the Countess de Voisins, lies beside her husband the count in Division 94 at Père-Lachaise. Oddly enough, she rests in relative peace near Alice B. Toklas and Gertrude Stein. Rarely have a light foot and a heavy hand resided so close to each other. A tomb is a tomb is a tomb.

Not really. There's no doubt about Nijinsky's tomb, a hundred yards or so from Gautier. His monument must be one of the most strangely wonderful conceived. A squatting gnome in fancy dress protects but does nothing to project the memory of this phenomenon of nature drawn to Paris by its Romantic heritage.

Aimé Millet, the sculptor—not Jean-François Millet, the painter—created the touching statue *Youth Picking Petals Off Roses* that marks the monument in Division 5 of Henry "La Bohème" Murger. It may be my favorite tomb of all. The youth is a comely young woman, Mimi arisen raining rose petals for eternity. Many times I have found opera tickets, bouquets of violets, and images of Mimi and Rodolphe left in homage.

Up and down crumbling staircases, hidden behind towering trees on curving quiet lanes lie the tombs of Degas, Zola (a cenotaph), the Goncourt brothers (buried side by side), Berlioz, Madame de Récamier, Adolphe Sax, Ary Scheffer, Stendhal, Gustave Moreau, Horace Vernet, Alfred de Vigny, and a more recent resident, François Truffaut, a latter-day Romantic whose movies helped broadcast the myths and magic of Paris.

Why should any of this matter? Why spend hours in graveyards instead of sipping something refreshing at a café, gazing at masterpieces in museums, or strolling in parks?

When in Paris you don't need the explanation. You feel the answer. The past and its people are as ubiquitous and penetrating as the microwaves you don't see, the DSL communications you don't hear when you talk on the telephone. I had this high-tech epiphany one day not long ago standing by Gautier's tomb looking up at the artists' studios across the way and the antennas on their roofs. Strands of thought, feeling, and intuition came together, forming cables or fiber optics in my mind. The city's hundreds of *lieux de mémoire*—those "places of memory" found only in ancient places— are broadcast towers. For some, the wavelength is intermittent and the message garbled, while for others, being in a cemetery on a premodern street, in an old building, monument, or park or café or museum is like hooking onto broadband or picking up five-bar Wi-Fi. Whether you're reading Paris loud and clear or imperfectly, you can't help being transfixed by phenomena in part beyond your ken. Unless you're insensate you're tapping into the emotions, brain waves, and other vibes emanating from those around you. Some people are relay towers sharing the magic. The more you know about history and culture and art and architecture and people living or dead, the more attuned you become to what the ancients called the "spirit of place" both good and bad. Paris possesses this in spades.

PART EIGHT

Open Endings and Musings on the
Looping Lanes That Link the Balzac
House and the Great Romantics to
Their Unwitting Descendants
and Modern-Day Paris

42

THE LONG AND WINDING ROAD

From atop his marble hill Balzac rules at Père-Lachaise while Gautier lords it over Montmartre. Their potency remains impressive despite broadcasting at lower wattages than Hugo and Dumas in their Panthéon acropolis. Unlike the great secular trinity of French literature, Gautier doesn't have a museum of his own. His voluminous archives and manuscripts, the charcoal sketches and oil paintings of his youth, and a handful of keepsakes reside beneath the same slanted slate roof as those of his friend, mentor, and colleague at the Balzac House Museum. It is to this shrine of skepticism hidden in a sunken garden in Passy near the Seine in western Paris that I pay homage to both men, a literary twofer.

"He wore the monk's habit of white flannel or cashmere," Gautier wrote, recalling his first encounter with Balzac the living legend. "Perhaps it symbolized to his eyes the cloistered life to which his work condemned him. . . . The gown was flung back, disclosing the neck of an athlete or a bull, round as the section of a column . . . of a satiny whiteness contrasting with the stronger tones of the face . . . blood glowed a healthy crimson in his full cheeks and warmly colored those lusty lips, thick and curved, and ever laughing, which a slight mustache and imperial tuft defined without concealing."

Like Gautier, who was a boxer and weight lifter, Balzac gave the lie to the image of the Romantics as shrinking violets. Both men enjoyed rude good health, food, wine, and sex. Balzac's apparent robustness and voluble bonhomie hid the complex, many-layered personality of an artist whose behavior at times bordered on insanity. "The forehead was handsome, vast, noble . . . His thick hair was long, wiry, and black, thrown back over his head like a lion's mane. The eyes, there were never any like them. They had a life, a light, an inconceivable magnetism, the white of the eyeballs pure, limpid, with a bluish tinge like an infant's or a Madonna's, enclosing two black diamonds flecked here and there with gold—eyes to make an eagle drop his lids, eyes to read through walls and into hearts or terrify an enraged wild beast, the eyes of a sovereign, a seer, a subjugator."

Gautier did not specify what Balzac's legs looked like, presumably because the author of *The Human Comedy* wore pants under his signature monk's robe. But like Baudelaire, Hugo, Nerval, and Gautier, Balzac was also a pathological walker, an addict of the cityscape born to lope. It stands to reason he had good calf muscles.

With this in mind, on a lark I decided to head on foot to his former digs, a meandering five-mile walk west from the Marais. Descriptions of Balzac's looks, his novels, and his life played through my mind as I marched along, a paperback copy of Gautier's *History of Romanticism* tucked in my pocket.

From my office near the Bastille I made a slow U-turn around Balzac's virtual garret near the Arsenal Library, then slalomed across the Marais to pass half a dozen places where Balzac or his clan lived, and probably about 1,001 he used as backdrops for his hundred or so books. No, that isn't right. Paris was more than a *backdrop* for Balzac. Paris was human, alive a presence that penetrated the soul of those who lived there. Every corner, every café, each bend in the Seine was a madeleine baked with epiphany yeast.

I knew that if I continued detouring to follow Balzac's trail I would never reach my goal far off in the 16th arrondissement. Picking up the pace along the Seine, I exited an hour later at Iéna, then mounted the high-rent heights of the Chaillot district. They are now known for the Palais de Tokyo and Trocadéro, with Passy lying immediately beyond. Balzac always said he wanted to live in airy places atop hills with a view. That's why the wily Rastignac made his dare to Paris at Père-Lachaise Cemetery, from the spot where Balzac was thoughtfully buried, belatedly fulfilling his wish.

Happily, while alive Balzac also enjoyed several fine views, the fanciest of them on what was at the time rue des Batailles. The tilting semi-rural street is no longer. It was folded into Avenue d'Iéna and most of its man-

sions were demolished. The one where Balzac lived stood near today's palatial Shangri-La Hotel. That would certainly please the novelist. His
ambition was to be famous and loved, in that order. Did he succeed?

If the silver or flat screen are a measure, the movies made from Balzac's
books currently top sixty in French and English, not counting dozens of
spin-off adaptations, with at least as many TV series some of them very
recent. To say he "influenced" or "shaped" everyone from Karl Marx and
Dickens to Flaubert, Zola and Proust, Wilde and James or Simenon is understatement. Beyond the Balzac main line, side tracks lead to J. K. Huysmans and Louis-Ferdinand Céline (*Journey to the End of the Night*), plus a
thousand foreign writers who applied Balzac's techniques to their own societies. Balzac is the ecumenical, apolitical enigma who introduced sui ge-
neris realism and telling details—at times an overabundance of them—into
the early modern novel.

Before entering the Shangri-La Hotel, for instance, were he alive today
Balzac would pause to remark upon the mild gradient of the hill, the as-
phalt and stone composition of the streets, sidewalks, and stairs, the type
of material the building was made of, its provenance and color, the height
of each floor, the kind of architectural detailing, the fact that you could still
detect in the current façade the traces of an earlier, turreted building, and
more, much more.

It was the overabundance of detail and the roughshod modern style—
or lack of style, which is equally modern—that led Flaubert the supreme
stylist to make his famously venomous remark: "How great Balzac would
have been had he known how to write." It was all the more wounding for its
accuracy. But it missed the main point. Flaubert was a wealthy landlord and
could afford to spend five years writing and polishing each of his masterpieces. He produced only a few books, one more timeless than the next.
His work is Balzac perfected and elevated and naturally leads to Proust.

Gautier was perhaps more perceptive in his reading. He celebrated Balzac's "original understanding of modern beauty" and saw that, to him, style
was coarse of necessity because artifice and speed trumped everything.
Modernity is why Baudelaire hailed Balzac as the century's genius. An
anti-Classicist with a hidden Romantic heart, Balzac gloried in the fascination
of fashion, life on the street, food, drink, entertainment, crime, prostitution,
murder and violence, in all things living, changeable, and contemporary no

matter how ugly, gross, offensive, or absurd. His plain-Pierre writing and cinematic technique fit the subject matter and the punishing time constraints of his publishing plan: His books read like movie or TV serial treatments and were indeed serialized, making him a marathon wordsmith. Debts and ambition kept him running.

Whereas Balzac's friendly rival Victor Hugo harked backward, Balzac was an unapologetic man of his times. Hugo gradually grew away from *The Hunchback of Notre Dame* and *Hernani* toward Balzac's conception of modernity. He described the poverty, crime, and politics of his day. But Hugo and the others—Musset, de Vigny, even George Sand—no matter what the subject wrote in a lyrical, rhetorical, high-sounding Romantic style.

Daubed with sweat I entered the posh marble-paved lobby of the Shangri-La Hotel on muddy tiptoe, prepared for ejection. My remarkably casual dress didn't distress the doormen. Billionaires often look like bums these days. Balzac, a master of disguise, went about in the uniform of a factory worker or cross-dressed as an aging widow. The hotel's gleaming Second Empire style interior with crystal chandeliers and gilt ironwork looked a little like chez Balzac, an ambiance guaranteed to please pashas and parvenus.

Honoré de Balzac was both, and his name tells all. He had more than a small dose of Rastignac in his blood. The fictional character was based largely on Adolphe Thiers but also on Balzac's own father, the adaptable peasant Bernard-François Balssa from the South of France. Balssa rose to riches, changing his tainted name—his brother was convicted for murder—and adding an aristocratic *de* to compete with other arrivistes. The fact that Balzac was the first to write extensively about the great taboo—the French obsession with money—reflected society as a whole then and reflects it now. Greed began close to home. He might well have declared in the mold of Louis XIV and Flaubert, "Rastignac, *c'est moi.*"

It was here at Chaillot that the already famous, temporarily rich, but imperfectly loved Balzac rented his apartment in the name of the Widow Durand, the nighttime wanderer of the Seine's banks often seen leaning on a heavy cane. When he stripped off the disguise, underneath he might be found wearing his blue velvet coat with solid gold buttons, the one reserved for the opera and theater. The cane doubled as a cudgel, its pommel encrusted with gold studded with turquoise. This was Balzac's dandy period. Fascinated by fashion, he believed clothes made the man, and fine

clothes and a fine address also induced publishers to pay him bigger advances and royalties. Perhaps that was a good reason to rethink my ward-
robe and lodge at the Shangri-La.

Jules Sandeau, healing from another broken heart, lived with Balzac at
Chaillot for a time, as he had in the old days of George Sand and Marie
Dorval. Few others were welcome. The faithful Gautier was a privileged
guest, however. It was he who left the most amusing description of the prem-
ises, adding to the picture Balzac himself painted in the novella *Girl with the
Golden Eyes*.

The Shangri-La's security is nothing in comparison to Balzac's. Fearing
interruption by admirers and creditors, he posted three guards and issued
passwords to intimates. "To the porter we said, 'The plum season has arrived,' at which he allowed us to cross the threshold," Gautier recalled. "To
the servant who rushed to the staircase when the bell rang it was necessary
to murmur, 'I bring some Brussels lace.' If you assured the third servant that
'Madame Bertrand is quite well,' you were admitted forthwith. This nonsense
amused Balzac immensely."

Inside Balzac's "boudoir," the look was pure Shangri-La. He had decorated with precious silk fabrics and pillows, thick curtains and red wall hangings, antiques, a clock and candlesticks of marble and gold, a wide Turkish
sofa and a fireplace of white marble veined with gold. A chandelier hung in
the center of the gilt, molded ceiling. Twin candles held by vermilion arm-
shaped sconces stuck out from the walls. One end of the vast salon had
been refashioned into a semicircle, so the room was horseshoe-shaped.

Like a child on a treasure hunt, Balzac opened a secret door and led
Gautier through a narrow corridor into two nooks hidden between the walls.
One nook was equipped with a cot, the other with a writing desk and im-
plements. This was the sanctum where the wicked monk with solid gold
buttons hid out and labored up to eighteen hours a day, rising at midnight,
drinking quarts of tar-like coffee, and working until dawn, then correcting
and editing his words until evening. The specially built boudoir was sound-
proof, Balzac boasted, instructing Gautier to go back into it, shout and
scream. Mystified, he did. Balzac soon reappeared, displeased. He could
still hear faint noises.

The mystery of the soundproofing was soon revealed. Balzac was the
first known "method writer." He incarnated his characters with a wider range

than Vishnu, Gautier claimed, dressing like them, speaking like them, going to the places they worked or lived, imagining larceny, rape, and murder until fiction and reality blended. When Gautier showed up, Balzac was working on *Girl with the Golden Eyes*. He said he wanted to be sure the neighbors couldn't hear the screams of Paquita Valdes.

Who was she? Balzac explained everything as if sexual violence and strangulation were perfectly normal. In his monk's robe he must have looked like the perverse prelate in Matthew Gregory Lewis' famous 1796 Gothic novel *The Monk*, a touchstone among Romantics. In Balzac's novella, the debauched antihero Henri de Marsay, infatuated with Paquita, was preparing to seduce and corrupt her in the fictional-real apartment at Chaillot in the most diabolical way.

"He had only so far feasted his eyes on the marvelous wealth of perfections Paquita Valdes presented him," Balzac wrote, "but the drive of passion was nearly dead in him. Constant satiety had weakened in his heart any feelings of love. Like old men and the disillusioned, he had no longer anything but extravagant foibles, ruinous tastes and fantasies that, once satisfied, left his heart empty."

So blasé Henri de Marsay decides to ravish Paquita for the thrill of it. He discovers she is already the mistress of another and plots to kill her in the apartment, only to find she has just been brutally murdered by her lesbian lover—de Marsay's own sister!

If Balzac's extraordinary apartment had been preserved, I couldn't help thinking as I slipped out of the Shangri-La, it could have been remounted at the Carnavalet Museum or the Balzac House. Both were founded too late. I was as perplexed as Gautier by Balzac's convoluted tale. What did it mean at a deeper level? After digesting a square yard's worth of dusty books and scuffing the sidewalks for a decade, I began to think I understood. *Girl with the Golden Eyes* was about the innate nobility or ignobility of people and the effect society had upon them. *Innate* is the operative word here. Man is innately awful for Balzac. An extraordinary progression of perversion became clear to me: Balzac described primitive impulses in order to denounce them without apparently judging them or showing his hand—he did not want to write the kind of agitprop George Sand dispensed.

The progression of thinking on this subject starts with Jean-Jacques Rousseau and Bougainville's ideas of the goodness and nobility of primitive societies. From there it runs to the Marquis de Sade's impotent sadistic fantasizing at the Bastille about the rightness of the irrepressible, primitive urge. Then it leaps to Balzac at Chaillot and from Balzac to Baudelaire lucubrating with the Black Venus on the Ile Saint-Louis, reaching its apex with J. K. Huysmans, Verlaine, and Rimbaud experiencing extremes all over Paris. Onward the march of literature went from these forebears to scores of twentieth- and twenty-first-century authors of noir, scarlet, and rose. Some of them delighted in the squalor, while others sought to show why repression—by the church or the authorities—was essential to civilization. Balzac never preached, he claimed; he belonged to what we call the "show, don't tell" school. But Baudelaire and De Sade made similar claims. Few take them at their word. The chiaroscuro ambiguities keep people guessing to this day.

Balzac is sometimes tarred as a reactionary royalist who hated the poor and downtrodden. In reality he bequeathed his democratic oeuvre to everyone, underscoring in volume after volume the dark nastiness and corruption above all of the rich and greedy.

"True, there is no lack of despicable characters in *The Human Comedy*," wrote Gautier in the kicker to his moving biography of Balzac. "But is Paris peopled exclusively by angels?"

If it were, how boring Paris would be.

43

QUIET DAYS IN PASSY

In pre-Revolutionary times, hilly Passy was dotted with the villas and gardens of the aristocracy. When the bourgeois kingdom of Louis Philippe came along, so did factories, mills, and the first apartment buildings. Persecuted by repo men from Paris, Balzac sought respite in this far-flung hodgepodge outside the city limits. Legally he was beyond their reach. Paris ended at his doorstep. A stone plaque marking the boundary is still affixed to the building where he lived, his penultimate residence.

The spacious five-room apartment Balzac found in the former garden annex of a much diminished princely property suited him perfectly. As a precaution, he rented it in the name of his housekeeper and sometime bedmate, Madame de Breugnol. He was still courting but had not yet married a wealthy Polish widow, the mysterious Madame Hanska, who Franz Liszt was also pursuing.

Built on a slope Balzac's eighteenth-century folly was fronted by a row of recent apartment buildings. They screened it and the small terraced garden from view. When entering, Balzac pushed through the heavy carriage door of a banal apartment house, opened a back door, climbed down several stories and did a dogleg through the garden to reach his front door. In case of need, a winding staircase led another three stories down from his apartment to a maze of doors on the ground floor, giving out onto a gated courtyard and a narrow country lane. The lane did not dead end but at the city limits became an alley less than an arm span wide. It was impassable by horse or carriage, and is impassable today by cars. Balzac felt safe. From his terrace far above the lane he could see Paris' western edge on both sides of the Seine and could spot enemies approaching. Approach they did.

By the time he moved to Passy, Balzac was mired in debt. He had lost his savings, art collection, furniture, and Les Jardies, a property he had bought across the river at Sèvres but did not have the resources to develop. (It now houses a small museum to Balzac and a later resident, Léon Gambetta.)

If miracles are the result of vigorous human intervention, then it might be accurate to say Balzac's bizarre pavilion has been miraculously preserved. It, the courtyard, country lane, and alley are still here, the winding staircase, terraced garden, and city limits plaque as well. The factories and satanic mills have been replaced by castellated Art Déco luxury apartment complexes worthy of Rockefeller Center in Manhattan. After decades of research, many of Balzac's belongings as well as a dozen painted or sculpted portraits of the artist have been reassembled in the suite of wax-scented top-floor rooms where he lived. This is one of the city's enclaves of enchantment, saved from the wrecker's ball in the nick of time. The row of apartment buildings out front on rue Raynouard was demolished, and one of Paris' most egregious early cast-concrete modernist buildings rises next door. Yet once you're in the magical garden and Balzac's curious cliff house, you no longer notice or care.

In his writing Balzac was obsessive about details. But it's not the creaking parquet and the antiques, the multiple portraits of the author and his family members, or the didactic displays that cast a spell for me. It's the overall ambience, the atmosphere, the setting, the view, and the tangible history that combine to seduce visitors. It's the knowledge that Balzac worked and received in his rooms or in the perfumed garden with its bent-metal chairs and stone benches, gazing at Paris and the Seine, verbally sparring with Sand and Delacroix and too many others to list. The house still has green shutters and a provincial air, as it did in Balzac's day. What could be better than setting up your bathtub in the garden and soaking while you gazed at the view? That is what Balzac did in fine weather.

There are a few details, a few items of special interest, however. The dashingly Romantic bust of Balzac by Pierre-Eugène-Emile Hébert and especially the painted enameled head by Rodin are compelling. When I stand alone before them in the quiet of a winter's day, I can hear Balzac insisting, as he famously did to painter Louis Boulanger, "Pay attention to my nose, my nose is a world!" Balzac's nose *is* a world, a leonine and large-lobed nose it was, the nose of a con sniffer who could scent cant a mile off. No wonder Rodin was bewitched.

While creating his head of Balzac and the full-size sculpture now on Boulevard Raspail, Rodin became a slave to a dead master. Balzac had been buried for nearly half a century by then. To research the commission, Rodin did not so much adopt Balzac's method-acting method as he did succumb to a kind of feverish possession. Rodin's quest to capture the essence of the man became a Proustian exercise in reliving a life and a heroic, Faustian struggle to resuscitate Balzac through art. Rodin spent years reading Balzac's works and every biography about him, starting with Gautier's highly personal portrayal. Convinced he needed a look-alike, a doppelgänger, Rodin traveled to Balzac's birthplace at Tours to find an avatar, a cousin, a secret son or descendant. The haunting polychrome expressionistic portrait he created is more than modern. It is contemporary and could have been made yesterday. That may be why copies of the head and the statue are in so many cities and museums across the world. Isn't it strange? The most profound evocation of Balzac was made postmortem. It would not have seemed so to Balzac. Like Hugo and Chopin and the rest he is not actually dead—not to Parisians, in any case.

Visitors with object fetishes always stand in rapture before Balzac's writing desk, a squat Louis XIII style dark wooden table with coiling legs, seemingly built for a child. Balzac was thick of neck and waist but short in the leg and tiny by modern standards. The museum's other cult objects are Balzac's scepter-like cane and coffeepot. I once asked a solicitous young guard whether forensic analysts had examined the cane's gold pommel for traces of scalp, hair, or human blood. The guard seemed startled but then nodded enthusiastically and followed me around the house museum, nodding and discoursing. Paris was dangerous throughout the Romantic Age, he confirmed. Canes and fans often concealed knives or derringers. Balzac could swing with the best of them. He had whacked many a horse flank and cracked more than one human shank—and head—with that cane. The pommel is slightly battered. Forensic analysis was something to consider, the guard added, his eyes twinkling.

It is Balzac's curious coffeepot that seems to draw the biggest crowds. Made of white porcelain with bands, swooping stripes, and Balzac's initials in bloodred, the pot was conceived much like a contemporary drip coffee-maker with a heating element underneath. Balzac brewed his coffee in the pot like tea, adding grounds and water. The result must have been toxically acidic and dangerously caffeinated, the worst truck-stop brew imaginable. Coffee killed him, experts claim. It ruined his digestive tract. It may have provoked ulcers or colon cancer. No wonder Balzac considered switching to hashish to knock the coffee habit. But he loathed and detested smoke and once told Gautier that if he could, he would chop the heads off all tobacco users. Balzac would have had to set up a thousand guillotines in his day and even more of them now, and run them 24-7 for several years.

Like a true addict, when Balzac recruited the innocent young Gautier to write for him at his magazine *La Chronique de Paris*, he tried to inculcate into the eager protégé the master's graveyard-shift schedule and his habits, including the use of caffeine. Gautier duly had himself awakened at midnight, swallowed several cups of pestilential coffee, began to write, and promptly fell asleep. He was too healthy and normal for Balzac's routine, delivering only his classic spoof *La Morte amoureuse* by using Balzac's method.

What of Gautier? As in life, he lives in death in Balzac's shadow. There is little or nothing on view in the museum's public areas to evoke this unsung hero of Romanticism. One day I discovered that his archives were in the reserves, so I made an appointment to visit the library. I was treated en route to a spiraling descent down the stairs Balzac used when fleeing through the lower courtyard. The museum occupies the entire building. Iconographers, researchers, curators, and administrators inhabit a warren of unseen rooms. A cordial curator librarian led the way, then opened the archives for me.

It was in the ground-floor reading room of the Balzac House that I confirmed the "impeccable poet" had impeccable handwriting. Gautier wasn't just neat and aesthetic in his penmanship. He rarely made corrections or changes and didn't need to, the opposite of hesitant, tortured, endlessly self-critical Balzac, who wrote, rewrote, corrected, and added to his proofs up to a dozen times, a ruinously expensive and time-consuming process. If Gérard de Nerval pioneered Surrealism and automatic writing, Gautier was the master of the perfect first draft and Balzac the king of cut-and-paste.

Gautier's manuscripts were gorgeous. But I had to admire Balzac's wild proofs. They beat the best word collages and were unplanned masterpieces of printed and quilled prose, with extra snippets pinned on, a typographical map of the author's labyrinthine mind.

Unsurprisingly Balzac was galled by Gautier's effortless, joyful ease with writing. He could find nothing to correct in Gautier's magazine submissions but goaded him to work harder and try rewriting at least four or five times. "It would be even *better,*" Balzac, the envious editor, commanded. Luckily Gautier did not obey.

Sitting in the library looking through Gautier's manuscripts and keepsakes—a porcelain inkpot and silver-plated cup, among them—I had a sudden inspiration. I realized why Baudelaire had dedicated *Les Fleurs du Mal* to Gautier and not Hugo or Balzac. The reason was clear. Baudelaire knew the modest, erudite "impeccable poet" had decrypted the puzzle of the title of his life's work, *Les Fleurs du Mal.* Gautier speculated in a review of the collection that Baudelaire had found inspiration in an 1844 short story by Nathaniel Hawthorne, "Rappaccini's Daughter." It was another tale of American influence: white socks and black cats. Poe via Baudelaire had helped shape French literature and, it now dawned on me, so had Hawthorne. Gautier was right in his guess. Baudelaire was flattered that he had been found out. *The Flowers of Evil* bloomed on the page.

Another revelation came to me later in the garden as I sat under a sweet-smelling viburnum bush leafing through my cheap paperback copy of Gautier's *History of Romanticism.* The edition I own includes a booklet titled *Forty Romantic Portraits.* As I read for a second or third time parts of the concise biographical study of Balzac in the booklet, an example of cross-pollination I had never seen cited occurred to me. All the way back in 1858, Gautier compared Balzac's struggle as a writer to wrest characters from his imagination with *Jacob Wrestling with the Angel.* Delacroix had by then sketched and painted his small-scale studies for *Jacob* for the mural at the church of Saint-Sulpice. Gautier was a leading art critic, and perhaps he would have seen the studies. So it's not surprising the image of the artist-writer struggling to summon the powers of creation should become a theme in Gautier's sketch of the life of Balzac.

But here's the twist: Delacroix completed the painting three years after Gautier's biography was published, so the painter may well have had Gautier in mind as he labored at Saint-Sulpice. I have returned to the church several times since this idea came to me, but I can't claim the handsome muscular brown-haired Jacob resembles Balzac in any perceptible way. The struggle is within. All three artists—Gautier, Balzac, and Delacroix—were fascinated less by externalities than by inner turmoil. They used surface reality to indicate what lies below.

A final telling detail in the Balzac-Gautier saga also came to me as I prepared to leave the house museum and head back across Paris. Gautier keeled over and died while writing his history of Romanticism; Balzac fell fatally ill and managed to scribble one final, barely readable line. It was addressed to Gautier in a farewell letter: "I can no longer read or write." The subtext was clear: Therefore I can no longer live. He was barely fifty years old, financially comfortable at last, and married to Eva Hanska, the love of his life. The coffee got him.

Forged from stainless steel, Victor Hugo buried them all. He composed and read the funerary oration for Balzac at Père-Lachaise. Some thought it fitting Hugo was nearly crushed by the wheels of the hearse and knocked into Balzac's yawning grave. "All of his books made a single book," Hugo declaimed, "a living, luminous, profound book where one sees the whole of contemporary civilization coming and going, walking and stirring with that je ne sais quoi of the frightful and terrible mixed with reality."

It still does.

44

SENDING OUT AN SMS:
FROM BALZAC WITH LOVE

eandering down the alleyway toward Paris as Balzac loved to do, my
arms out and fingertips brushing the scabrous sides, I gazed up at a
wild grapevine and a bunch of grapes hanging over my head. Should I jump
like the fox and pick them or leave the décor intact? I left the grapes for
others to see, not that many visitors to the Balzac House were likely to wander down the lane or risk going into the alley, the kind of long, knife-slit
passageway it would be suicide to walk through in most big cities. Luckily
curiosity is not an act of self-destruction in Paris' 16th arrondissement. I
had five scenic miles and the rest of my life to work out a few more mental
connections, starting with the unusual items I had learned from the affable
librarian in charge of the Gautier archives.

We had talked at length of Paris then and now, of romance and Romanticism and Gautier and Balzac in love. Was there really still a connection
between Balzac and the hundreds or thousands of digital-age schoolchil-
dren who visited the museum each year? I asked. Without hesitation she
said yes, Balzac was no institutional writer French schoolkids were forced
to read. Free e-books helped. But it was the movies, TV, and computer
screens that had kept him alive for the young, for the generations that no
longer read print books. The librarian said young French boys and girls
were reading the Romantics off the handheld devices that seemed to be
extensions of their arms.

"We encourage teenagers to read Balzac's beautiful love letters to Eva Hanska," she added in a jocular tone. "We tell the boys especially that if they want to learn how to seduce with words and send amazing SMS messages, there is no better teacher."

This I could not make up. All the youngsters need do, it transpires, is find the magic words on the Internet, copy and paste them into a message, and then change the names to suit their needs. Reportedly a Balzac SMS works like a charm.

I loved it. This was plagiarism of the kind Hugo, Musset, and Flaubert practiced: Victor recycled his ecstatic phraseology from Juliette to Léonie; Alfred copied his love letters to Sand, reusing them in his novel *Confession of a Child of the Century*; and in *Madame Bovary* Flaubert reappropriated verbatim words and experiences he had shared with Louise Colet in the intimacy of their correspondence and life. These three writers were at least as powerful in the realm of seduction and romance as Balzac.

"Ugly is beautiful," I imagined a pimply adolescent pecking out on his smartphone, quoting Hugo. "Eternal love is in the mind of the hero," and "Your melancholy is a charm, your unhappiness an attraction."

As I emerged smiling from the alleyway into rue Marcel Proust, descending toward the Seine, an earworm from the late 1970s dropped from a shade tree. My ears rang with the irrepressible, tuneful reprise from that old Police top-ten single "Message in a Bottle." I had listened to it a thousand times. "Sending out an SOS," sang the young Sting, lyrical on vinyl. Sending out an SOS? Why?

Over and over I heard Sting singing in my head, SOS morphing to SMS, then back again as I crossed the Bir Hakeim Bridge on the Seine and paused to admire the miniature Statue of Liberty the French had kindly shipped from the Old World to the new. It instead made me think of blasé Henri de Marsay and Balzac's *Girl with the Golden Eyes*. Did tired old blasé Paris need someone to send out an SOS and bring over the happy pills? Did Paris need help from irrepressible optimists? Probably not, I reflected, certainly not from outsiders with bleached teeth and elephant trains.

It was clear to me that Balzac would love the mess of modern Paris—the bumper-to-bumper traffic on the Seine-side Pompidou Expressway, the late-twentieth-century high-rise towers thrilling for their hideousness, the shantytowns under the lacework spans on the Seine, bridges where blissful foreign couples in nineteenth-century revival black designer outfits were having wedding pictures taken. Balzac would be fascinated by the padlocks spreading like a rash along the parapets. Seeing them, he would quickly plot a potboiler of passion, revenge and crime. Balzac would not be walking, however. He would be at the wheel of an SUV or in the back of a stretch limousine talking on his cell phone to his agent, or taking snapshots of the newlyweds and the padlocks for later use in a ghoulish sitcom.

Etching the jagged cityscape, I could see both the novel Eiffel Tower and the familiar domed Panthéon—novel and familiar to George Sand, for instance, who died before the tower was built but lives on as an "idea," according to Victor Hugo. If she was alive in body and not just in spirit, George would be gleefully tilting at the last vestiges of chauvinistic male domination but would nonetheless stop on the bridge to check out the sexy groom or the pretty bride and perhaps invite them over for drinks. Dressed in dark men's fashions and chain-smoking cigarettes, cigars, or joints, she might become a contemporary terrorist and blast a hole in the side of the Panthéon, then occupy it with other feminists. She would tweet en route to her millions of followers about rotten Alfred de Musset, adorable Marie Dorval, nasty Marie d'Agoult, ditzy Franz Liszt, and weedy Frédéric Chopin, each of them still alive, saved by antibiotics, steroids, and gene therapy. Perhaps Sand would do like other lustful Parisians these days and rush naked into Notre Dame or fornicate in public on a bench in the Luxembourg Garden for a lark. It was easy back then but is hard today to be shocking in Paris.

What about Victor Hugo? If not at the Place des Vosges working in his attic, he would be at the Luxembourg Palace in the Senate, wrestling Euroskeptic England and pig-headed Germany toward that idealized United States of Europe that still hasn't happened, or he would be resisting the continuing destruction of old Paris by militating with a contemporary NGO he had inspired. Between sessions Hugo would visit his backup mistresses, behaving like a contemporary French politician while Juliette Drouet sends out SMSs and waits patiently in their Marais love nest.

Paris does not need help, I repeated to myself. It is securely anchored in the Romantic Age.

As I wandered home in crazy zigzags I imagined Gautier at the Comédie-Française watching his *Giselle,* sitting in his usual spot on new upholstery or attending the latest revival of *Hernani.* Musset and Murger would be dead drunk and shouting with the rowdies in the alleys of the Latin Quarter. Baudelaire, his pink gloves glowing on the damp green quays of the Ile Saint-Louis, would fit in with his acolytes reciting melancholic lines to the thumping of bongo drums and gangsta rap. Dumas and his friends would be dancing in Square d'Orléans at four a.m. while the neighbors phoned the cops.

I could see Gérard de Nerval with his lobster and Modigliani comatose atop Montmartre or in a Montparnasse nightclub. Meanwhile, Nadar would have swapped his tattered old balloon for a new one or a blimp or perhaps a Pterodactyl Ascender ultralight and have switched to digital photography. He could hover overhead and take a group portrait of all his friends and a selfie of himself high above Paris.

Adept at dodging horses, carriages, and road apples, everyone would feel perfectly at home once they got used to the newfangled motor vehicles, sidewalks, and dog dirt. They'd be able to find their way home down familiar streets to many of the cafés and restaurants, theaters, gardens and parks, government offices, museums, train stations, mansions, villas, and apartments they'd known when alive. They could go to the opera for Murger's masterpiece reworked by Puccini in *La Bohème* and pick up a copy of *Les Misérables, The Three Musketeers,* or *The Flowers of Evil,* all still in print and sold at Galignani, booksellers on rue de Rivoli since 1855. Napoléon III and his sidekick could gloat over their boulevards and tour the sewers, perhaps slipping in. Comfortingly, most Parisians would still be dressed in deep unisex Romantic black, especially in the Marais and existentialist Saint-Germain-des-Prés, or in wildly colorful carnival outfits headed to that party at Dumas'. Opening the pages of *Le Figaro*—the same broadsheet many of them wrote for and read—they might discover the current president of France had been photographed in flagrante with a second or third mistress while the first lady or official mistress had been hospitalized to avoid the paparazzi. So what's new?

What's new is we could herd all the great Romantics, the gods of Paris' cultural Panthéon, onto the Pont des Arts with the Asian and African and

American lovers and their padlocks and get Hemingway, Picasso, and Stein to come along singing "a myth is a myth is a myth is a myth." With Nadar focusing from above, the final word would go to Alphonse Karr.

Dites fromage!

KEY DATES

1789–1799: The French Revolution

1793–1794: The Terror

1799: The Consulate; Napoléon Bonaparte is First Consul

1803–1815: The Napoleonic Wars

1804: Napoléon Bonaparte becomes Emperor Napoléon I

1815: Waterloo and final defeat of Napoléon I

1814–1830: The Restoration of the Bourbon Monarchy, Louis XVIII
(reigns 1814–1824) and Charles X (reigns 1824–1830)

1830: The Battle of Hernani and the July Revolution

1830–1848: Reign of King Louis Philippe I, Citizen King of the July Monarchy

1831: Victor Hugo's *The Hunchback of Notre Dame* (*Notre Dame de Paris*) and Honoré
de Balzac's *The Magic Skin* (*La Peau de chagrin*)

1848: February Revolution, creation of Second Republic, Louis Napoléon
Bonaparte elected president

1851–1852: Coup d'état, Louis Napoléon Bonaparte becomes Emperor
Napoléon III

1852–1870: Second Empire

1870–1871: Franco-Prussian War, Siege of Paris, Commune

1870–1940: Third Republic

KEY CHARACTERS

Marie d'Agoult (1805–1876)

Marie Catherine Sophie de Flavigny, Comtesse d'Agoult, novelist alias Daniel Stern, celebrated for literary salon, lover of pianist Franz Liszt, mother of three of Liszt's children.

Léonie d'Aunet (1820–1879)

Madame Biard, writer and explorer, had seven-year liaison with Victor Hugo.

Honoré de Balzac (1799–1850)

Novelist, playwright, authored a hundred novels, most grouped into *The Human Comedy* (*La Comédie humaine*).

Charles Baudelaire (1821–1867)

Poet, critic, essayist, and translator of Edgar Allan Poe; authored *The Flowers of Evil* (*Les Fleurs du mal*) and *Artificial Paradises*; decades-long liaison with Jeanne Duval (the Black Venus).

François-René de Chateaubriand (1768–1848)

Early Romantic poet, writer, diplomat, politician, author of *René* and many other works.

Frédéric Chopin (1810–1849)

Polish composer and pianist; nine-year liaison with novelist George Sand.

Auguste Clésinger (1814–1883)

Sculptor and painter; married Solange Dudevant, daughter of George Sand; sculpted funerary monument to Chopin at Père-Lachaise Cemetery.

Louise Colet (1810–1876)

Née Louise Révoil, poetess, artist's model; lover of Victor Cousin, Gustave Flaubert, Alfred de Musset, Victor Hugo, Alfred de Vigny, and other great Romantics; inspiration for the character of Emma Bovary in Flaubert's *Madame Bovary*.

Eugène Delacroix (1798–1863)

Painter, colorist; leading Romantic celebrated for *Liberty Leading the People* (*La Liberté guidant le peuple*), 1830, and murals in the church of Saint-Sulpice.

Marie Dorval (1798–1849)

Leading Romantic actress; lover of Alfred de Vigny, George Sand, Victor Hugo, Jules Sandeau, and others.

Juliette Drouet (1806–1883)

Artist's model, actress; personal secretary to and longtime lover of Victor Hugo.

Alexandre Dumas (1802–1870)

Novelist and playwright; authored *The Count of Monte Cristo, The Three Musketeers*, and seminal revolutionary Romantic play *Henri III et sa cour* (1829); entombed in the Panthéon.

Jeanne Duval (1820?–1862?)

Alias the Black Venus; mixed-race dancer and actress; longtime liaison with Charles Baudelaire.

Gustave Flaubert (1821–1880)

Novelist, author of *Madame Bovary, l'Éducation sentimentale*, and other works; nine-year liaison with poetess Louise Colet.

Théophile Gautier (1811–1872)

Leading Romantic artist, poet, novelist, playwright, critic, essayist, travel writer, historian; father of modern ballet criticism; wrote the libretto for the ballet *Giselle*.

Georges-Eugène Haussmann (1809–1891)

Aka Baron Haussmann; prefect of the Seine responsible for Second Empire remake of Paris.

Victor Hugo (1802–1885)

Leading playwright, poet, and novelist; statesman, hero of the Romantic Age, enemy of Napoléon III; author of *The Hunchback of Notre Dame, Les Misérables*, and others; married to Adèle Hugo; fifty-year liaison with actress Juliette Drouet and contemporaneous seven-year liaison with writer Léonie d'Aunet; entombed in the Panthéon.

Alphonse Karr (1808–1890)

Novelist, critic, essayist; newspaper and magazine publisher; playboy; celebrated for quips including "The more things change, the more they stay the same."

Franz Liszt (1811–1886)

Hungarian composer, conductor, and pianist; friend of Chopin and George Sand; lover of novelist Marie d'Agoult.

Prosper Mérimée (1803–1870)

Novelist, historian, archaeologist, author of *Carmen*; inspector general of historic monuments; hired Viollet-le-Duc et al to restore Notre Dame Cathedral, Sainte-Chapelle, and Carcassonne.

Henri Murger (1822–1861)

Writer, journalist, playwright; author of *Scenes of Bohemian Life*, better known as opera *La Bohème* by Giacomo Puccini; trailblazing bohemian; founder of the Society of Water Drinkers.

Alfred de Musset (1810–1857)

Leading poet, playwright, novelist; author of *Confession of a Child of the Century*; celebrated liaison with George Sand.

Félix Nadar (1820–1910)

Pseudonym of Gaspard-Félix Tournachon; artist, caricaturist, journalist, and leading portrait photographer; inventor of aerial and flash photography; pioneering bohemian.

Napoléon I, Emperor (Napoléon Bonaparte, 1769–1821)

Revolutionary general; first consul, emperor of First French Empire 1804–1814.

Napoléon III, Emperor (Louis Napoléon Bonaparte, 1808–1873)

Nephew of Napoléon I; dictator, emperor of Second French Empire 1852–1870.

Gérard de Nerval (1808–1855)

Writer, poet, playwright, translator; proto-Surrealist; leading Romantic spirit.

Charles Nodier (1780–1844)

Novelist, intellectual, librarian; host of Romantic salon at Arsenal Library, birthplace of French Romanticism.

Louis Philippe I d'Orléans (1773–1850)

Alias the Citizen King; reigned 1830–1848.

James Pradier (1790–1852)

Romantic sculptor celebrated for his literary salon; lover of Juliette Drouet and other Romantic women.

Charles Augustin Sainte-Beuve (1804–1869)

Literary and theater critic, journalist, novelist; celebrated for adulterous affair with Adèle Hugo.

George Sand (1804–1876)

Pseudonym of Amandine-Aurore-Lucile Dupin, Baroness Dudevant; controversial writer, essayist, journalist, playwright; author of *Lélia* and nearly eighty other novels; pioneering feminist; lover of Alfred de Musset, Frédéric Chopin, Jules Sandeau, Prosper Mérimée, and others.

Jules Sandeau (1811–1883)

Novelist remembered today for his collaboration and love affair with George Sand, whose pseudonym derives from his name.

Ary Scheffer (1795–1858)

Dutch-German painter; introduced Romanticism to court of Louis Philippe; lived in today's Museum of Romantic Life.

Alfred de Vigny (1797–1863)

Poet, playwright, novelist; author of *Chatterton*; longtime liaison with actress Marie Dorval.

Eugène Viollet-le-Duc (1814–1879)

Architect; restored, re-created historic French buildings and cities, including Notre Dame Cathedral, Sainte-Chapelle, and Carcassonne.

IMAGE CREDITS

ABOUT THE AUTHOR

David Downie, a native San Franciscan, lived in New York, Providence, Rome, and Milan before moving to Paris in the mid-1980s. He divides his time between France and Italy. His travel and arts features have appeared in over fifty print publications worldwide. Downie is co-owner with his wife, Alison Harris, of Paris, Paris Tours custom walking tours of Paris, Burgundy, Rome, and the Italian Riviera. He is the author of the critically acclaimed *Paris, Paris,* and the bestselling *Paris to the Pyrenees.* Please visit his Web sites www.daviddownie.com and www.parisparistours.com.